Recovering From Incest

Recovering From Incest

Imagination and the Healing Process

Evangeline Kane

SIGO PRESS
BOSTON

Workshops and Lectures
Evangeline Kane offers seminars, lectures, and training workshops on topics related to incest and sexual abuse; she also conducts support groups for incest/abuse survivors and their families. If you would like to attend one of Dr. Kane's upcoming lectures or workshops or invite her to speak in your area, please write to Sigo Press.

SIGO PRESS
25 New Chardon Street, #8748
Boston, Massachusetts 02114
Publisher and Editor: Sisa Sternback
  Associate Editor: Marc E. Romano

Excerpts from *The Assault on Truth* © 1984, 1985 by Jeffrey Moussaieff Masson, reprinted by permission of Farrar, Straus & Giroux, Inc.

Library of Congress Cataloging-in-Publication Data: 88-15845

Kane, Evangeline.
  Recovering from incest.

  1. Incest victims—Mental health. 2. Psychotherapy.
I. Title.
RC560.I53K36 1989 616.85'83 88-15845
ISBN 0-938434-42-X
ISBN 0-938434-43-8 (paperback)

To my daughter, Nicholette, sparkling with life.

TABLE OF CONTENTS

FOREWORD

I was thrown into the most astonishing confusion after receiving the invitation to write a foreword for Evangeline Kane's *Recovering From Incest,* an invitation I greedily accepted in the spirit of an anxious father wanting to tell the world of his new child. While it may be indiscreet to admit publicly, Evangeline will not be surprised if I claim some paternity to this work of hers. However, as is true of most fathers, my contribution over these past years of our work together has been but a fleeting moment compared to the endless hours of torment and struggle, as well as joy and pleasure, that Evangeline Kane has experienced in conceiving and carrying this creation, and now giving it birth.

Like all proud fathers, as I look now upon this most strange yet wonderful book, I'm unexpectedly set to anxious wondering: is this mine? Or is the "real" father elsewhere? To see the work finished, to see just how much of Evangeline's soul and her passion marks these pages, humbles me completely. No, I cannot claim it. Let me be content to proclaim it.

Yet even this has been hard for me. After trying too many hours to find the right words to stand as foreword to the book, nothing would come except despondency at my seeming failure at this task. In the midst of that melancholy mood I dreamed that the foreword had to be written by a woman. Yet, in asking whatever feminine aspect I have available in me to speak, I was greeted only by continuing silence. And as the deadline to sending off these words approached, I felt more and more paralyzed, stupefied, frozen.

And then I understood.

I couldn't speak because I needed to experience something (however minor by comparison) of the silent agony of the many women and children who have suffered the most horrible incestuous and sexual abuse at the hands and bodies of men. I needed to experience something of the experience Evangeline describes so well, where the incest victim's tongue becomes frozen in mute witness to the crimes of failed masculinity. My tongue, even my pen, became ice.

Evangeline has written a work many women will listen to knowingly, as if they had ears in their bones, in their blood. She has written nothing less than a revelation of the failures of the masculine spirit. And what are these failings? A long list. The rape of the feminine body. The rape of the feminine mind. The rape of feminine reality. The rape of the feminine psyche. Yet these rapings are but symptoms of failure; the failure itself is the failed initiation of the masculine spirit. In contrast to many feminist claims, Evangeline rightly and importantly argues that this initiation *cannot be accomplished by women.* Clearly, the answer is not for men to become more feminine, but to become more masculine, more truly and genuinely masculine. That is the task of the fathers among us men, a task we all too often fail now, a task sadly not even *known* as a task among most modern men.

Evangeline's book will appeal quite naturally to women. Unfortunately, most men will turn away from it. How can you ask a man to read such chapters as "The Absence of the Masculine Spirit," "Little Red Riding Hood Cries Tears of Flowers," "Embracing the Good News of the Fish Tail"? How can you ask a man to "fall down and kiss the earth"? What man today knows anything of the "secret of the forest's heart"? Will any man today know of the redemption of the masculine spirit from its "patriarchal lustful snifflings," enabling the perfume of the primal forest to draw out the Beast, the Beast that leaps the borders with "arching and rippling strength" which is not the pseudostrength of the compulsive and brutish rapist, nor the "staggering and arrogant stumbling strut of him whose only tool is the 'weasel word' that sucks life out of Logos," but rather the rush of "savage, bristling potency that is at once profound light and utter blackness" seeking "relief from itself through an objective relationship with the other"?

I doubt many men will know what Evangeline is talking about. I wish

I could challenge them, cajole them to read her words, because I know of no one who has written with a better sense of the character and necessity of masculine eros than she has, even if this was not her intention in this work. So to any man I can say: if you want to know what is wrong with men today, read this book. And to any man I can say: if you want to know what can be right with men, read this book. And to any man I can say, do not be put off by being seen by a woman, but realize deeply that women cannot accomplish what men can only do for themselves. Men must seek their soul *in their own ways.* Women's ways will not do. It's up to us.

As Evangeline makes so clear, the outcome of a man's sexual violence and incestuous abuse is the denial of soul life not only to the victim, but to the victimizer as well, with both becoming mired in frozen fantasies, losing all access to the life and warmth of genuine imagination — that true path to soul that is also the much-needed medicine for relationships between men and women.

I wouldn't ordinarily suggest how to approach a book, but in relation to *this* book I would like to tell Evangeline's readers — particularly the men — *not* to approach it in the usual way, but just to open it at random and *begin,* treating the book as a circle, or even a lake. I did this myself, and came upon that passage in Chapter Three in which Evangeline describes that incredible case of the man who forced his wife to have sex with animals, and if she refused he would shoot them — to end up finally forcing his children to watch his wife help him have oral sex with himself. What I like so much about Evangeline's sensitivity in relationship to these "crude realities" is that she sees through the most obvious pathology to what the psyche is yearning for, even in the most horrific reality. Here a man is desperately trying to connect his feminine aspect with the animals as a step toward union with himself. But, as Evangeline notes, the whole process is lost in literality and acted out externally, thereby crippling the man's wife and children and the discovery of his own soul. Evangeline shows all these images to be absolutely necessary, but necessarily requiring an *imaginal* interiority which, in this particular case and so many others like it, has failed horribly.

Perhaps this is sufficient to quicken the reader's curiosity about what lies ahead in these pages. I hope so. One thing I know for sure: Evangeline's words are psychoactive. Last night, as I tried to finish this foreword, I reread the words in the *Epilogue* and I dreamed a poem, only the first line of which I can now recall. The rest I must seek to recover, but for this hint I thank Evangeline: *The Beast dreams of reality in the*

caverns of the damned.
And to you, dear reader: forward with courage!

Russell Lockhart
Port Townsend, 1989

ACKNOWLEDGEMENTS

I am deeply indebted to Dr. Russell Lockhart who, over recent years, has maintained a quiet and deeply receptive sanctuary in the heart of the forest into which I have stumbled and danced. Here I have been slowly able to gather the courage to find my own voice and my own stance.

I appreciate, beyond the measure of words, all the imaginal journeys of those who have laboured beside me in healing from patriarchal woundings. I am touched daily at their willingness to suffer "the wound" allowing it to transform into a window through which to perceive greater depths of Life's mysteries.

I would also thank Marion Woodman and Dr. Joel Elkes for receiving my work, encouraging me, and suggesting ways to improve on "the vessel." My thanks to Josephine Elkes for sharing with me valuable stories about breastfeeding mothers — stories that were never previously published because of war time conditions. I am also very grateful to Linda Bright for her labour of love in checking references, and to the staff of Sigo Press for the gracious way they have pruned and weeded an overfull flower bed.

Finally, I thank my husband, Franklin, for enriching my life so deeply, bringing reverence and ritual into the mundane details of daily life, as well as for his stalwart courage in living his own masculine mysteries.

Recovering From Incest

CHAPTER I

Soul Abandoned

Introduction

Healing from the effects of incest, sexual abuse and the basic demise of feminine consciousness—all endemic in our society—is the goal of this work. As such it will be an account of the imaginings of the soul arising from an awakening heart. Psychologically speaking, incest occurs when individuals fail to use their imagination for their own creativity, but unwittingly project their images onto others. This imposition can in the more unconscious individual lead to exploitation, abuse and physical incest.

Carl Gustav Jung discovered that loss of imagination and denial of the feeling function are the true result of the abandonment of the incest taboo—a startling and profound conclusion that transforms our understanding of incest in our culture. Despite the obvious physical and emotional pathologies of incest, the victims' imagination suffers, since it too is rooted in the body. Where connection with the body has been lost through trauma, so too has imagination. This causes the victim to retreat into the realm of fantasy, which results in unrelatedness and ironically leaves her open to further exploitation. However, the awakening of the heart allows images to be released that previously have been sealed in a tomb—the heart turned to stone.

* * * * *

During April of 1982, a young girl of twelve in rural Alberta was facing a terrible dilemma. She was being continually sexually assaulted by
her stepfather, and no matter what she did, her mother did not seem
to get the message and take steps to prevent the abuse. The girl tried
running away, she tried stealing money from her stepfather, still no one
knew, no one would guess that her night-times had become living nightmares. The girl was frightened. Things were out of control. She desperately needed friends, but who could possibly understand her with her
terrible secret? One day she was cutting paper and kept the scissors moving into the flesh of her hands until blood was drawn. Her body had
stopped feeling. She had lost any sense of boundaries, and physical pain
was almost a relief.

In complete desperation one day, rather than attend school, she took
one hundred-fifty dollars from her stepfather and went out to buy
presents for her friends. Her mother, puzzled by rebellion in her once
amenable daughter, drove to find her, took her home and instructed
her to wait in her bedroom for her stepfather to come home. The girl
panicked, barricaded the bedroom door, and quietly jumped out into
the deep snow. She made her way to a riverside campground on the
outskirts of the little town, knowing that there she could be alone and
perhaps think clearly.

It was early spring, still bitterly cold, but the river-ice was thawing.
As the girl watched, close to her a chunk of ice broke away and she
stepped back. But then the ice she was standing on cracked away from
the banks, and the girl found herself trapped, barely afloat, and beginning to move downstream to the faster moving water and gathering ice
blocks midstream. The girl knew that to do nothing would mean certain death. There were no more towns she knew of downstream. The
river would flow on across the Canadian tundra and empty itself into
the Arctic Ocean. The girl knew that to do the inevitable was almost
as dangerous. But she jumped in anyway, risking being crushed between
the iceblocks and disappearing into the water. Straining every muscle,
lunging, seared with cold, fighting the numb blackness, she dragged
herself up onto the nearest islet. Her clothes began stiffening into ice.
She shouted for help, but who could hear? A man who had also been
walking around the campground was surprised to hear cries for help.
He spotted the young girl stranded on the island, waving her arms and

shouting. He ran to the first farmhouse and borrowed a canoe, then ran back with it to the river. Very soon he was deftly steering the canoe through the ice.

Even now, long after the incident took place, the girl is still not warm and still does not feel safe. She tells me of the blackness that threatens to encase her with icy fingers if she dares to relax her vigilance for a moment. Her stomach seems to have remained shrunken in fear and pains her. No one will be her friend, she says, though her teachers call her a ringleader. She has developed what doctors call "epilepsy," but she tells me she just hasn't finished shaking with cold. This patient also told a story that she said didn't interest her in the slightest though she had read it five times. It was the story of a blind boy whose dog saved him from the eruption of Vesuvius. The dog had sensed danger, and tugged and cajoled his young charge into movement, and led him away from the molten rock that turned everything in its path to stone. At some level the girl seems to understand that after the shock of her trauma, she has to heed the sensings of her instinctual body (the dog), letting her fear quiver through her being, breaking the icy chill of deadened feelings that threatens to invade her.

This young girl carries the burden of our times, symbolizing the terrified Soul dejected, unheard, contemplating her fate and finding herself adrift and panic stricken, mustering her last ounce of strength to take the plunge, knowing that she must live. But a year later, the young girl disappeared again. Weeks later her unrecognizable body was found and finally identified by an old break in her arm bone. The girl had been murdered. Her body had been dumped outside the city, beside the prison, under a real estate "For Sale" sign. The policeman I talked with could not understand why she had been dragged there, of all places, within view of the large search lights. But she had remained invisible long enough for her body to rot. Victims tend to be revictimized.

This story illustrates the torture and abandonment of young Psyche. At the worst end of this continuum, there are inappropriate sexual acts by one family member against another. Most frequently, we see this in the patriarchal family system. The father, in impotent ploys of abusive power, is dependent upon the young daughter (sometimes as young as two or three years of age) for bearing his soul consciousness, thus robbing her of her childhood and forcing her into a prostitution of herself. The father frequently appears as bristling with autocratic willfulness, often well camouflaged, though in fact he defends both for and against his own hurt inner child. He has lost his own imaginal connection with life. His daughter becomes obliged to carry his fantasy life. The family's feminine element has deteriorated into manipulative, masochistic passivity. The young boys in these troubled families are trapped in the maternal womb with no potent masculine role models. The family vessel is cold and depleted, and individual family members show an absence of personal boundaries and mutual respect.

In the story above, we see a present day enactment of the themes of betrayal and abandonment. In addition to case studies, over the following chapters we will look at the myths which pertain to our themes. Myths enable us to see ourselves in vast archetypal structures from which we may slowly gain some objectivity, as we seek to break away from ancient and destructive patterns and move towards the emergence of our own personal myth.

In Greek mythology, black-winged Night, a goddess of whom even Zeus stood in awe, was courted by the wind and laid a silver egg in the womb of Darkness. Eros hatched from that egg and set the world in motion. Night lived in a cave with her son Eros, and she manifested herself in a triad—Night, Order and Justice. Before the cave sat the inescapable mother Rhea, playing on a bronze drum, and compelling man's attention to the oracle of the goddess. Eros created earth, sky, sun and moon, but the triple goddess ruled the universe until her mantle passed to Uranus.[1]

This is an Orphic creation myth of a time when many believe there was a remarkably homogeneous system of religious ideas throughout much of Europe.[2] It may come as a shock to us that there was a time of goddess worship which lasted five times as long as recorded history. The stones, carvings and statues of this era range anywhere from three to thirty thousand years old; they constitute the earliest form of art known. In the time of the matriarchy, the Mother Goddess was supreme, feared and obeyed by man, who in some sense was her frightened victim. Occasionally she would take him for her own erotic pleasure, not as a father for her children; her impregnation came from elements such as wind and fire. The Mother lived with her son and there seems to be no proof of an adult male god for the son to stand beside.

Into this matriarchal world came the Hellenic Greek invaders. Many scholars have extolled the gifts that this age brought us—gifts of grace and beauty, and profound philosophies. But its shadow side seems to haunt the feminine soul. Uranus, the sky god, was husband of Gaea, the deep-breasted earth mother. Between them they gave birth to the Titans, Cyclopes and monsters, all of whom Uranus hated and banished to the center of Earth Mother's body. Gaea first mourned for her children, then became angry. Drawing a flint sickle from her breast, she gave it to one of her sons, Cronus, telling him to cut off the genitals of Uranus and cast them into the sea. Uranus' blood fell to the earth and gave rise to the Furies; his genitals were thrown into the sea to encourage fish to breed, and Aphrodite the goddess of beauty and sexuality later arose from them. Throughout this book we will focus on Aphrodite/Venus, who emerged from violent beginnings, and whose childhood was lost in a watery world such as the one which threatened my young patient.

The generation after Uranus and Gaea was no better. Recalling what he did to his own father, Cronus feared that his children would usurp his power, so he ate them. His wife, Rhea (who was also his sister), became desperate as one by one her newborns disappeared into the belly of the father. She asked her earth-mother to help her. Gaea, probably recalling her own earlier plight, came up with a scheme to protect Zeus, Rhea's son. Significantly, it is the earthmother who helps protect Zeus, the new father-god of the Greeks. Gaea knows that it is important that the intellectual soul of the patriarchy be ushered into consciousness out of the maternal world. What is now needed is that the individual form an objective relationship to both the maternal and paternal principles in order to release the hurt child from captivity and victimization.

Gaea protected her grandchild by instructing Rhea to wrap a stone in swaddling clothes and present that to Cronus instead of their son. Cronus swallowed the stone, and the child was saved. Rhea had gone to the island of Crete to give birth to Zeus in a cave dedicated to the goddess of childbirth and death. Some say this same cave was used for male initiatory rites, and that the clanging of young men's shields muffled the infant's cries, so that Cronus did not suspect he was being outwitted. The boy has the potential to emerge with a war-cry, yet remain closely connected with the goddess of birth and death. However, this potential rarely flowers. On the one hand there are many aggressive, ithyphallic men in our society, and on the other, all too many who remain mama's boys locked into impotence and timidity. There are few who can retain their grounded potency from within the goddess's dark cave of death and renewal.

Zeus was born to guard the sanctity of marriage, yet he never tired of pursuing and raping virgins. He also disposed of his father. His erotic adventures, like those of other Greek heroes, seem to have been political and religious in design. He was appropriating pre-Hellenic local moon goddesses and their priestesses by violating their sanctuaries with his rapine authority. Women gradually lost their full power and became chattels. The only significant thing left for them was prophesy—and we shall see later that the power of prophesying is heightened and distorted by sexual abuse and subsequent denial of the body. Zeus' wife Hera is frequently described as a nag, as bitter and as exhibiting conservative religious feeling. Yet surely this is understandable when we consider that what had been severely tampered with was her right to choose her own lover, her spiritual freedom, and her own connection with her children.

The next generation of children gave rise to increased psychological complexity. Hera reverted to earlier custom, according to some, and produced Hephaestos parthenogenetically[3]—that is, without male help. Zeus was so enraged by Hera's independent birthing of Hephaestos that he determined to follow suit. To balance the matriarchal son, he took a secret love—Metis (meaning "counsel"), daughter of Oceanus. He had first met her when he wanted advice on how to release his siblings from his father's fearful belly. She had suggested the use of an emetic to be added to Cronus' honeyed drink, and that Zeus should be the old man's cup bearer.

We learn that Zeus lusted after Metis, and that to avoid him she kept changing forms, though finally he impregnated her. Zeus had been warned that Metis would produce wise children. Since Zeus had no desire of being supplanted by a son, one day, as she sat beside him enchanted by his honeyed words, he opened his mouth and swallowed her. Zeus did not merely banish his children as had his father and grandfather. He also devoured mother counsel to save his own position of power, though later he conceded to listening to her counsel from the inside. Walking by a mountain peak, Zeus suffered great headaches on account of his devoured feminine counsel. Finally Hephaestos was asked by Hermes to intervene. Using a wedge and beetle, Hephaestos opened Zeus' skull and Athena, fully armed, sprang out with a war-cry. A girl child was not as threatening to Zeus.

Where Hera relied on the old form of parthenogenesis, Zeus moved to a new parthenogenesis of violent and unnatural birth. In neither case was there cooperation between the parents. Athena and Hera were constant enemies, and conflict between Zeus and Hephaestos regularly flared. In the absence of a sacred marriage between husband and wife, there can be no profound bond between father and son, or mother and daughter.

Athena became Zeus' mouthpiece—his complement, not his rival.

She was the Goddess of the Law Courts. Remaining a virgin, she participated in war because it was man's activity and would encourage the Greek heroes to superhuman feats. In her temple she employed only priests, not priestesses. She is seen as the birth of man's anima, a man's inner feminine principle released from its regressive mother roots.[4] The birth of Athena is an important turning point in human consciousness. In many ways she has become the most revered feminine archetype in our culture, aligned with the father's world but unfortunately oblivious of her own history.

At one time Athena was also called Medusa or Metis, and was served by priestesses in her temple. Each priestess wore a goat's shield, or Aegis, ornamented with the oracular serpents which served as aprons and chastity belts. The Aegis was considered a badge of divine power. Death was the punishment for a Libyan man who removed the Aegis without its owner's consent.

Athena rejected the Medusa principle in Greek times. The story goes that the banishment and degradation that Medusa represents in mythology was brought about when she dared to make love to Poseidon in Athena's temple. True to form, Athena did not punish Poseidon. Medusa's action might be looked at as a very progressive move to integrate the forces of the unconscious with spirituality and Logos. However, Athena, in her over-identification with her father, dealt with Medusa's integrative action in a manner that is often reenacted by present day Athenas when they become alienated from their body, their sexuality, and their mothers—that is, banishing them to the realms of the unconscious, preferring to live over-intellectualized lives reflecting the chauvinism that dominates their milieu.

Thus we see the Greek, patriarchal archetypal family as incestuous and not united by the sacred marriage of masculine and feminine, or culture and nature. We see the rape of the feminine, the devouring of the mother wisdom and the disruption of the mother-daughter bond. Susan Griffin, author of *Pornography and Silence: Culture's Revenge,* suggests that it is the chauvinist mind that must separate nature and culture. Human reason must control lust: men own the head realm and women the body realm. The chauvinist mind, in man or woman, can be seen as senex logic (the logic of old patriarchal man) controlling woman's body, which becomes mindless and submissive.

To teach and speak with psyche's voluptuous passion is generally not a quality of the intruding and undifferentiated senex/puer (old man/boy) archetype. Perhaps the best way to help others learn may be by displaying the "raw chunks of one's developing understanding, with all their sloppy edges dangling and all the ego-danger this involves."[5] Such a teacher is still within a learning process herself—there is thus more likelihood of a mind-body-soul connection left intact. As Rachel Carson wrote in the preface to her book *The Edge of the Sea* (1955),

> To understand the shore, it is not enough to catalogue its life. Understanding comes only when, standing on the beach, we can sense the long rhythms of earth and sea that sculptured its land forms and produced the rock and sand of which it is composed; when we can sense with the eye and ear of the mind the surge of life beating at its shores. It is not enough to pick up an empty shell and say "This is a murex" and "that is an angel wing." True understanding demands intuitive comprehension of the whole life of the creature that once inhabited the empty shell.[6]

C.G. Jung explains the value, among primitive peoples, of the many rituals surrounding the separation of the son from complete dependence on only mother/wisdom and his move into masculine consciousness through impressive initiations in the "men's house" and ceremonies of rebirth. The son, at this time, receives instruction about those things which threaten from the dark side of consciousness, from which the mother normally protects him.

> Because the mother is the first bearer of the soul image, separation from her is a delicate and important matter of the greatest educational significance.[7]

He is then in a position of being less psychologically dependent on mother's protection. Civilized man has had to forego this initiation, and thus his anima can be transferred (unconsciously, of course) to any situation that betokens the dark aspects of the psyche. The undifferentiated old man/boy, as well as the trapped virgin, will then tend to thrash out against the unknown with too much logic, order and light because there are no sacred rituals involved in leaving the mother-son symbiosis. The result is a proliferation of concepts wrested away from mother wisdom, and the loss of culture. As a latter-day substitute for rites of separation, education becomes both petrified and abusive in its never-ending thrust for mere clarity. In matriarchal times, education from books and letters was not separated from charm, mystery, images, bodily nourishment, nor from death. Returning scholarship to the realm of culture involves a return to the oceanic motherhouse of wisdom, to revalue her and relieve ourselves of the compulsion to both thrust away from and dominate her.

In *Centuries of Childhood,* Philippe Aries has suggested that until the end of the middle ages the weaned child was considered to be merely a small adult. And although the twentieth-century work of such psychologists as Piaget and Bruner has alerted us to how different child and adult worldviews are, it appears as if our society has, in fact, not made a conscious step in seeing that difference. The result is that the very concept of childhood, to say nothing of the child, is in danger of disappearing. David Elkind has made impassioned pleas for us to look seriously at this phenomenon—how we hurry children relentlessly, and force them into our conceptual straitjackets. I often hear, in the course of my work, how beneficial it can be for some young incest victims to testify against their assailants in the court room. I have yet to hear anyone talk about the shadow side of articulation under spotlights, at so young an age. What effect does this have on the child? The cruelty of incest is often alarmingly present in the courts, whose true function ought to be securing justice for incest victims. Lawyers defending those accused of incest have used many tactics to question the credibility of the victim's testimony. There has been at least one bar group sponsoring a training seminar on how to undermine young witnesses. "The message: intimidate, mock or confuse the child who, for the moment, is an enemy."[8] This is a horrendous experience that adds to the problem the victimized child already has about trusting his or her own senses and his or her own truth.

Children being used as bait by both parents and lawyers is another way in which the child, and his or her developmental needs, is victimized. A lawyer once suggested replacing a five year old child in the abusive situation to see if it would happen again, in order to obtain even clearer legal documentation of the abuse.

Many of our children are forced to abandon childhood prematurely. A report from Washington says that one hundred and seventy million of the world's children are "unwillingly" or "unwittingly" involved in child prostitution, trafficking and pornography. Examples are drawn from Melbourne, Australia, where Filipino boys are imported; from Amsterdam, where children are bought and sold in auctions; from West Germany, the Netherlands, Japan and the U.S., where child "sex tours" are organized to visit Sri Lanka, Thailand, and the Philippines.[9] Adult sexual needs are forced onto children, often with a highly organized efficiency.

Precocious sexual activity seems to result in never-fully attained adulthood. It is significant to note that the Greek goddesses generally appear in maiden form, and thus leave us bereft of any images of the holy girl child. Athena appeared as a fully armed warrioress. And we are told nothing about Aphrodite's struggle at the bottom of the sea to release herself from the straitjacket of Uranus' disembodied phallus. Traditionally we only meet her as she emerges from the sea, radiant and fully grown.

Hillman writes that "Freud's fantasy of the little girl's mind becomes a Freudian fantasy in the little girl's mind."[10] The Freudian fantasy is that children are sexual in a genital, adult, erotic sense. In my experience, this is a surprisingly widespread belief—particularly among schooled male professionals whose contact with real children is limited. This act of imposing adult sexuality onto the child can be done in remarkably subtle ways. For instance, in a recent T.V. advertisement for diapers, it is the father's finger that is inserted into the diaper to test for wetness, and the father's voice used at that moment. The rest of the advertisement uses a woman's voice. All this can be rationalized extremely well through reference to the new "androgynous childrearing." The trouble for me is that I know many situations where child abuse started with the compulsive applications of cream to the girl child's genitals. I also recall an offender being asked why he abused his child. His reply was, "Well, what do you expect, she was running around with her diapers hanging off."

Another glossy advertisement asks, "Do you know who your daughter is sleeping with tonight?" The picture shows a little girl hugging her teddy bear. Thus children become sex-objects, linked to the acquisition of money and commodities, and child pornography becomes acceptable.

The loss of the child parallels the cultural loss of heart and wholeness, and thus in the pornographic mind the child must be sacrificed. The real child remains locked in the earth, like earth mother Gaea's first children and like Medusa banished from human consciousness by the overly brittle intellectual soul that must forever separate the body from true culture.

* * * * *

Property, Money, War, and the Feminine

Associated with the early rise of masculine power, patriarchal society, and the male priesthood was the accumulation of personal rather than communal property.[11] Woman too became seen as man's property.

Ancient Hebrew law, for instance, viewed rape as a property crime of man against man.[12] Criminal rape, as a patriarchal father saw it, was a violation of the new way of doing business. It was, in a phrase, the theft of virginity, an embezzlement of his daughter's fair price on the market. Even today it is often the male relatives of rape victims who speak of being most upset and incensed by their property being violated. Frequently their outrage is most upsetting to the woman, who is characteristically unable to express a justified and healing anger towards her assailant.

The scientific revolution further undermined the organic cosmology of the female earth, and was paralleled by a market-oriented culture in early modern Europe.[13] Gradually Mother Earth was conceived of as "passive and docile, allowing all manner of assault, violence, ill-treatment, rape by lust, and despoilment by greed." And "digging into the matrices and pockets of earth for metals was like mining the female flesh for pleasure."[14]

Walter Ben Michaels makes an important point by saying that an increased investment in personal autonomy will naturally be accompanied by an increased insecurity about the status of that autonomy; a self that can be owned can also be stolen away or gambled. Seeing ourselves through the window of a "market economy"—owning or being owned— can be considered as the root of pornographic sadomasochism.[15] Unless the ego can be relativized by a healthy immersion in Self, one will live in a constant state of insecurity and threat of power battles.

Gradually, as mass-produced goods replaced homemade ones, women's domestic production lost its commercial value. Men left farms to work in offices and factories and women were advised to concentrate on mothering. Housework became a science and the domestic sphere became a sacred calling.

Paradoxically, as interaction with real matter became less and less, more and more was said about its "sacredness." Mother was both more imbued with superhuman powers, and more blamed for causing all our ills.

Money

Both the very rich and very poor find it difficult to value true exchange, and thus to understand money's connection with transformation. Hillman calls money the ultimate taboo. He refers to a survey of analysts regarding what they feel they must never do with a patient.[16] It was discovered that touching and holding, shouting and hitting, drinking, kissing, nudity and intercourse were all less prohibited than lending money to a patient. Yet where women work with women, money is often given away—for gas money, bus fare to come to the clinic, to help offset a stolen purse, and so on. There is something so different in the feeling tone of these gestures of giving, as compared with that of a comment from the head of the government agency that evaluates a program in my area. He said, "We want the biggest bang for our buck." Both feeling-toned statements tend to polarize and constellate each other. Both display a certain naivete about the place of money in the realm of psyche. Indeed, I find that as women individuate, the aligning of money with psyche becomes an essential task.

Early gold and silver coins were minted in the Roman temple of the Great Mother Goddess, Juno Moneta. Her coins were valuable not only because they were of precious metal, but because they had been blessed by the Goddess herself, and could thus effect healing.[17] Coined money is a highly cultural phenomenon. It came into history with the Greeks and belongs to the muses of imagination, and to the devil when the imagination is not valued (as in Christianity).[18] The problem with money is that it has been severed from the gods and goddesses from which it came. Again we are back to the ocean with Medusa, the banished dark feminine. James Hillman writes that

> ...money is as deep and as broad as the ocean, the primordially unconscious, and makes us so. It always takes us into great depths, where sharks and suckers, hard shell crabs, tight clams and tidal emotions abound. Its facts have huge horizons, as huge as sex, and just as protean and polymorphous.[19]

War

It is impossible to discuss the patriarchal treatment of women, and of the feminine in general, without taking modern-day warfare into consideration; like the realm of money and property, the realm of war is emblematic of the wholesale degradation of the archetypal feminine (and by consequence, often of actual women as well) that characterizes our psychically one-sided culture. It is certainly true that among certain Celtic and Germanic tribes women fought in wars alongside men, and also that prehistoric war-gods were often female. But the very nature of modern war and of the modern patriarchy makes any comparison with archaic warfare fatuous.

Like incest, war is a symptom of undifferentiated, incomplete masculinity; its violence is the product of inner fear much more than it is of any external threat, however "rationally" evaluated.

The life/death battle, when seen consciously, is ultimately in the service of life renewal. Violence, as archetypal energy, can spontaneously arise when rebirth is called for in an erstwhile stagnant situation. There was a time when life-renewal could have been a realistic, albeit semiconscious objective. When aggression and violence served the greater glory of emperor, church or fatherland, they were integrated into a moral and ethical system. Even warfare had its rules and rituals where pockets of compassion were sacrosanct. Of course, terribly barbaric acts can be committed for some ideal when ritual is desacralized. But these are gentle ripples compared with what we are now capable of. The "motherland" and "fatherland" can increasingly be only inner archetypes whose recognition necessitates looking at the images of war that overshadow our world. Violence has not only its own terror, but its own fascination. It is a profoundly moving experience, and one that is closely linked with sexuality and creativity. In fact, aggressive and sexual or erotic pathways are interlinked in the lower brain stem. Soldiers and criminals have been observed to have seminal emissions at the moment of inflicting or suffering death.

The male anguish about defeat in war is partially over the rape of their own women, their property, by the invading army. For instance, in 1937 the invading Japanese committed an estimated twenty thousand rapes within the first month of their occupation of Nanking; in 1971 Pakistani troops raped anywhere between twenty and forty thousand Bengali women. The Germans raped Jews and Russians; the Russians in turn raped German women.[20] And American servicemen raped Vietnamese women. It is hardly surprising that the raping animus is such a feature of women's early therapy dreams. Collective norms become quietly ingested. However, they cannot be dismissed collectively. We must deal with actual wounds of individual women in order to first connect with soul and then to see the release of potent spirit, the logos of meaning, from the wounded masculine.

Certainly in our modern warfare there is virtually no face-to-face encounter. Missiles can be launched from an underground control room by pressing a button. This is a most graphic picture of the masculine whose Eros feeling functions like that of a child, "whose organism sleepily or tyrannically flourishes"[21] from the underground matriarchal control room. It is important to see the Holocaust not as an event in the past, but as a dynamic in our daily lives. The image of the raping, brutalizing Nazi certainly lives in the souls of most hurt women with whom I work.

Hitler placed tremendous emphasis on the will to patriarchal power, another boy-Eros tyrannically flourishing in the maternal embrace — mama's loyal son, but with rage. He never grows up. We know too, that Hitler was repeatedly and severely beaten by his father; later, he saw the masses as being feminine and crying out for fatherly authority.[22] Yet Hitler also thought that Nature gave him her orders. Though afraid of women, he would ask prostitutes to tie him up and beat him. There are other sources which claim that Hitler demanded lovers to humiliate him by urinating on him.[23] Thus he continued to hate women and exploit and undermine the Feminine. Nazi propaganda accentuated feelings of heroism and attempted to uplift the masses from mother earth so that eventually illusions replaced perceptions.[24]

Dr. Sam Janus of New York has published a seven-year study of "high class" call girls and prostitutes.[25] The majority of the customers are politicians or top executives who may pay up to ten thousand dollars a year on prostitutes — who themselves are paid to dupe the men into believing that they are proving their masculinity through sexual performance. Many clients asked to be bound and flagellated, feeling that the need to be hurt is atonement for their compulsive sexual needs. One highly placed politician could only have sex after his arms and legs were bound into the shape of a cross.

Hitler's description of the Jews as a virus — contagion, plague, pestilence, poisoning — against which he and others of the pure race had to defend at all costs is an apt metaphor for the incestuous family situation, where anything new is perceived as virulent and must be excluded. The outer conglomerate throng is always perceived by the patriarchal authority with heavy emotional judgments. This authority does not recognize that it is denying its own dark body reality. And in truth the fundamental incestuous situation is always an archetypal potential in the patriarchal family.

In an article in *Esquire* (December 1984), William Broyles, a Vietnam veteran, explains men's hate/love relationship with war. He states first that the veterans had no way to tell anyone about their experience, not only because of shame but because

the language failed them: the civilian-issue adjectives and nouns, verbs and adverbs, seemed made for a different universe. There were no metaphors that connected the war to everyday life.[26]

The shame had to do with the possibility of loving war. To admit doing this would be to mock the values one was supposedly fighting for.

It would mean admitting being an insensitive brute. The patriarchal world cannot allow this sort of honesty.

Broyles spends the rest of the article trying to make meaning of the fact that—although he had not fought since grade school, was not a hunter, and had seen enough of war to know that he wants neither himself nor his children to ever be involved in it—at the oddest times he finds himself pulled back to the war he never believed in nor wanted to fight. He misses and he also loves the war for complex and contradictory reasons. It was, first of all, an experience of great intensity, and provided much opportunity for "the fundamental human passion to witness"—the marines called it "eye-fucking." Interestingly, *testis* means "to witness," and such an activity is necessary, in a sacred sense, as initiation into manhood. The beauty they witnessed was often so intense—"divorced from all civilian values, but beauty still."

Broyles tells us that war removed the "fear of freedom, and like a stern father, gave both the security of 'order and discipline' and the irresistible urge to rebel against it." The fear of isolation was the greatest fear of all—"a terrifying prelude to the final loneliness of death." The bond that developed with fellow soldiers as a result of this fear was, in fact, "brotherly love" and it could give rise to deeds of classical heroism. The duties of "ordinary life" tended to disappear: there were many excellent warriors who had little adaptation to civilian life.

And finally, war heightens sexuality and cloaks men under "a collective power, an almost animal force." Sex becomes "the weapon of life. War thrusts you into the well of loneliness, death breathing in your ear. Sex is a grappling hook that pulls you out, ends your isolation, makes you one with life again."

At the beginning, Broyles had *War and Peace* and *The Charterhouse of Parma* stuffed in his pack. They were soon replaced by the *Story of O.* This is the story of a beautiful woman, a fashion photographer, slowly unlearning the knowledge of her body, supposedly for the man she loves. In the last scene she appears in an owl mask, her humanness unrecognizable. No one speaks to her, but they form a silent circle around her, staring, "threatening her like a real bird, deaf to human language, dumb." She has become nature, entirely separate from any civility. She has become the jailed bird.

Broyles said that it was in sex even more than in killing that he could see the beast, crouched, drooling on its haunches, mocking him for his frailties, knowing he hated them himself, but that he couldn't get enough and that he would keep coming back again and again.

Then Broyles tells of a beautiful orphaned Vietnamese girl with whom he fell in love. He says he wanted her desperately but her tenderness and vulnerability, the torn flower of her beauty, frustrated his death-obsessed lust. He didn't see her as one Vietnamese. He saw her as all Vietnamese. She was the suffering soul of war, and he was the soldier who had wounded it but would make it whole. However, like her former lover, he also abandoned her. Yet, some fifteen years later she and the war are still on his mind, leading him back through the hundreds of labyrinths to the essential truth that the power of war and the power of love, alike, spring from the heart of the individual.

It seems that war is one of the few experiences that provides the patriarchal man an opportunity of finding his roots in the blood of the earth, where language once again becomes "all darkness humming with portent."[27] But without sacred ritual, the warrior is merely a murderer. In being unable to face and combat the inner beast, he subjugates the feminine with his death-obsessed lust, pushing her into the world of nature devoid of cultivation. The suffering soul of war is there to remind us that the battleground can now only be on the inside. Any future war threatens to destroy all boundaries for ever.

Living with and relating to our images requires new forms of discipline, with their own rigorous and ethical demands, so that the traumatized soul's jungle of complexity and horror may become exactly the place where individuation may begin and our own myth emerge. The suffering soul of war beckons us to connect with Eros.

Notes

[1]Robert Graves. *The Greek Myths,* Vol. 1. Harmondsworth: Penguin Books, Ltd., 1983, section 26
For an excellent explication of the role of Greek mythology in the realm of contemporary psychology, see James Hillman's *Revisioning Psychology,* especially p. 27.

[2]*Ibid.,* p. 13

[3]John Layard. *A Celtic Quest.* Appendix II, "Anima and Animus." Dallas: Spring Publications, 1985, Appendix II, p. 211

[4]*Ibid.,* pp. 211-222

[5]Michael Rossman. *On Learning Social Change.* New York: Vintage Books, 1972, p. 66

[6]Rachel Carson. *The Edge of the Sea.* Boston: Houghton-Mifflin, 1979.

[7]C. G. Jung. *CW* VII, par. 314

[8]"The Youngest Witness." *Newsweek,* February 18, 1985

[9]Garry Trudeau. "Child Sex Trade Big Business," *Edmonton Journal,* November 24, 1984

[10]James Hillman. *The Myth of Analysis.* New York: Harper & Row, 1978, p. 243

[11]Esther Harding. *Woman's Mysteries.* New York: Harper & Row, 1976, p. 31

[12]Susan Brownmiller. *Against Our Will: Men, Women and Rape.* New York: Simon & Schuster, 1975, pp. 8-9

[13]Carolyn Merchant. *The Death of Nature: Women, Ecology, and the Scientific Revolution.* San Francisco: Harper & Row, 1983, p.xvi

[14]*Ibid.,* pp. 39, 41

[15]Walter Ben Michaels. "Masochism, Money & McTeague." In *The Threepenny Review,* No. 16, Winter, 1984

[16]Russell Lockhart, James Hillman, *et al. Soul and Money.* Dallas: Spring Publications, 1982, p.37

[17]Barbara Walter. *The Women's Encyclopaedia of Myths and Secrets.* San Francisco: Harper & Row, 1983, p.667

[18]James Hillman. *Soul and Money.* Dallas: Spring Publications, 1982, p. 40

[19]*Ibid,* p. 36.

[20]Susan Brownmiller, *op. cit.,* p. 31

[21]Bradley TePaske. *Rape and Ritual: A Psychological Study.* Toronto: Inner City Books, 1982, p.74

[22]Susan Griffin. *Pornography and Silence.* New York: Harper & Row, 1982, pp. 156-199

[23]*Ibid.,* p. 177

[24]*Ibid.,* pp. 156-199
Hitler's first task on entering the German Workers' Party was to take over the management of propaganda, which allowed the German masses an opportunity to live in a cultural fantasy. His speeches, "his high point of fulfillment and happiness," swept impressionable listeners off their feet and allowed them to feel heroic. People were told, nonsensically, that war was made for peace and pain was sought for pleasure. This is another example of the distortion of the logos principle that pervades a patriarchal society.

[25]Matthew Fox. *Compassion.* Minneapolis: Winston Press, 1979, pp. 64-65

[26]William Broyles. "Why Men Love War," *Esquire Magazine,* December 1984

[27]C. G. Jung *Speaking: Interviews & Encounters.* William McGuire and R.F.C. Hull, eds. Princeton: Princeton University Press, 1977, p. 189
Jung equates the joy of imminent massacre, seen in trains full of soldiers leaving for the front in 1914, with the joy of finally achieving union with blood and death, i.e., the unconscious.

CHAPTER II

Psychotherapy and Incest

In his book *The Assault on Truth*, Jeffrey Masson explored the controversial question of why Freud abandoned his initial theory on the actual sexual abuse of many of his patients (male and female) during childhood, and that this trauma was the cause of their hysteria and other psychological problems. Masson's research in the Freud archives led him to conclude that Freud changed his mind through a "loss of courage," and then went on to develop "psychoanalysis as a science, a therapy and a profession."[1] In place of his seduction theory, Freud claimed something entirely different, what has been called "the more basic truth of the power of internal fantasy, and of spontaneous childhood sexuality."[2] According to Masson, Freud's abandonment of the seduction theory was camouflaged by later analysts in order to protect readers from Freud's early doubts and hesitations.

Masson raises issues that are critical for our discussion. In abandoning the seduction theory, Freud made a profound shift away from his view that neuroses can be the result of sexual abuse and exploitation. Children became not innocent victims of abuse, but precocious sexual beings capable of indulging in sexual fantasies. Abandoning the theory, Freud also abandoned the victims of childhood seduction. Using Masson's work as a point of departure, I will address two main issues, the differentiation of fantasy and imagination, and the value of death and disintegration in the healing process.

The Differentiation of Fantasy and Imagination

Freud's Theory of Seduction and Its Abandonment

Freud started his discussion on the etiology of hysteria not by following Charcot, who believed that heredity alone caused hysteria, but by building on Breuer's "momentous discovery" that

The symptoms of hysteria (apart from the stigmata) are determined by certain experiences of the patient's which have operated in a traumatic fashion and which are reproduced in his psychic life in the form of mnemic [memory] symbols.[3]

Freud added that he was

inclined to suppose that children cannot find their way to acts of sexual aggression unless they have been previously seduced. The foundation for a neurosis would accordingly always be laid in childhood by adults.[4]

Even at this time, Freud thought his listeners would be disinclined to appreciate the "powers emanating from a mnemic image which was absent from the real impression."[5] Early in his career he was clearly supportive of the hysteric, saying that his or her reaction is only *apparently* exaggerated; "it is bound to appear exaggerated to us because we only know a small part of the motives from which it arises."[6] He also clearly realized that the child in an incestuous situation was always physically and psychologically in a tragic and grotesquely imbalanced state.

Freud listed all the reasons to believe that the patients had in fact been abused — they were reluctant and distressed at discussing the abuse; recalling the event, they experienced violent sensations of which they were ashamed and tried to cover; there was a uniformity of certain details; they described as harmless events whose significance they did not understand, or mentioned details without stressing them; information on the abuse was often like the last piece of the jigsaw puzzle in pulling together a case history; and finally, the abuse could sometimes be confirmed by others.[7]

Freud reported that the presentation of his paper *The Aetiology of Hysteria* met with an "icy reception," and that Krafft-Ebing (distinguished professor and head of the Department of Psychiatry at the University of Vienna) commented that "It sounded like a scientific fairy tale."[8] Freud defiantly declared that his colleagues could all "go to hell"; he would maintain his views.

However, in 1905 Freud publicly retracted the original seduction theory, and this opened the way for the formulation of Freudian psychoanalysis. The standard explanation for this shift has been that clinical research led Freud to conclude that he had made a mistake. And ever since, Freudian psychoanalysts have been told to believe that patients' so-called memories are lies — though Freud never actually used that word. Freud said that he was "at last obliged to recognize that these scenes of seduction had never taken place, and that they were only fantasies which [his] patients had made up,"[9] and which often dominated a woman's life thereafter. He elaborated that these fantasies of the father seducing the daughter in childhood were the daughter's attempt to hide or repress the infantile sexual activity of masturbating. The "grain of truth in the fantasy," according to Freud, was that the father's "innocent caresses" had unwittingly "awakened the little girl's sexuality" (the same dynamic applies to the little boy and his mother) and these "same affectionate fathers" would then endeavor to break the child of the habit of masturbating.[10] Furthermore, Freud dismissed adults' violence towards children and replaced it with the idea that "children had aggressive impulses against their parents;" and thus he drew near to the Oedipus complex. Masson suggests that if children had been abused, then aggressive impulses would have been a healthy sign of protest. He continues that

It was not only the aggressive acts of a parent that were attributed to the fantasy life of a child; now aggressive impulses too were the products of the child's *imagination*.[11] [Emphasis added]

In taking this step, Freud seems to have fictionalized certain facts about the abuse of children, and childhood traumas were said to have been invented by young women to postpone adolescence, as well as to repress childhood masturbation. Sexual abuse by the father became labeled as an excess of parental affection which later caused harm because the child could not cope with the loss of love. Love and abuse had been perversely twisted. If the basic view of the analyst is that women lie, then the patient would be placed in a double bind. In order to claim any feeling of acceptance, she would have to lie in order not to lie in the analyst's frame of reference. Again the woman would be having her truth fictionalized, and this could only add to her rage. The victim would somehow get the feeling that "it's happening all over again" (that is, her reality is being denied, again) but she would probably be unable to articulate exactly what was going on.

Certainly, it was not only women's and girls' traumas that were disregarded or ignored. Masson reports on Ruth Mack Brunswick's reanalysis of "Wolf Man" (at Freud's request)—one of Freud's most famous later case studies. She had been astonished to learn that as a child Wolf Man had been anally raped by a family member and that Freud had not known this.[12] Freud wrote that the Wolf Man suffered from the delusion that the great Paul Flechsig wanted to castrate him. Masson maintains that Freud knew that castrations were performed by Flechsig on hysterical and obsessional patients in the very asylum where the Wolf Man was held.[13]

In response to Masson's suggestion that Freud was wrong to abandon the seduction hypothesis, Anna Freud wrote him (Sept. 10, 1981) that

> Keeping up the seduction theory would mean to abandon the Oedipus complex, and with it the whole importance of phantasy life, conscious or unconscious phantasy. In fact, there would have been no psychoanalysis afterwards.[14]

Masson's work centers on the Freud/Fliess relationship and their relationship to a mutual patient, Emma Eckstein, who had been sexually abused as a child. Masson attempted to show that this case was influential in Freud's major decision at this point in his life. Masson also maintained that up to the end of his life Freud had never been entirely convinced he had made the right decision.

Ferenczi's Confusion of Tongues

Masson devotes a chapter to Ferenczi's last paper, "Confusion of Tongues," an impassioned defense of the abused child. For more than twenty years Ferenczi had been Freud's closest analytic colleague (Freud often addressed him as "dear son").[15]

However, as a result of failure in his clinical practice, Ferenczi began to believe more and more strongly that the "source of neurosis lay in sexual seductions suffered by children at the hands of those closest to them." Ferenczi's paper bore a strong similarity to Freud's *Aetiology of Hysteria*, though Ferenczi's paper has some important new insights. However, the response to it was also uniformly negative.[16]

Ferenczi explained that the child's desire for tenderness can be exploited by an adult's need for sexual gratification at any price; if this abuse occurs, the child becomes paralyzed by fear. For Ferenczi it is clear that seduction is hatred, not love, and that the love/hate split is still foreign to the child's consciousness.[17] The child brings to bear in the traumatic situation a "pathogenic defense mechanism" that Ferenczi was the first to name—"identification with the aggressor." The aggressor disappears as external reality and becomes intrapsychic instead of extrapsychic.

The intrapsychic phenomenon can be shaped into positive or negative hallucinations, and through the trance-like state the child maintains his pre-incestuous trust at the expense of trusting his own senses and losing his hold on reality. In addition, the child as victim takes on the parent's guilt, because no one else in the family will, and so the child is "already split—innocent and guilty at the same time."[18] Furthermore, the adult frequently becomes harsh after his abuse of the child, and plagued by remorse and anger, which is projected onto the child—who becomes even more confused. Not infrequently, the aggressor becomes overly moralistic or religious after the event. Ferenczi says that generally the child's relationship with another trusted person, such as the mother, is "not intimate enough to provide help."[19] The child becomes mechanically obedient (or deviant) without knowing why.

At the end of the paper (presented at the International Psycho-Analytic Congress, Wiesbaden, Sept. 1932), Ferenczi reserved for further investigation how much sado-masochism in the sexuality of our time is determined by culture, and how much develops spontaneously as an independent phase of development. Ferenczi responded to a patient's questions about why she cannot remember being raped, though she dreams of it constantly, with the following (July 30, 1932):

> I know from other analyses that part of our being can "die" and while the remaining part of our self may survive the trauma, it awakens with a gap in its memory. Actually it is a gap in the personality, because not only is the memory of the *struggle-to-the-death* effaced, but all other associatively linked memories disappear...perhaps forever.[20] [Emphasis added]

This appears to be true for those who have been sexually abused. Certainly it often takes months for repressed contents to surface, and when they do the patient has the opportunity of integrating new material into consciousness. It is my opinion that women can dream of being raped

yet may never have in fact never been physically raped or genitally abused
as children or at any other time in their lives. Such dreams are unconscious expressions of fear and anger toward the raping patriarchal values
and practices of our society, emotions of which we may be totally unaware in our conscious minds. Indeed, these raping values and associated archetypal images can impinge on a soul even in therapy, or whenever
one's personal truth is negated.

Function and Fantasy

The Gray-Wheelwright Personality Type Test is based on Jung's description of the four functions in his theory of typology. Of the four functions, two are rational (i.e., thinking and feeling) and two are irrational
(i.e., sensation and intuition); these functions constitute one way of referring to the structure of the personality. This test was administered to
twenty-four female victims of sexual abuse as children and/or rape as
adults. With the exception of two women, every woman's primary function was found to be on the "irrational" axis. That is, her primary mode
of functioning would be through the senses, either directly through "sense
data" or via the unconscious. My impression at this point, though still
very tentative, is that the more severely abused the woman, the more
highly intuitive she becomes, and the more fantastic her symbols and
visions. Non-genitally abused women may have a high intuitive score
but may not be given over to fantastic visions in the same way as those
who had been genitally abused. This would throw light on their difficulties with reality orientation and the frequently bizarre images and symbols with which we start work. It is as though the wound in the victim's
"ego body" is so deep and profound that the unconscious pours through
it. But it is contaminated, as it were, by the personal unconscious and
is therefore not to be trusted in the sense of being a definitive statement.

In addition, because the rational feeling and thinking functions are
not well developed, the victim has no way to mediate or value her outpourings. They simply tear her apart again, or lead her into the wilds
of fantasy. The abused woman's inferior function is often deeply buried
in the unconscious. It would also explain why during truly integrative
therapy the woman will frequently experience violent sensations—
shaking, nausea, even urination—as her inferior sensation function comes
into play.

In 1932 Ferenczi said "we often speak of a split personality, but we
do not seem to appreciate sufficiently the depth of the split."[21] Indeed
there is evidence to suggest that a large percentage of so called "split

personalities" are victims of sexual abuse[22]: there are no mediating possibilities as yet within the wounded soul. Where Freud concentrated on hysteria, Jung concentrated on schizophrenia and laid down a conceptual framework that promised some hope of treatment. He urged us not to foster an ego that is rigid and defensive against intrusion by other archetypal potentials. Many sexually violated patients, however, have egos so rigid as to appear almost nonexistent. And although therapy must involve some aspect of ego strengthening to stand strong in the face of the flood from the unconscious, these patients offer a most profound opportunity to witness the healing potential of the many-sided personality, and the sterility of society's rigid insistence on egocentric values. The challenge of the therapist is to trust the individual's psychic leads and follow them, believing in the objective psyche's balancing potential. If the therapist has not experienced this within herself, she will always tend to subvert the other's journey.

Working with the hurt, repressed feminine, it becomes essential to distinguish *fantastica* from true imagination, a distinction that Jung also found in the alchemical text *Rosarium Philosophorum* (1550):

> . . .And take care that thy door be well and firmly closed so that he who is within cannot escape, and — God willing — thou wilt reach the goal. Nature performeth her operations gradually, and indeed I would have thee do the same; let thy imagination be guided wholly by nature. And observe according to nature, through whom the substances regenerate themselves in the bowels of the earth. *And imagine this with true and not with fantastic imagination.*[23] [Emphasis added]

The imagination is the real and literal power of soul to create images — compared with fantasy, which means a mere conceit, something ridiculous and insubstantial. Imagination is the

> . . .*active* [emphasis added] evocation of (inner) images *secundum naturam,* an authentic feat of thought or ideation, which does not spin aimless and groundless fantasies into the blue — does not, that is to say, just play with its objects, but tries to grasp the inner facts and portray them in images true to their nature. This activity is an *opus,* a work.[24]

Overly developed intuition pertains only to the realm of fantasy. It is ungrounded because it lacks the balance of sensation and the mediation of the thinking and feeling functions. Sexually abused women have been given over to the realm of fantasy, abandoned to the unconscious primarily because their bodies, and hence their very necessary childhood and adolescent egos, have been stolen away from them. They have been robbed of their imagination and creative outreach. They have been robbed of soul.

The seriousness of this dilemma is extremely difficult to appreciate in a society that does not value imagination, and in a discipline where the distinction between *fantasy* and imagination is rarely articulated. Furthermore, the prevailing norm in society would likely be thinking/sensate—the total opposite of most of my clients. Hence their utterances would seem at best strange but interesting, and at worst, deluded and nonsensical.

The true work of the therapist of sexually abused women is to allow fantasy to be transformed into authentic thought or ideation, true imagining. Nature is responsible for the regeneration of substances deep within the bowels of the earth. Retrieval of imagination and renewal within the body of the earth are deeply connected processes.

But this balancing of intuitive with sensate powers does not happen by jumping from one polarity to the other, from primary to inferior functions. It can only be approached through one of the other functions of feeling and thinking, which are less undeveloped than the inferior function.

Differentiation of the Feeling Function: the Healing Path

In the *Aetiology of Hysteria,* Freud wrote that when patients recall scenes of infantile seduction, they suffer from violent sensations, but they attempt to withhold credence from them by saying that they have no memory of the scenes. Masson interprets Freud as saying that "permission to remember seemed to be also permission to feel, and the feelings apparently absent from the original assault were then experienced—the anger, the disgust, the sense of helplessness and betrayal"—all emotive words.[25] Hillman states in *Jung's Typology*[26] that neither Bleuler nor Freud clearly separated feelings from emotions, from passions, from affectivity, when as early as 1921 Jung had differentiated feeling as a function of consciousness equal in importance to and different from thinking, sensing and intuiting. Within the feeling function, according to Jung's framework, both negative and positive feelings are important. This function has to do with the basic response "I like" or "I dislike" which relates, makes judgments (not in the intellectual sense), connects, denies and evaluates. The feeling function brings personal value to an experience; it relates events to consciousness. Its roots are laid in childhood.[27] The more differentiated the feeling function, the longer it takes to formulate a "feeling" about something. The development of the feeling function leads to an increasing differentiation of values and value-systems. What an event feels like is always complex; thus feelings may offset the pinching of consciousness brought about by the reductive nature of the Western mentality.

The healing of abused women does not consist in simply emoting and blaming others for one's misfortunes. If women find that their therapy becomes stuck at this level, they become extremely angry. They prefer to work at attempting to stay within the sacred and protected circle of the therapeutic encounter, at reclaiming their voice and stance with regard to their experience of patriarchal abuse, and at bringing value to inputs from the unconscious—the minute sensings, the visceral changes, the visions and dreams. In this way, their feeling function becomes a conscious reality. This input is slowly woven into a picture that becomes important to the individual; she begins to apprehend her personal myth. Events have been enlarged into experiences: the individual slowly becomes ensouled.[28]

Reclaiming the Beauty of Thinking: the Healing Path

Masson suggests that before writing his *Aetiology of Hysteria,* Freud had probably been influenced by work then being conducted in France, namely in the areas of child physical and sexual abuse. Ostensibly he had gone there to study with Charcot, but it is likely that he was exposed to the work of Tardieu, described as "the most eminent representative of French legal medicine,"[29] who was commissioned by the courts to examine cases from a forensic point of view. Tardieu's first work has been ignored for one hundred and twenty years and, at the time Masson was writing, had never been quoted in psychoanalytic or psychiatric literature. Tardieu considered the abuse of children by their parents to be "one of the most terrifying problems that can trouble the heart of man."[30] Tardieu was aware that society at large, and medical practitioners in particular, preferred to deny the reality of the problem. He also found that the victims (mostly girls) were participating in the denial.

Masson gives a summary of one of Tardieu's cases—the abuse of Adelina. This young woman of seventeen was kept sealed in a coffin away from the outside world. Her blankets were covered with pus which oozed, up to a liter a day, from her body. Intermittently her father had tied and beaten her, burning her with coals, and her mother had washed her wounds with nitric acid. The girl said that the father had made advances of a vulgar kind. One evening the parents tied the girl's legs apart and forced a block of wood from a elder plant into her body. However, the investigating physician, Dr. Nidart, discovered to his evident puzzlement that Adelina would "invent stories" of what had happened to her in order to cover up the crimes of her parents against her own person, "imagining" falls and accidents rather than allowing others to know the horrible truth of what had been done to her.[31]

This is a very common occurrence and can only be understood in terms of the fear the child experiences. There are frequently threats made that if the child tells, then she will be killed, or someone else will get sick, or her mother would not be able to stand it, or the father would be sent to prison and it would be her fault. And so the child "lies"— to protect her life and that of others, including that of the perpetrator. She learns early to disassociate from her experienced reality and thus becomes embroiled in a general distortion of the Logos/thinking principle, characteristic of sexually abusive homes. This is not only seen in the denial of the reality of the abuse, but also in a tendency to use evasive language in general. Indeed young victims, particularly those in teenage years (who should be moving into a deeper appreciation of Logos at this time anyway) are incredibly relieved in family therapy sessions when someone else spots these verbal distortions. Sometimes relief over this issue seems to be more profound than over the disclosure of the physical abuse itself. Freud did comment on the hysteric's constant establishment of "false connections" between his or her most recent "convulsive attack" and "the most recent cause"— which could be the physician's inadvertent intrusion upon a wounded self-image. Freud believed that when the physician knew more of the patient's conscious and unconscious motives, the response was entirely justified. It would seem that initially Freud was attempting to understand the undermining of Logos in victims of past sexual abuse.

Ferenczi proposed a similar view. He said that "the unconscious patient is in his trance really a child that can no longer respond to intelligent clarification, but at most can respond to maternal warmth." Ferenczi thought that the patient needed to be brought to the point of being able to "reproduce in thought" past events without losing emotional equilibrium.[32] The point is, this is a clarification that comes *from the client*, not from the therapist. For this to happen, Ferenczi makes his last plea in this, his last paper, for all of us to

pay closer attention than [we] have in the past to the strange, much veiled, yet critical manner of thinking and speaking of [our] children, patients and students, and, so to speak, loosen their tongues. [We] will hear much that is instructive.[33]

To listen like this means being able to stop talking—both inwardly and outwardly—thus relinquishing a role that is very difficult to escape from.

The more an analyst or therapist can listen with this quality of devotion, the more apparent will be the value of the simple word in all its potency. This would challenge that illusory mode of thinking and speaking in which seduction is labeled as "too much loving," and where acts of sexual abuse and incest are relabeled the "daughter's seduction," placing the blame upon her. Incest, along with other forms of sexual abuse, wreaks havoc on the victim's conception of the truth and on her ability to later reclaim her own shadow and negative animus—both essential to her wholeness.

Jung describes the sort of truths that the daughters need.

They are the truths which speak to the soul, which are not too loud and do not insist too much, but reach the individual in stillness—the individual who constitutes the meaning of the world. It is this knowledge that the daughter needs, in order to pass it on to her son.[34]

This son may be her outer, physical son, but also the budding of her own inner masculine potential—her animus. Jung knew this quality of "word"—gentle yet powerful. He also knew that all coercion—be it suggestion, insinuation, or any other method of persuasion—ultimately proves to be nothing but an obstacle to the highest and most decisive experience of all, which is to be alone with and comprehend one's self. The patient alone must learn how to regain control over life; such an experience can give an indestructible foundation of inner strength.[35]

It is imperative that the truth about what happened be restored to an abused person, so that a clear understanding of the experience, however painful, can begin to replace the more painful and debilitating unconscious outpourings of hysteria.

Transformation

It is the recovery of a sense of truth and a recognition of the emancipating power of clear thinking and feeling that allows the sexually abused woman to engage in the life of potent, grounded imagination. She can then express long-repressed memories and relieve herself of the burden of guilt and shame that has silenced her for the years since she was abused. In coming to appreciate her inability as a child to protect herself from a grown man and to see that she no longer needs to carry blame and guilt, the woman takes a decisive step toward healing. Paradoxically, she cannot deal with her personal shadow until she has stepped away from the enormous projected patriarchal shadow. This awareness of the value of the truth must not be lost sight of, and must be pursued creatively in analysis. The abuse victim's struggle to make connections from the ego to everyday life must be seen in context of the struggle to retrieve the memories of the abuse, placing them in a healing perspective. The dream images gradually transform. The internalized aggressor, the very negative animus, becomes less dominant as the woman begins to inform him that there is a perspective other than his. If the outer abusive man can no longer be confronted, the introjected animus certainly can. It is this that allows the victim to be freed of ego-strangulation, enabling her to understand and release her pent-up anger and grow stronger, and to lay claim to some choices for herself.

The Victim's "Precocious Intelligence"

Masson reports Tardieu as saying that the sexually abused:

> . . . reveal the deepest sadness; they are timid and apprehensive, often they look dazed and the expression in their eyes is lifeless. But sometimes, often in fact, it is very different: they have a *precocious intelligence* which only reveals itself in a dark fire in their eyes.[36] [Emphasis added].

Freud, too, noted a frequent precociousness in the sexually abused — this time in terms of somatic sexual development, which, he postulated, could have been promoted by too much early sexual stimulation.

Ferenczi comments that his sexually abused clients displayed "a strange, almost clairvoyant knowledge of the thoughts and emotions of the analyst"[37] (particularly with respect to any hypocrisy), even though they might not be able to give expression to their superior knowledge.[38] He continues saying that there can be no shock or fright without traces of a personality split, and that the individual will likely regress to pre-traumatic bliss in seeking to undo the trauma. Otherwise, according to Ferenczi:

> The sexually violated child can suddenly bring to fruition under the pressure of traumatic exigency all future faculties which are virtually performed in him and are necessary for marriage, motherhood and fatherhood, as well as all feelings of a mature person. Here one can confidently speak of *traumatic* (pathologic) *progression or precocity* in contrast to the familiar con-

cept of regression[39]

Ferenczi explains that to protect herself from people without self-control, the child must first know how to identify those people. Thus the child becomes pseudo-mature, often becoming in his or her own right a parental figure within the family. The abused have an acute grasp of the emotional life and motivation of all family members, as well as shrewd insight into the shortcomings of the therapist and others. These children are often struggling to understand some of the enormous ethical and moral problems pertaining not just to their own personal situation, but also of a more general nature. Many of these attributes we could indeed marvel at were they not the product of victimization, and thus laden with brittle and harsh or sentimental overtones.

To see the problem at this depth helps us to understand the extent of the difficulties facing abused women and children. In my experience, it takes many months of intensive therapy before adult victims of early sexual abuse even get to the point of realizing that they have never had their own feelings, their own thoughts—even their own fantasies—because their body, their very being, was never fully theirs. These are all issues of personal boundaries. The victim's efforts at self-preservation have led to the loss of personal power in the extreme, though to a casual observer it could often appear that someone with so much insight into others, so capable of running a home at such a young age, is indeed a powerful person. This power is a pseudo-power of willfulness, and its foundation is one of loss, as well as of burden—the burden of carrying the unconscious problems of others, indeed of a society that demeans and devalues the feminine and the victim.

Of Witches and Devils

The dreams, visions and play therapy scenes of victims of sexual abuse of all ages frequently center around the archetypes of the witch and devil, both of which carry tremendous power and frustration. The less the therapist understands the archetypes, the more likelihood of the therapist exacerbating the woundedness of the victim.

The secretive and shameful nature of the crime against the young child or woman makes it difficult for her to share her reality with anyone, and the ensuing loneliness causes a great deal of heartache to victims. Jung explains that

Isolation by a secret results as a rule in an animation of the psychic atmos-

phere, as a substitute for loss of contact with other people. It causes an activation of the unconscious, and this produces something similar to the illusions and hallucinations that beset lonely wanderers in the desert, seafarers
and saints. That is why primitive man has always believed that lonely and
desolate places are haunted by "devils" and suchlike apparitions.[40]

The more the victim feels herself alone, the more "the devil" and "the
witch" are constellated.

Masson gives us some of what he thinks were Freud's attempts at ex-
onerating Fliess from his bungling operation on Emma Eckstein's nose
in an effort to cure her of masturbation. This exoneration was, in Masson's opinion, very much entwined with Freud's having been propelled,
through work with Emma, into the lonely territory of witch and devil,
for he wrote to Fliess that "Emma has a scene where the Diabolus sticks
pins into her finger and puts a piece of candy on each drop of blood."[41]
Freud connected Emma's fantasy to witchcraft—linking it with his newest
theory, which involved the abandonment of the reality of children's abuse.
Freud writes:

> What would you say, by the way, if I told you that my brand new theory
> of the early etiology of hysteria was already well known and had been pub-
> lished a hundred times over, though several centuries ago? But why did the
> devil who took possession of these poor things invariably abuse them sexu-
> ally and in a loathsome manner? Why are their confessions under torture
> so like the communications made by my patients in psychological
> treatment?[42]

Freud did not provide the answer to these crucial two questions. Masson maintains that

> . . . it matters very much whether one says that the reason the devil invaria-
> bly abuses the witch sexually is that this is a fantasy on the part of the witch,
> originating in a childhood wish to be possessed by the father, or whether
> one says that this is a distorted memory of a real and tragic event that is
> so painful it can only be recalled via this subterfuge.[43]

Certainly Masson's distinction is of critical importance. But even this
does not do true justice to the depths of the problem, which, as I see
it, makes us realize that something is constellated in the child which
is really beyond our understanding. Freud's view of Emma's problem
(and thus of hysterical women in general) was ultimately that she almost bled to death after the inappropriate nasal surgery because of her

"perverse imagination."[44] The sins of the patriarchy (both those of her childhood assailant, and those of Fliess, and Freud in covering for Fliess) were forgiven and, indeed, ennobled by Emma's predicament. But to conceive of abused women as witches, involved in seduction out of longing, and to liken therapy (however obtusely) to their torture and murder is enough to make any woman with a slight vestige of self-worth run away from therapy. The faster the better!

It would seem that the devil and witch archetypes appear to be constellated in abused women and children, and any therapist must do *inner* battle with them. In my experience, I have found that an abused woman's "devils" are associated with her outer assailant, whom she has introjected and unconsciously united with herself. Her witch is frequently a powerful but terribly lonely soul who resorts to casting spells and making scenes because nobody will take her seriously. Both archetypes are tremendously powerful and cannot be dismissed by a merely intellectual understanding. Any therapy that does not confront the power issues of the victim, still mindful of the wound, has, in my opinion, barely begun.

An Appreciation of Death and Disintegration on the Healing Path

The Victim's Difficulty in Embracing Death

I have come to realize that sexual assault is an imposed death experience for the victim. That is, the victim experiences her life as having been taken by somebody else. Paradoxically, until the victim is strengthened through a fully conscious *psychic* death-experience, she is never free to enter a relationship—either with an inner or outer male (animus) figure. The loss of a willing and conscious death experience is at the root of much of the masochistic behavior of victims. The victim knows the need for a conscious experience of death. However, for the descent to be renewing it must be activated and supported by Self—not by the memory of coerced death.

Ferenczi seems to have had a similar thought when he referred to the loss of the memory of "the struggle-to-the-death," intimating that the assault was a death-like experience.[45] Masson records the case history of a Mrs. Severn, who was analyzed by Ferenczi. Here a woman, abused as a child, dreams of her own funeral as a child, being conveyed to the grave, and of simultaneously being her own mourner. Masson suggests that this is a remarkable representation of [the child/woman's] helplessness and loneliness and a powerful indictment of her mother's acquiescence in the partial murder of the child.[46]

Several dreams by abused clients of mine in early therapy were similar to the case of Mrs. Severn. In a sense, only the individual can really see his or her own voluntary death process. The therapist can at best intuit the process and support it. But the inner witness needs to have come of age. The inner child of the abused adult needs releasing into life, love, spontaneous playfulness and centered discipline in order to grow up sufficiently to become that adult witness of conscious disintegration.

Perhaps Freud early on experienced the "inevitability" of the dark side of the feminine as he entered into the study of sexual abuse and the resulting hysteria. He wrote to Fliess that:

I am as isolated as you could wish me to be: the word has been given out to abandon me, and *a void* is forming around me.[47] [Emphasis added]

Freud felt as though he were despised and universally shunned because of his initial paper. Indeed he was. I would suggest that one countertransference phenomenon with the sexually abused is a death experience for the therapist. One way of dealing with it is to avoid it and cling to an insurmountable superego. Anyone who takes this route would automatically be compelled to deny another's own death/rebirth cycle(s). In particular, the feminine polarities would have to be repressed. It appears as if Freud took this route. For instance, in addition to glossing over facts and distorting the Logos/thinking principle, he eventually maintained that Fliess (and by implication, himself) was completely without blame as far as "the blood" was concerned. Eventually his reasoning allowed him to maintain that Emma's bleeding had nothing to do with Fliess's bungled surgery. For Freud, it had to do with Emma's "perverse imagination," as previously shown, and it was also described by him as an effort of Emma's to bring him to her side. One might ask what it was that Emma was trying to show Freud by repeatedly coming so close to death. Freud aggrandized himself by assuming that Emma's response was out of seductive longing for him.

Masson quotes Ernest Jones on Freud's relationship with women:

[Freud] found the psychology of women more enigmatic than that of men... Freud was interested in another type of woman, of a more intellectual and perhaps *masculine cast.* Such women several times played a part in his life, accessories to his men friends though of a finer calibre.[48] [Emphasis added]

Emma was listed among these women. It is interesting to note that Irving Stone's biography of Freud shows him leaving Europe because of the Nazi regime, and taking with him an exquisite sculpture of Athena. Maybe the father's daughter was indeed Freud's preferred archetype of the feminine.

The abused woman's desperate flight into the world of the patriarchal ego could be nothing but exacerbated by a therapist unable to willingly join with the woman in death, without considering this a female seduction. In reality, the woman needs her therapist to help her descend into her own body and to let her old self die.

Incest and Fantasy

Jung tells of his developing empathy for Babette[49], a schizophrenic woman sequestered in a mental hospital for twenty years. She would introduce herself with the phrase "I am the Lorelei." The doctors trying to understand her would invariably admit that "I don't know what it means." But Jung made the connection: "I know not what it means" was the first line of Heine's famous poem "Die Lorelei." It was as if this imprisoned Lorelei were attempting to draw someone into the Rhine waters to gain new perspective. This was a clue for Jung that the schizophrenic's strange distortion of tongues indeed had a meaning—if the doctor had a bridge. Jung began to realize that

> At bottom we discover nothing new and unknown in the mentally ill, rather we encounter the substratum of our own natures.[50]

Jung introduced Freud to Babette during his 1908 visit to Zürich, and Freud was interested in Jung's discovery. However, Freud wondered how in the world Jung was able to spend hours and days with that "phenomenally ugly female." This idea had not occurred to Jung, who wrote:

> In a way, I regarded the woman as a pleasant old creature because she had such lovely delusions and said such interesting things. And after all, even in her insanity the human being emerged from a cloud of grotesque nonsense.[51]

Jung then proceeds to write about his work with a young woman of seventeen, a victim of brother-sister incest and other sexual abuse. She had withdrawn from other people, heard voices, refused food, and became completely mute. Overcoming resistances after many weeks with Jung, she finally told him that she lived on the moon where she had at first seen only men. She had learned that this territory was inhabited by a vampire that kidnapped and killed women and children, so that the moon people were threatened with extinction. The moon men had therefore taken the woman to the sublunar dwelling where they hid their women and children.

Jung's patient decided to help the moon people: she would kill the vampire. After some nights she saw him approaching from afar; she took her sacrificial knife, hid it in her gown, and waited until he suddenly stood before her. He had several pairs of wings. His face and entire figure were covered by them, so that she could see nothing but feathers. Wonderstruck, she was seized by curiosity to find out what he really looked like. She approached, hand on the knife. Suddenly the wings opened and a man of unearthly beauty stood before her. He enclosed her in his winged arms with an iron grip so that she could no longer wield the knife. In any case, she was so spellbound by the vampire's look that she would not have been capable of striking. He raised her off the platform and flew off with her.

After this revelation the woman was able to speak unabashedly. But new resistances emerged, brought about by the telling of her inner fantasy life, which closed the door on her escape back to the moon. At this time she suffered "a relapse into her catatonia" and Jung had to have her admitted to a sanatorium. She was discharged two months later, when she became communicative again, and gradually realized that it was best for her simply to go on with her life.

Some time later she took a nursing job in a sanatorium, where an assistant doctor rashly approached her. She responded with a revolver shot, which fortunately only slightly wounded him. She apparently carried a revolver constantly, and only handed it to Jung at the end of their last interview. She explained to Jung that she would have shot him had he failed her.

The woman married, had several children, survived two world wars, and never suffered a relapse.[52] Jung explained this as follows:

> As a result of incest she felt humiliated in the eyes of the world, but elevated in the realm of fantasy. She had been transported into a mythic realm; for incest is traditionally a prerogative of royalty and divinities. She became

"extra mundane" as it were, and lost contact with humanity and met the winged demon. She projected this figure onto me during treatment. By telling me her story she had in a sense betrayed the demon and attached herself to an earthly human being. Hence she was able to return to life and even marry.[53]

After this encounter with the lost woman on the moon and her inner devil, Jung, as he mentions in *Memories, Dreams, & Reflections,*

> regarded the sufferings of the mentally ill with a different light. For I had gained insight into the richness and importance of their inner experience.[54]

Jung had intuited that the hurt moon woman, in her desperation to see the Spirit face-to-face, was willing to be taken into the arms of the blood-sucking vampire devil because she had lost her own grounded feminity. He knew too that the patient would not take her own psyche seriously if the doctor did not take his seriously. He also realized that the patient would lose that part of the psyche which the doctor could not understand within himself. He must know those subterranean territories for himself. Without that, the farthest reaches of human consciousness and experience cannot be retrieved and made meaningful.

Notes

1. Jeffrey M. Masson. *The Assault On Truth*. New York: Farrar, Strauss & Giroux, 1984, p. xix

2. *Ibid.*, pp. 252-253

3. *Ibid.*, p. 269

4. *Ibid.*, p. xxii

5. *Ibid.*, p. 273

6. *Ibid.*, p. 278

7. *Ibid.*, p. 266
   The last point is more possible today, but even now workers in the field are frequently thwarted in their attempts to find corroborative information— particularly when the child is a preschooler.
   I am well aware that children once assaulted are frequently drawn back to the flame, giving perhaps the impression that they like it. Certainly many love their assailant, who is often "gentle" in the assault. The child may never have experienced any other family lifestyle. It often takes months before a child or young person can begin to get in touch with the confusion and circumstances such a family lives within.

8. *Ibid.*, p. 9

9. *Ibid.*, p. 11

10. *Ibid.*, pp. 12-13

11. *Ibid.*, p. 113
    Note that "imagination" is used here, whereas I would use "fantasy."

12. *Ibid.*, p. xix

13. Janet Malcolm, "Archives II," In *The New Yorker*, December 12, 1983, p. 105
    Malcolm wonders whether Freud knew of Fleschsig's treatment only after he had published his own paper. In any case, Freud apparently did not alter his opinion.

14. Masson, *op. cit.*, p. 113

15. *Ibid.*, p. 145

16. *Ibid.*, p. 151

17. *Ibid.*, p. 295

18. *Ibid.*, p. 290

19. *Ibid.*, pp. 290-291

20. *Ibid.*, p. 147

[21]*Ibid.*, p. 288

[22]Kluft, Richard, and Braun, Bennett. "Multiple Personality and Intrafamilial Abuse." In *International Journal of Family Psychiatry*, 5, 4:283-301, 1984

Kluft, Richard. "An Update on Multiple Personality Disorder." In *Hospital and Community Psychiatry*, 38, 4:363-373, April 1987

Coons, Philip M. "Child Abuse and Multiple Personality Disorder: Review of the Literature and Suggestions for Treatment." In *Child Abuse and Neglect*, 10, 4:455-462, 1986

[23]C.G. Jung, *CW* XII, par. 218

[24]*Ibid.*, par. 219

[25]Masson, *op. cit.*, p. 10

[26]M.-L. von Franz and James Hillman. *Jung's Typology*. Dallas: Spring Publications, 1971, p. 83

[27]*Ibid.*, pp. 90-91

[28]James Hillman. *Archetypal Psychology*. Dallas: Spring Publications, 1983, Chapter 4

[29]Masson, *op. cit.*, p. 15

[30]*Ibid.*, p. 19

[31]*Ibid.*, p. 120

[32]*Ibid.*, p. 286

[33]*Ibid.*, p. 294

[34]C.G. Jung, *CW* XIV, par. 233

[35]C.G. Jung, *CW* XII, par. 32

[36]Masson, *op. cit.*, p. 19

[37]*Ibid.*, p. 288

[38]*Ibid.*, p. 286

[39]*Ibid.*, pp. 292-293

[40]C.G. Jung, *CW* XII, par. 57

[41]Masson, *op. cit.*, p. 103

[42]*Ibid.*, p. 104

[43]*Ibid.*

[44]*Ibid.*, p. 106

[45]*Ibid.*, p. 147

[46]*Ibid.*, p. 166

[47]*Ibid.*, p. 10

[48]*Ibid.*, p. 233

[49]C.G. Jung. *Memories, Dreams, Reflections.* New York: Vintage Books, 1965, pp. 125-126

[50]*Ibid.*, p. 127

[51]*Ibid.*, p. 128

[52]*Ibid.*, p. 130

[53]*Ibid.*

[54]*Ibid.*

CHAPTER III

Towards An Imaginal Therapy

Introduction
The intellectual soul has a strong inclination to conquer material and articulate its every nuance. Imagery is enraging to the intellectual soul. The opening of von Eschenbach's *Parzival* addresses this issue:

> If inconstancy is the heart's neighbour, the soul will not fail to find it bitter. Blame and praise alike befall when a dauntless man's spirit is black-and-white-mixed like the magpie's plumage. Yet the man see blessedness after all, for both colours have a share in him, the colour of heaven and the colour of hell. Inconstancy's companion is all black and takes on the hue of darkness, while he of steadfast thoughts clings to white. This flying metaphor will be much too swift for dullards. They will not be able to think it through because it will run from them like a startled rabbit.

The intellectual soul cannot follow imagination in its haphazard and frantic dartings. For true consciousness of soul to emerge, one can only sit quietly and allow the images and ideas from within to surface.

In psychology, we talk of projection as the unconscious transferal of psychological material belonging to one person onto another. This is done because it is difficult to recognize the material as one's own.

Projection involving inner images burdens the person receiving the projections, for he is obliged to carry them, usually in an unconscious way. Thus men will usually project or transfer their inner feminine soul images, their anima, onto the women they know. Similarly, women project their animus onto men. When one family member unconsciously projects his inner animating function onto another, the two keep each other in bondage. In the more unconscious individual, this can lead to acted-out incest.

Allowing the images to surface can at first be startling enough, but more so when feeling is brought to the images. Secondly, relating to the images on an inner imaginal level is stunningly revelatory of one's life patterns. The first task is to discover what images we do in fact carry with us, and then slowly to allow ourselves to see how they govern our lives through our very unrelatedness to them.

* * * * *

Jung as Alchemist

A close look at the texts which drew Jung into a profound research of alchemy reveals that the end point of the alchemical process (the opus) was the hermaphrodite (half man, half woman) of supposed wholeness. Jung considered the hermaphrodite to be "still a hideous abortion and perversion of nature," of "crude embryonic features."[1] These pivotal studies by the alchemists contributed to the creation of a phenomenology of the unconscious long before the advent of psychology. By projecting their imaginations onto the materials in their retort vessels, the alchemists practiced an early form of self-analysis. In his study on the alchemical work *Tabula smaragdina*, Jung wrote that the alchemical mystery is a sacrament of maternal *matter*, rather than a sacrament of paternal mind:

> Had the alchemists understood the psychological aspects of their work, they would have been in a position to free their "uniting symbol" from the grip of instinctive sexuality where, for better or worse, mere nature, unsupported by the critical intellect, was bound to leave it. Nature could say no more than that the combination of supreme opposites was a hybrid thing. And there the statement stuck, in sexuality, as always when the potentialities of consciousness do not come to the assistance of nature — which could hardly have been otherwise in the Middle Ages owing to the complete absence of psychology. So things remained until, at the end of the nineteenth century, Freud dug up this problem again.[2]

Much of Jung's life was devoted to showing the value of what nature could teach us, in comparison with the spirit that believes that "light is born from light" and which gives rise to all the clarifying and accumulation of aggressive critical analyses. The end result is the aggrandizement of "consciousness"—spirit, light and good—and the unconscious entrapment of critical intellect, or intellect that is essential, in unvalued matter. Jung considered the wealth of animal symbols in alchemy suggestive of *mater natura,* Mother Nature, reminding us of what Christianity had left behind with its bias in favor of light and spirit and its simultaneous tacit depreciation of matter.

Perhaps most familiar to us is the female's change of status among the Israelites. It was against the moon mother who had reigned in Sinai before Jehovah's coming that Judaic monotheism waged its greatest struggle. The Feminine was more reviled in Judea than she ever was in Greece. The serpent, which used to be associated with mystery and numinous energy, now became Eve's tempter. Eve slides into being a mere woman, marked by sexual self-consciousness and bodily shame. Like Medusa, she becomes lost in matter. There is little recognition that Eve's rebellion caused spiritual progress: afterwards, there could no longer be ongoing blissful, unconscious innocence. What developed in Palestine was the first male god who had no female consort—at least, this is how the patriarchal doctrine had thus far been generally expounded.

There was already a tendency in Egyptian and Greek times for the virgin anima to gravitate towards or to be taken up by the ruling father, as we saw with the Athena/Medusa archetype. But it was not until 1950 that Pope Pius XII proclaimed the dogma of the Ascension of the Blessed Virgin. The declaration of the physical ascension of Mary leads to the presumption that mother nature can be received into the metaphysical realm, which according to the earlier views was reserved for the masculine principle. From the historical viewpoint, Jung says this equality needs to be metaphysically anchored in the figure of a divine woman. The Christian version of the feminine principle was thus *lifted* to a radically new position.[3]

In 1954 Jung asked what had become of the "characteristic relation of the mother image to the earth, [to] darkness, [to] the abysmal side of the bodily man, with his animal passions and instinctual nature, and to 'matter' in general."[4] Spirit may no longer reign absolute, but we are in danger of completely losing true valuing of matter because of our insistence upon light and elevation. In moving Mary upwards, we are in danger of leaving Eve ever further behind, though the idea of her still exerts a fascination because she can bear the projection of man's own animal nature.

Mary has "usurped the qualities of pagan goddesses, and she therefore embodies far more of the dark feminine than the patriarchy has allowed her."[5] But to become *conscious* of the inherent unity of Eve and Mary requires a totally new conception of consciousness. A new *coniunctio* heralds the union of God and beast, Mary and Eve.

Jung elaborates that Christianity attempted to deal with incest in one way:

> The conflict between worldliness and spirituality, latent in the love-myth of Mother and Son, was elevated by Christianity to the mystic marriage of sponsus (Christ) and sponsa (Church). [This] Christian solution of the conflict is purely pneumatic, the physical relations of the sexes being turned into an allegory or—quite illegitimately—into a sin that perpetuates and even intensifies the original one in the Garden.[6]

A few sentences later, Jung saw alchemy dealing with incest another way:

> [It] exalted the most heinous transgression of the law, namely incest, into a symbol of the union of opposites, hoping in this way to bring back the golden age.

It seems that both doctrines are an attempt to return to the original, conflict-free Edenic experience. "For both trends, the solution lay in extrapolating the union of sexes into another medium." Christianity, which ruled on the surface, abandoned matter, making physical sexuality a sin and marriage a mystic affair. Jung continued by saying

> It certainly seems today as if the ecclesiastical allegories of the bridegroom and bride, not to mention the now completely obsolete alchemical coniunctio, had become so faded that one meets with incest only in criminology and the psychopathology of sex.[7]

By this he means that the archetypal and mythological underpinnings have been lost to consciousness—there is no awareness of the psychic task required for a *true* union of opposites, not merely an aberrant form. He also maintains that the "incest problem is practically universal and immediately comes to the surface when the customary illusions are cleared away from the foreground." Alchemy, which ran like an undercurrent to Christianity, glorified the unconscious and incestuous hermaphrodite. It is hardly surprising to see these two projected forces in clinical work. On the surface this is manifested as the offender's compulsive moralizing and/or frequent church-going, and in the victim's compulsive and primitive relationship with a God figure — an abstract God who is often the only friend she has. Below the surface, there is compulsive identification with an acted out, materialized, unconscious hermaphrodite of incest. In today's society, this figure constantly appears, most obviously in the form of hermaphroditic pop heroes and early dreams in psychotherapy. Thus we see that the patriarchal Church with its emphasis on Spirit, and alchemy with its aggrandizement of matter, represent the poles of the problem. According to Jung, "neither of them located the problem in the place where it arose — the soul of man."

Jung thought that the sexuality of the unconscious, lying dormant since the time of the alchemists, was instantly taken with great seriousness and elevated to a sort of religious dogma by scientific enquiry. Because it cannot "push its way over the threshold of consciousness," Jung suggests that the very problem which defeated the alchemists threatens to defeat us — that is, how is the profound cleavage in man and the world to be understood, how are we to respond to, and if possible, abolish it?[8]

Jung found alchemy helpful because of its attention to matter, which the Church had abandoned. Although he chose to use alchemy to talk about transference, he remained dissatisfied with where the discussion ended. He maintained that he had never come across the hermaphrodite as a personification of the goal, but more as a symbol of the initial state,[9] expressing an unconscious identity with anima or animus. Jung intimated that the latter hoped-for stages could not be attempted until nature and the feminine were reclaimed from the middle ages. It would seem as though the knight's valuing of the lady never reached full maturity.

Jung states that a different symbol for the goal of the opus, more appropriate to our time and age, would be one of a more "objective" nature — such as the mandala, where opposites are united under the sign of the *quaternio,* intimating the possibility of wholeness, where contradictions are reconciled. Such symbols point backwards to the original and primitive order of human society, as well as forward to an inner order of the psyche.

Jung describes the effect of the healing alchemical opus on the man's anima — his inner feminine soul qualities. The anima left unconscious "is a creature without relationships, an autoerotic being whose one aim is to take total possession of the individual,"[10] leading, of course, to all sorts of illusions and complications. However, if the ego has released itself through a deep acknowledgement of and relationship with the

anima, then the anima gradually ceases to act as an autonomous personality and will become a function of relationship between conscious
and unconscious. She becomes objective — not objectified as in
pornography — and can thus support many acts of creation. What seems
to happen is that

> The withdrawal of projections makes the anima what she originally was: an
> archetypal image which, in its right place, functions to the advantage of
> the individual.[11]

Jung's break with Freud seemed to revolve a great deal around the
two men's relationship with the psyche and with women, although Jung's
reason was that he could no longer stand the "constricting atmosphere"
of Freudian psychology, particularly the "reductive causalism"[12] of the
whole outlook. In Jung's *Symbols of Transformation*, which poured out
of him at his parting from Freud, he starts with a reminder that from
Freud's perspective the Oedipal legend, with its supposed incest fantasy, is the root of individual conflict. Jung goes on from there to make
some radical departures from Freud. But towards the end of the book
Jung says:

> Freud's incest theory describes certain fantasies that accompany the regres-
> sion of libido and are especially characteristic of the personal unconscious
> as found in hysterical patients...[Freud's theory] is just as unconvincing as
> the ostensibly sexual trauma of hysterics.[13]

Jung seems to be saying that the hysterical person has had no real sexual trauma, thus maintaining Freud's abandonment of the seduction theory. Indeed, he maintains that it was he who introduced Freud to the
Schreber case, and although he felt that Freud wrote it up unsatisfac-
torily, he himself appears not to have realized, either, that Schreber had
been a victim of physical abuse and threats, and that a "soul murder"
had indeed been committed.[14]

Yet much later in his life Jung seemed to maintain with a certain
equanimity that incest does and did occur.

> The violent repudiation of Freud's original discoveries gets us nowhere, for
> we are dealing with an empirically demonstrable fact which meets with such
> universal confirmation that only the ignorant still try to oppose it.[15]

Jung also unearthed the psychic underpinnings and behaviors of incest
victims, presenting a picture that comes closer than any other to the

clinical experience with which I have become familiar. In addition, Jung stated that children's well-being was very much dependent on the psychology of their parents, and any wrong, albeit unconscious, attitude was bound to affect the child. If father and mother remain unconscious, the power of the divine pair grows in proportion to the degree to which they remain unconscious.[16] Jung stated clearly that children not given *real* love would develop premature sexual symptoms because they would be carrying the parents' unresolved issues. He went on to say that children need love, tenderness, and understanding.[17] In healthy families, according to Robert Stein, the child is continually allowed the

> crucial formative experience of the incarnation of the harmonious connection and interaction of father and mother; and through repeated experiences of its own wholeness in relation to both parents. When the fundamental connection between husband and wife is obstructed, the child's formative experience of the Royal Marriage is also obstructed . . . (As a result) an unconscious spiritual marriage is formed between father and daughter, and between mother and son.[18]

Sexual Drive to Libido

Over time, Jung radically changed his views on libido. Tracing his ideas from *Symbols of Transformation* (possibly completed in 1916) through to *The Psychology of the Transference* (completed in 1945), the most obvious and perhaps most fundamental shift was in developing the concept of the libido. Jung noted that:

> Despite his definition of libido as sexuality, Freud does not explain "everything" in terms of sex, as is commonly supposed, but recognizes the existence of special instinctual forces whose nature is not clearly known, but to which he was bound to ascribe the faculty of taking up these "libidinal affluxes."[19]

Earlier, in *The Psychology of Dementia Praecox,* Jung used the term "psychic energy" (i.e., libido) because more than erotic energy was missing from these patients. Jung felt that it was more important to have a psychological theory of neurosis than a sexual one,[20] and he saw instinct as a very mysterious manifestation of life, partly psychic and partly physical in nature. Importantly, he also saw the drive towards the life of ensouled spirit as a human instinct—in fact it was what distinguished them from other primates. Thus spirituality had a physical aspect.

Anima and Animus

Jung's conception of an inner, animating contrasexual component led to his particular understanding of the complexities of the transference phenomenon. Since all women have inner animus figures and all men have inner anima figures, all of which are largely unconscious, they will be projected onto outer individuals. The therapeutic relationship is not the only one in which this transference occurs, but it is special because it is the arena in which the projections can be moved into consciousness as the inner figures are related to and valued. The therapeutic relationship is sacred because it allows for both therapist and patient to move into areas of consideration far beyond the confines of the personal. This can only happen when inner images are brought to consciousness and related to — being neither concretized nor inappropriately etherialized.

Fear of Regression

Jung moves from the Oedipus complex to the Jonah in the Whale myth and the fear of being devoured — not ultimately by the personal mother, but by the unconscious, the creative matrix of the future. Descent into the unconscious is inevitable if life is to become animated, for it is here in this dark cavern that Jonah, from the light of a pearl, was able to see all that was in the seas and in the depths. It is in this creative matrix that modern Jonah discovers what images he carries within him. Here, the food necessary for the second half of life is to be found — in the animation of underworld images which bring soul-life renewal.

This understanding has important ramifications for male/female relationships — both inner and outer ones. I constantly hear women complaining that the men they are involved with only want mothering. The women say they are tired of Peter Pans; they have enough children. For Jung, the term *incest* means

> the urge to get back to childhood. For the child, of course, this cannot be called incest; it is only for an adult with a fully developed sexuality that this backward striving becomes incest, because he is no longer a child but possesses a sexuality which cannot be allowed a regressive outlet.[21]

It is the incest taboo which normally cuts the adult off from "the security of childhood and early youth, from all those unconscious, instinctive happenings that allow the child to live without responsibility." If the incest taboo is broken the child remains in "a state of unconscious identity with the mother [or father], still one with the animal psyche

[and] just as unconscious of it."²²

Very often the men these women complain about are indeed caught in an unconscious incestuous relationship with their personal mothers. But what is so hard to understand, at the heart level, is that ultimately the man is reaching beyond the human woman to the lap of the Great Mother, the ocean of the unconscious, in order to redeem his full animation. For a woman to appreciate her partner's need to return to a great ocean-wisdom, she must have her own knowledge of the inside of the whale's belly, the inside of the tomb. Then she must be willing to allow it to become her partner's home also. I have come to see that a woman's intimate and conscious encounter with death is her spiritual gift to her family and her community. A woman in whom the victim/offender syndrome is resolving into simplicity is able to be the non-aggressive leader in the family by assuming her rightful role as carrier of soul qualities and the necessary appreciation of symbolic death.

In the final analysis, because of the reality of the animating archetypes, Jung posits that incest is

> ...the hiding place for all the most secret, painful, intense, delicate, shame-faced, timorous, grotesque, immoral, and at the same time, the most sacred feelings which go to make up the indescribable and inexplicable wealth of human relationships and give them their compelling power.³²

The effects of incest could best be described as "possession," for important mythologems are relegated to the unconscious and the individual experiences a loss of soul, and a parallel loss of creativity. Our whole civilization with its cult of consciousness—our soulless paradigm, with a Christian stamp which means that neither anima nor animus is integrated but still in a state of projection (i.e., expressed by dogma)—manifests this very state of possession. Jung continues by saying that:

> ...incest symbolizes union with one's own being, it means individuation or becoming a self, and, because this is so vitally important, it exerts an unholy fascination—not, perhaps as a crude reality, but certainly as a psychic process controlled by the unconscious, a fact well known to anybody who is familiar with psychopathology. It is for this reason...that the first gods were believed to propagate their kind incestuously. Incest is simply the union of like with like, which is the next stage in the development of the primitive idea of self-fertilization.²⁴

Our task is to become conscious of the inner bipolar hermaphrodite so that we are no longer encased in the animus or anima, but can through conscious separation communicate with that part of ourselves. Jung maintains quite categorically that the drive to wholeness begins by presenting itself under the symbol of incest, and that unless a man seeks that wholeness within himself, reclaiming aspects of his consciousness from the women in his family, he will invariably find it in the women close to him.

One example that perplexed clinicians was a family whose condition had deteriorated so badly that they were living in a barn. Knowing northern winters, that fact in itself was astounding. For five years, the man had been attempting to coerce his wife into sexual activities with animals so that he could watch. For five years she resisted, though it became more and more difficult for her because every time she refused, the man would shoot the animal in front of her. In her role as victim, the woman finally capitulated. The final straw came when the man lined the children up in front of him and forced the woman to help him have oral sex with himself.

The example clearly shows a "crude reality" and a desperate attempt, on the man's part, at union with himself. Instead of having an inner relationship with "the animals," being redeemed from unconscious entrapment in the animal psyche, the man was compelled to *outwardly* recreate the link between woman and *mater natura*. When this was denied, he responded with a coerced death which he imposed, in rage and frustration, on the natural order of things. There was absolutely no understanding that these very necessary aspects of the *opus* should take place inwardly. The whole situation was utterly lost in nature — there was no critical or essential intellect, no relationship with inner images to redeem it, even though the setting was the same as that of the birth of the Divine Child. The archetypal mythologems had fallen completely into the unconscious, but there they continued to rumble and rage and eventually entrap the family in what became psychopathic acts of brutality, and a profane and devilish enactment of the serpent that fertilizes and gives birth to itself.

At a different psychic level, before the mythologems have disappeared completely into the unconscious, the same archetypal themes have to be related to. We will look at the inner work of a thirty-five year old professional man called Chris. The first dream he shared was of himself turning into a wolf and of then being confronted by a man with a menacing trickster quality. In his third working session with me, he told me he had dreamed that he was on his knees in front of a woman he knew, begging her to understand, begging her to yield, but she remained stone-faced and withdrawn. The man awakened sobbing and feeling his heart wrenched out of him.

When we reentered the dream together, I wondered what might happen if he stood up. The woman immediately shriveled and began to disappear. Obviously that approach would simply end the relationship, so Chris quickly got to his knees again and the woman resumed her former stony aloofness. I encouraged Chris to try to explain to the woman what he was working towards—some sort of mutual understanding. And as he watched, the woman changed to a tiger, then a sphinx. The man became a small boy as the sphinx-like-figure grew in size, and the boy knew he could be completely overpowered by such a creature.

Then we talked about the riddle the Sphinx posed to Oedipus on the way to Thebes, a riddle whose answer is "man." Chris had a problem with this because his "felt experience" at that moment was of being a young boy.

Here was a man who knew very well that his relationship with his personal mother had robbed him of some of his vitality—that in some senses he remained a boy. In *Puer Aeternus,* von Franz points out how a mother, like the Sphinx, asks the philosophical question at the moment when action is needed, and thus keeps her son from learning to have a foothold on life.

> ...for instance, a youth wants to go skiing or go off somewhere with his friends; he is filled with the élan of youth, which carries one out of the nest, eager to be with others of the same age. The boy tells his mother what he plans to do. That is just youthful exuberance, but the mother begins to worry about his being away from home. The boy is living and learning about life in a natural way, if only the mother does not hang onto him. But if she does, then she starts, "Ought you to do this? I don't think this is the right thing. I don't want to prevent you. I think it is quite right for you to go in for sport, for instance, but I don't think you should go just now!" It is never right "just now." Everything must be thought over first—that is the favorite trick of the devouring mother's animus. Everything must be discussed first. On principle, says she, there is nothing against it, but in this case it seems a bit dangerous. Do you really want to do it? If he is at all cowardly, he begins to wonder, and then the wind has gone out of his sails. He stays at home on Sunday while the others go off without him, and once more he has been defeated in his masculinity.[25]

This dream image was not of Chris's mother. The dream image was originally of a woman who had rejected Chris, which led him to attempt suicide. She had married someone else and recently Chris had met her and tried to reach an understanding and release from her. But she had turned on him with a viciousness Chris had not expected. It now seemed as though outward resolution was to be denied Chris—at least at this time. He was being obliged to pull the energy inwards (not negating his hurt, anger and frustration) to the place where the outer woman assumed inner archetypal dimensions. It seemed as though there were other questions that required attention before he could be released from hurtful relationship into a relationship of mutuality and understanding with the feminine. The frigid virginity of the sphinx image within him was ensuring that we would have to press to a deeper layer of understanding. Virginity of soul is to be respected. It guards a treasure.

The mother-complex is fully resolved only when the man gains access to her "symbolic equivalent," through bending or kneeling in humility to a force greater than himself. He is required to psychologically enter the earth tomb of *mater natura.* Only then will he be free to be reborn.

Two weeks prior to the emergence of the sphinx-image dream, Chris told me about his dream of a small boy in diapers, a precocious child lying in crib, playing with matches. Chris saw this and wanted someone from the other room, preferably the mother, to come and look after the child. Upon reentering the dream, with no prompting from me, it was quickly apparent that the one called to witness this sight was Chris—not the mother. This surprised him greatly, since he felt himself to be addicted to her approval.[26]

Upon looking again, the child seemed older, sitting up, though he was still playing with matches. In guided active imagination, I wondered aloud if Chris could light a fire for the boy, since I know how much young children usually enjoy such shared activities.[27] The fire was lit and the boy, huddled in a blanket, sat beside Chris. The child was obviously delighted by this turn of events. But there were two aspects of the scene that bothered Chris. First, he did not really like the look of the child—he seemed so undifferentiated as he huddled in the blanket. The other was that Chris discovered that he couldn't hear the fire crackling, although he knew the boy could. Try as he might, there was nothing Chris could do to reclaim his hearing loss. The undifferentiated child could hear a sound of nature that was imperceptible to Chris.

Several things were happening at once. Chris knew that part of his libido had been trapped by his personal mother—he had learned to perform for her, to be clever for her. And he was slowly becoming conscious of the fact that any sign of undifferentiation was something to be avoided. Becoming a "blob" would seem too much like becoming encased in the mother. And yet, at a psychological level, he was presently so encased as to be unable to hear the sounds of nature with his inner ears. This was strange, because he was a man who spent much time in the northern wilderness. To be willing to become undifferentiated and descend into the mother-tomb would call for sacrificing independence.

Chris was surprised to see that a woman he knew became an unknown tiger-sphinx-woman who from behind her huge and stony aloofness could ask him the "ultimate" question. Perhaps it was now safe to meet her because the fire had already been lit. The child within was being attended to appropriately. As his therapist I could have attempted to stay at the level of the personal mother, yet this would have been a denial of the imaginal facts as they were presented to me. I could easily have come between Chris and the movements of his own psyche.

Jung suggests that had Oedipus, on the road to Thebes, been sufficiently intimidated by the frightening appearance of the terrible devouring mother personified by the Sphinx, he might have avoided the tragedy of unknowingly killing his father and marrying his mother.[28] This is because he could conceivably have been drawn into an awareness that the unfriendliness of the conscious mind towards the unconscious usually results in the appearance of terrifying monster-animals. Oedipus walked right into the Sphinx's trap, "overestimating his intellect in a typically masculine way, and all unknowingly committed the crime of incest. The riddle of the Sphinx was *herself*—the terrible mother imago,"[29] half beautiful woman, half fearsome and hideous beast/serpent. She is the image of soul, and Oedipus could not solve her deeper riddle nor ultimately conquer her. As Jung puts it, a psychic factor of the Sphinx's magnitude cannot be "disposed of by solving a childish riddle." Oedipus could not take her as a warning and allow himself to fear and feel dwarfed in the way that Chris did.

Jung and the Sphinx

It appears that a sphinx-like image was exactly what Jung struggled with in his break with Freud. One of the issues between the two men was their relationship with the enigmatic Sabina Spielrein. One recorded anecdote is of Jung's complimentary responses to Speilrein's work as he was writing the second half of *Transformations and Symbols of the Libido* (later retitled *Symbols of Transformation*). Jung reassured the woman that her fear of being robbed of her ideas was unfounded:

The study is extraordinarily intelligent and contains excellent ideas, whose priority I am happy to acknowledge as yours.[30]

In fact he did just this. Writing to Freud about Sabina's work, he says:

desinat in piscem mulier formasa supere [What at the top is a lovely woman ends below in a fish—Horace, *Ars Poetica*]...She has read too little and has fallen flat in this paper because it is not thorough enough.[31]

It is worth noting that Jung writes, in the very section of *Symbols of Transformation* where he found Spielrein's work helpful, that certain wise women are supposed to have a fish's or serpent's tail.[32] A page earlier, he also reminds us that the hero will frequently be confronted by a split-off part of his own psyche—an anima figure that tends to "lead an obsessive existence of its own," often anticipating the thoughts and decisions of the masculine consciousness. Such a hero "is unconscious of his own intriguing feminine." Jung goes on to describe the "impotent rage of Wotan who cannot bring himself to recognize his own contradictory nature." He will invariably find his own rejected anima projected onto women close to him.[33]

It would appear that Jung was struggling to become conscious of his own contradictory nature—his inner woman with the fish tail. In the heat of the struggle, he was not able to make appreciative comments about the outer wise woman to the father figure Freud.[34] He betrayed Spielrein, projecting his own fish tail onto her. Indeed it is a tremendous challenge to throw one's connection with the world of the mother and its roots in the unconscious in the very face of the patriarchy, which must forever turn its back on such vitality and animation.[35] The soul-woman's task is thus to become conscious of her fish tail, valuing it and loving it because it gives her depth—a history and a future. Valuing her fish tail helps a woman to stop being a victim of patriarchal projection.

Role of the Incest Taboo

Although it has frequently been said that the taboo against incest has only to do with biological problems of inbreeding, this in fact is not entirely true. It remains important to look behind the taboo and find out what it fosters—what its purpose is in a positive sense. Jung,[36] Layard[37], and more recently Petchkovsky (1982)[38] write about this purpose as endogamous and exogamous enlivening essential to the human spirit.

Endogamous Enlivening

Having reclaimed nature through an alchemical transformation, and moving beyond the distorted and unconscious hermaphrodite, the reunion of the differentiated male/female, king/queen, light/dark, produces a new birth—something totally different. Natural transformations are so often non-linear—who would think, logically, that a butterfly had once been a caterpillar? Without true imagination one simply cannot conceive of this type of change in a rational step-by-step progression. Jung expresses such a development in the language of psychology:

> The union of the conscious mind or ego personality with the unconscious personified as anima produces a new personality compounded of both. . . Since it transcends consciousness it can no longer be called "ego" but must be given the name of "self". . .(It is) both ego and non-ego, subjective and objective, individual and collective. It is the uniting symbol which epitomizes the total union of opposites.[39]

Connecting with Self, giving birth to the divine child, is thus the goal of the alchemical opus, as well as of analysis. Constant awareness of the goal moves the healing relationship beyond the boredom of "my confessing to you" and "you telling me what to do next." The resolution of transference is the "religious care with the impersonal, the persons of the imaginal."[40] After this we become free to serve the stone, the touchstone at our center, the enlivened imagination.[41]

My experience with incest victims is that this turning point is very complex. There is, originally, an absolute dearth of creativity in incestuous families. The family energy is tremendously introverted and guarded jealously by the family patriarch. Neither new blood nor new thoughts must enter. The balance of flow and discipline, so necessary for creation, has been upset. I shall elaborate on this problem later, but at present I wish to suggest that resolution of the creative dilemma marks one aspect of the healing of the victim/offender syndrome, and that imagination is essential to this resolution. This kind of imagination is rooted in the ensouled body, and should not be confused with fantasy. It moves beyond praise or blame, whether it pertains to relationship where the other is a person, an idea or an object. Praise or blame only serves to keep one within the boundaries of the "other," and not free to respond from the basis of esthetic considerations alone. One can only arrive at this latter stance when one is released from the inner voices of praise and blame—when figures from whom the voices emerge no longer need to clamor for attention. Such an esthetic stance emerges when one can admit

> ...that I need all my patience, my love, my faith and even my humility, and that I myself am my own devil, the antagonist who always wants to be opposite in everything.[42]

Exogamous Enlivening

In our society it is easy to assume that the Self-love required for the release of imagination is narcissistic, because there is little outside encouragement to experience an understanding of the Self as distinct from ego. In many ways the process is frightening, since it cuts across too many of the status quo boundaries.

The anthropologist Layard describes the incest taboo as primarily intended to encourage new ideas and new blood to enter the family in the safest possible way. Of course, in primitive communities this is not necessarily clearly articulated. The taboo also introduces polarities — black and white, moon and sun, etc. — into primitive societies at the level of experiential, ritualistic interdependence.[43] For the most part, however, all barriers have gradually broken down in our society, and nothing remains except the incest taboo — without any of its underlying structures. Accompanying the breakdown of society is the rise of the idea of the State, along with various creeds and dogmas. These, however, do not take the place of felt, experienced kinship — that enlivening of society and that placing of the individual within a societal framework, both of which are exogamous results of the incest taboo.

The result of these changes is that we now have a society with a plethora of dogmas and creeds, and an all-pervasive mass consciousness that provokes individuals into various brands of narcissism in desperate attempts at self-fertilization. Jung suggests that the important kinship libido has been pushed so far into the unconscious through rampant state-mindedness that it can only be experienced in the immediate family circle, and even there, minimally. "Kinship libido — which could still engender a satisfying feeling of belonging together — has long been deprived of its object."[44] The individual craves that sense of kinship which can can never be replaced by consciously imposed creed devoid of *mater natura.* This, says Jung, is the core of the whole transference phenomenon. It is impossible to argue it away, because relationship to the Self is at once relationship to our fellow man, and no one can be related to others until he is related to himself. Indeed, non-resolution of inner incest issues is what generally destroys community life at a psychological level. Individuals craving kinship can only bring about community destruction if they have not *experienced* transformation in the style of mother nature. No matter how they maintain intellectual ideals, they will remain addicted to will power, devoid of a discriminating feeling function and disconnected from Self and the true potency of Eros.

Jung posits that the incest taboo, with its rituals of religion and spiritual significance, takes us into the instinctual forces of man's animal nature, organizes them, and gradually makes them available for higher cultural purposes. It is indeed a profound conception that the incest taboo should exist to facilitate the individual's life of ensouled imagining for the enrichment of culture. The integration of animal totems has a profound place in a healthy society. It follows that the rape of soul-consciousness and ignoring of the inner animals brings about a demise of true culture and a tacit aggrandizement of mass-mindedness.

The Healing Relationship

Since the healing relationship is at root a human relationship, the transference phenomenon is immediately constellated and must therefore be addressed.

One of my female patients, Anne, explained this situation as she perceived it. She cut through all the jargon with which we might have encumbered ourselves. She said that she had begun relating to her young son, who was mostly a challenge to her. She had tried every "technique" under the sun — active listening, positive affirmations, logical consequences, as well as the occasional swat on his bottom. One day she found herself visualizing releasing a love relationship between them and discovered, to her amazement, that she could then relate to him much more smoothly. This visualization was not one imposed upon her externally. It arose out of her own inner work. Now she tries to do this regularly and has found that "the rest just follows." She has noticed that her son is now sharing his own perceptions and ideas and that she is enjoying them as an expression of himself. Simultaneously, she is feeling freer to be herself and express her limits and boundaries.

Anne explained that this was what I had done for her, and so now she can do it for him. I asked her to tell me more exactly what she thought I had done! She replied, "You have created a safe place in which I can discover who I am." Obviously, it was a safe enough place in which to entertain a healing imagination *arising from within herself.*

Interestingly, at about this time Anne had a dream of sexually abusing her son. Because she has never genitally abused him, she was particularly shocked by the dream. It was as if, having found a creative way of improving their relationship, she was then free to look at how she had, in fact, been stealing his personal power, his libido in the broadest sense.

This woman was just beginning to move into a wider circle of experience. She took these steps very, very slowly, after lowering herself into her body through dealing with some terrible physical and psychological wounds inflicted on her as a child and adolescent. The struggle to enter her body, to enter a relationship with her Self, had been tremendously hard and bitter. However, as her relationship with her son entered a new level of consciousness, she had the following dream:

> My niece was going to be in a school play and I was going to watch. They needed one more actress for a small part. They asked me and I said yes. I only had two or three lines. The only line I remembered was "my name is Joyce and 'J' is for honey." Opening night came and hundreds of people arrived. I could not remember my few lines. I asked the director if there was a script. He said that there was but he knew a better way. We went upstairs to where his infant son was sleeping. The director's wife and son had been political prisoners in South America and had just returned safely to him. He told me to lie on a small bed beside the baby and that all I had to know would come to me.
>
> Of course, I thought it would be much easier if he simply gave me the script, but I trusted him. After all, he was the director, and if anyone was going to be embarrassed it would be him. I felt that if I did lie beside the child I would absorb the play's message to the audience.

The woman was deeply touched by this dream. It seemed as if a certain quality of effortlessness had emerged in her life now that mother and son had been released from unconscious captivity. Anne could now easily learn new roles, moving beyond a script, if she kept close contact with the peacefully sleeping child — a child who is more objective than her external son, and whose presence can only help to release the son yet further into his own sense of being. Anne could now imaginally contribute to a community cultural event — an enrichment of an exogamous nature. Her new name showed the shift she had experienced from bitterness to a new sweetness, filling out her identity.

The release of Anne's son into a greater expression of Self is similar to the release that Chris experienced when, in our third session, he shared the following dream (which occurred between the fire dream and the sphinx active imagination). In both situations, the boy is released from his suffocating personal mother and therefore becomes freer to actually relate to her. During his second session, Chris had expressed the fear of falling in love with me. We talked at some length about this, and he was able to say that he was actually afraid that I would end up doing his inner work for him. I appreciated his frankness and promised to try to stay alert to any possibility of my intruding, unwholesomely, into his work space. We also talked a little of his extreme loneliness and sense of isolation — loss of kinship — through coming here from another part of the country.

He dreamed that he was

...lying in a bed with a skylight over it. There is a huge storm outside — the elm trees are bent almost horizontal as they fly in the raging wind. My therapist is sitting quietly in the room. Suddenly, the skylight shatters and the glass falls onto the bed. The storm has entered: I can hear it now. Then my therapist's husband enters the room.

I asked Chris what meaning he found in the dream. He replied, "There has been a breakthrough between us." I was a little surprised at the response, since to me the image suggested that the breakthrough had been between him and mother nature. Chris described the atmosphere in the room before the breakthrough as one of relaxed intimacy — like that between husband and wife. He was not at all perturbed by the breaking glass. I asked how he felt about my husband entering the room. His response was that it was particularly interesting to him — he felt he would be a reliable person who would help clean up the glass, but that in addition and more importantly, it was only through my husband's arrival that Chris had been able to truly ascertain my identity. Until that time I had been somewhat familiar, comforting and "wifely." When my husband arrived on the scene, the situation clarified and it was easier to see where the primary relationships lay. A healing quaternity had been established; therapist and husband, Chris and mother nature.

Of course, at one level Chris would feel the breakthrough as pertaining to his relationship with me: a man having an independent relationship with *mater natura* does indeed create a passage to a more satisfying relationship with an external woman. This is because he is no longer so free to project his anima onto the external woman. He is beginning to find his own fish tail. And he perceives me as having an inner husband. Establishing the *quaternio,* then, does not diminish the intensity of the relationship between patient and therapist. Prior to this dream, Chris had expressed not only fear of involvement with me but would also make belittling comments about our relationship — such as I have

frequently heard from patients burdened with a modicum of psychological sophistication. "Oh, it's just transference or something." Such
a statement is belittling because it tends to distance us both from the
intensity of the sacred task at hand. Chris would also easily dismiss any
of his own imaginations and my input by translating them, with considerable bitterness and adroitness, into "intellectual ideas." If I asked
if he had perceived any images, he would say "no," with a defiant grin.
Patients frequently distance themselves from others and from their images and a moral commitment to them—precisely because of the images' grounded intensity.

In four sessions, Chris imagined himself becoming an animal, then
he allowed himself to become a little boy and light the fire in the cavern of the whale-dragon-of-a-mother; he discovered he was inwardly deaf
to the sound of nature, and he had a terrifying encounter with the sphinx-
woman, who asked him an extremely difficult question. Interwoven with
these themes is the man's negative relationship with a devouring mother, as well as his relationship with his female therapist. Chris initially
saw this as somewhat alarming, in that he felt it could easily follow after the pattern of his relationship with his mother. There was the threat
of the therapist inappropriately invading the psychic space that was struggling to reclaim its male virginity in order to be strong enough to tolerate a more profound meeting with "the other." This last dream clearly
shows that the therapist's task is not to intrude upon the man's work,
but to support his more objective encounter with mother nature in order that his inner ears might be opened. Many months, sometimes years
of work may follow before such dreams can come to life, bringing their
images to an everyday reality. Having the dream is important, but without
bringing value to it, it remains a fanciful entertainment. Once the dream
has been imbued with meaning, the task is then to live the dream and
to actualize the potential of its message. Our task is to carry its images
to life. In allowing this process to take place within us, we can slowly
build bridges from Self to ego. Such bridges redeem us from narcissism
and enliven us into being moved by our creativity. Enslavement to oneself keeps us unconsciously trapped in *mater natura* while externally
violating her ways. This occurs because we remain narcissistic, devoid
of a relationship with our inner images, and unable to see ourselves as
creative and contributing members of an enriched, culturally enlivened
kinship network. We remain trapped, always waiting for an external and
incestuous fertilization, always unable to die.

Notes

[1]C.G. Jung. *CW* XVI, par. 533

[2]*Ibid.*, par. 533
Also *Ibid.*, par. 442
   Jung thought that the mandala, with its four-fold division, was a more appropriate symbol of wholeness. He postulated that the endogamous urge of the incest taboo might be trying to unite the different components of the personality on the pattern of cross-cousin marriage, but on a higher plane where "spiritual marriage" becomes an inner experience that is not projected and will not, therefore, disturb real relationships.

[3]C.G. Jung. *Word and Image.* Princeton: Princeton University Press, 1979, p. 211

[4]C.G. Jung, *CW* IX, I, par. 195

[5]Marion Woodman. *Addiction to Perfection: The Still Unravished Bride.* Toronto: Inner City Books, 1982, p. 82

[6]C.G. Jung, *CW* XIV, par. 106

[7]*Ibid.*, par. 107

[8]C.G. Jung, *CW* XVI, par. 534

[9]*Ibid.*, pars. 533-534

[10]*Ibid.*, par. 504

[11]*Ibid.*

[12]C.G. Jung, *CW* V, par. p.xxiii

[13]*Ibid.*, par. 654

[14]*Ibid.*, pars. 458, 459; also pp. 300-301ff

[15]C.G. Jung, *CW* XVI, par. 368

[16]C.G. Jung, *CW* IX, II, pars. 40-41

[17]C.G. Jung, *CW* XVII, pars. 218-222

[18]Robert Stein, *Incest & Human Love.* Dallas: Spring Publications, 1984, p. 29

[19]C.G. Jung, *CW* V, par. 190

[20]*Ibid.*, par. 199

[21]*Ibid.*, p. 235ff

[22]*Ibid.*, par. 351

[23]C.G. Jung, *CW* XVI, par. 371

[24]*Ibid.*, par. 419

[25]Marie-Louise von Franz. *Puer Aeternus.* Boston: Sigo Press, 1981, p. 176

[26]Chris presented another dream on this occasion. He saw a couple squatting cross-legged by the road. The woman's left breast was exposed. Three streams of milk from it combined into one which she collected in a bowl and offered to the man. He offered her a bowl of water. The dream left him with a feeling of wholeness, of "completing a circle close to the earth."
   Although I didn't include the dream in the main text, it was an important contribution to my sense that Chris could only find relief from his hurtful mother by moving to a deeper level of the feminine, and consequently a new conception of relationship between masculine and feminine.

[27]C.G. Jung, *CW* V, par. 311
   Jung refers to the Indian firebringer Matarisvan, called "he who swells in the mother." He suggests that "fire making is a preeminently conscious act and therefore 'kills' the dark state of union with the mother."

[28]*Ibid.*, par. 272
   Jung makes an interesting comment that "Mother complexes are extremely common in America and often very pronounced, probably because of the strong maternal influence in the home and social position of women generally. . . As a result of this conditioning many American women develop their masculine side, which is then compensated in the unconscious by an exquisitely feminine instinct, aptly symbolized by a Sphinx."

[29]*Ibid.*, par. 265
   In the same passage, Jung tells us that the Sphinx was a daughter of Echidna, a monster half beautiful maiden and half hideous serpent. She was born of Mother Earth, Gaia and Tartarus—personification of the underworld. The Sphinx was conceived incestuously by Echidna and her son, Orthrus the dog.

[30]Carotenuto, Aldo. *A Secret Symmetry.* New York: Pantheon Books, 1982, p. 183

[31]C.G. Jung in *The Freud/Jung Letters,* 310J. William McGuire, ed. Princeton: Princeton University Press, 1974, p. 498

[32]C.G. Jung, *CW* V par. 567; also p. 362ff

[33]*Ibid.*, pars. 553-565

[34]John Layard, "The Incest Taboo and the Virgin Archetype." In *Images of the Untouched.* Joanne Stroud & Gail Thomas, eds. Dallas: Spring Publications, 1982, p. 151.
Originally appeared in *Eranos Jahrbüche,* Vol. XII, 1945
   Layard maintains that Freud's rendition of the Oedipus myth is "a reflection of Freud's own psychology, and taken symbolically, represents an unconscious rebellion against his own patriarchal and over-intellectualized attitude as represented by the father."

[35]In light of this it is interesting that the hero in the novel *Manticore* (Robertson Davies) is facing a split in his anima—between a very analytical female Jungian analyst and the "bear woman" who takes him to ancient bear caves, and through a terrifying birth process through a long tunnel. The novel ends with the hero having to make a choice between the two women. Which one will be his guide? This suggests to me an archetypal question which we face both as a society and as a discipline.

[36]C.G. Jung, *CW* XVI, pars. 431-442

[37]John Layard, *op. cit.*

[38]Louis Steward, "Affect and Archetype in Analysis." In *Chiron Clinical Series*, 1987, p. 148
Perry's work with young adult schizophrenics shows that their relevant imagery has to do with the destruction of society, usually in its form as "kingdom" or city state, which is followed during recovery by the reconstitution of a new society.
Petchkovsky, in attempting to validate Perry's findings with his study of aboriginal Australians, found that the major etiological factor in the onset of the psychotic episode was the violation of the incest taboo, that is, marrying someone from a forbidden moiety. He concluded that "the radical disturbance of kinship structure through incest would seem to be an archetype for Aboriginal psychosis."

[39]C.G. Jung, *CW* XVI, par. 474

[40]James Hillman, "The Thought of the Heart." In *Eranos,* Vol. 48, pp. 155-156

[41]C.G. Jung, *CW* XVI, pars. 50, 531

[40]Ibid., par. 522

[43]Ibid., par. 433
Also, John Layard, *op. cit.,* pp. 154-164

[44]C.G. Jung, *CW* XVI, par. 445

CHAPTER IV

The Question of Hysteria

The Void in Our Scientific Paradigm of Hysteria

Starting with Freud and Breuer, psychoanalysis began as treatment for hysteria: the image of the analyst with his following of women is a common one. Even from Egyptian times, hysteria was seen as mostly affecting women.[1] To Freud's credit, he did bring the notion of male hysteria to Vienna from Paris. This male hysteria, though, could only exist in "men who show mental weakness, childish emotion and womanly emotion" (quoted from Dubas' textbook, 1910).

Hysteria was associated with the uterus; the term was first used in the Hippocratic *On the Diseases of Women*. This reference was quoted as late as the seventeenth century, with the uterus being "the cause of 600 evils and countless suffering."[2] Inherent in the root *hyster* is a strong association between the feminine and inferiority. The history of the "disease" hysteria has thus no conception of the womb as vessel of renewal, with a *minimum* of six hundred *blessings* emanating from it. Only its shadow has been identified.

> The womb [is thus] conceived to be self-moved, perhaps autonomous, and therefore a "living creature" or "animal." Hysteria was the effect of the

desirous animal in woman. It was a disease in which the autonomous animal dominates the human being, cutting her off from pneuma, respiration, spirit, and degrading her into the animality of her womb.[3] [Emphasis added]

The early hysterics were frequently branded as witches, and like witches on trial, they were prodded with pins and needles. The manifesto against witches, the *Malleus Maleficarium* (1494) derived the word *femina* from *fe* (faith) and *minus* (less). Women were defined as having less faith than men, and perhaps they were even soulless.

The first English work on hysteria was printed in 1603 by Edward Jarden, who was also an expert on matters of witchcraft for James VI of Scotland. Hillman describes Jarden's book, *A Brief Discourse On A Disease Called the Suffocation Of The Mother*, as "a watershed . . . moving the matter itself from an irrational, religious problem to one of secular explanation."[4] The evil witch became the poor patient. Her problem lay not with satanic forces but in her own womb; her own physiology was at fault. Now hysteria could be attacked through surgery. There were devices used for compressing or packing the ovaries in ice. There were ovariectomies and clitoral circumcisions. The brutalization of the body, the female body in particular, can once more be seen as an outcome of the dismissal of spiritual and soul issues and a parallel and profane descent into matter.

Psychiatric descriptions of hysteria frequently pointed to moral inferiority. In 1866 Falret says, "in one word, the life of the hysteric is nothing but one perpetual falsehood."[5] Kraepelin's four-volume psychiatric text, which was to remain the major psychiatric text for thirty years, was published in the middle of the First World War. The Latins, Slavs, and Jews ("burdened by long inbreeding") were considered to be more hysterical than the calmer, more sober Germans. Kraepelin also maintained that hysteria was

. . . the diseased form of the undeveloped, naive soul, which for men is a psychopathic disorder, but hysteria of women corresponds with a natural developmental direction; in some circumstances it is a remaining upon a childish level.[6]

It should be noted that Kraepelin's sample of hysterics had "an overwhelming preponderance of unmarried country girls aged fifteen to twenty-three, working in city households as serving maids and cooks,"[7] and that he himself was only twenty-seven years of age when his first volume was published.[8]

I have heard clinicians thankfully exclaim that women's and girls' hallucinations stop when family therapy starts. While I have no doubt that the patients are thankful to have been listened to, I have found that women's wild and crazy visions, coupled with their numb bodies, might perhaps give us some clues as to why hysteria has become the despised, if not forgotten, cornerstone of a discipline that is marked by its own forked tongue, its own Apollonian/Dionysian split. In our patriarchal society, there is no terrifying and valued encounter with the elemental feminine, with the dwarfing sphinx.

On the other hand, there is the simultaneous disappearance of woman into "mere nature"— elemental consciousness. This is reinforced by a patriarchal pornographic and sadistic worldview that coerces the feminine to disappear into animal form. Not only do women tend to disappear into elemental consciousness, but men who have abandoned soul will frequently find that their animae are, in early therapy, half-animal, or animal emerging into woman.

Abused women are frequently unable to sleep for fear of "an animal loose in the house," or of a snake or mouse entering their vaginas. Not infrequently, the dream is a recurring one dating from the onset of the woman's own abuse.

Olga was such a woman. Just after her marriage to Don, she dreamed of her husband's penis as a mouse, and she was terrified and could not allow it into her. E., another patient, would imagine being orally raped, and would picture herself toothless and dripping semen from her lips; she had nightmares of swallowing lots of mice. I have noticed that the response of many children to the lion and the mouse pictured in the *Children's Apperception Test* is a studious avoidance of the mouse hiding behind the lion's chair. Women and children tell me of becoming animals and plants when they feel frightened. For instance, a woman previously never beaten in her life was hit on the face and bruised by her husband. She dreams of being an animal and running as hard as she can to an enclosure in the forest, searching frantically for safety. She had never dreamed like this before. Lola, the daughter of a violent alcoholic father and a rape victim whose young daughter became an incest victim at three years of age, started to draw again after many years, though she had never had any formal training. The first drawing was of herself as a sleeping mouse, "still waiting to be connected" to another human being. A few weeks later the little mouse began to feed itself, though its hind paws were still buried deep in snow. It was to be another few months before any human form emerged—and that, only partially. Lola recalled as a child finding her dog dead, and its body thrown callously under the porch. It was the only friend she had. In some ways it was easier for Lola to be closer to the dog than to her mother. She had been so bereft and hurt at the loss of her dog that she had made a decision that she would live for the dog, and would also die with it. She began now to see that she had in a sense never lived.

It is not uncommon to find brutalized women seeing themselves or their children as half-animal. Halliday[9] recalls one patient who at sixteen was convinced that her baby would be half animal. She had been raped by her brother and locked in the basement with his Labrador retrievers. Certainly most sexually abused women and children I know are, in fact, extremely ignorant about their body functions, sexuality and reproduction. They dare not look and they dare not explore. But the fact of their having been lost, *psychologically,* in an elemental and animal world is rarely apprehended. This can be the case even if the woman has been through years of higher education. When women appear to themselves in their dreams as animals or Neanderthals, or are taken over by insects or men, it suggests a profound immersion of the inferior function in the unconscious, and therefore a denial of soul life — which I have come to see as the true outcome of violence and sexual abuse.

I know of an old woman whose family thinks her crazy and hysterical. But this old woman has also spent months alone on the prairie. Her husband was an operator of a "cat skinner," a huge machine, used in the tar sands oil industry, that rips and tears the earth. He would be away for months at a time. The woman lived in a single-room house. She tells of prairie fires that would sometimes rage around her for days. She would be trapped inside with her six crying, hungry children, only potatoes to eat, a little water and no power. She dared not let her children outside because of all the animals, including a cougar, that had taken refuge on her roof. She was also plagued by the memory of her wedding night when, upon retiring, her husband took out a picture of a former girlfriend and placed it on the dresser. I have come across no more apt and poignant image of the trapped, hurting, hysterical woman, surrounded by terrified animals, tormented by the image of the other woman, unable to allow her hungry children to play. She unconsciously must enact the Great Mother who cannot let the Son slip out of her grasp. A woman lost in an elemental world is generally addicted to mothering, but in a sense can only be a nymph-mother. She is not in a position to mediate the unconscious for her children, since she herself tends to be lost in it.

Well on in therapy, Lola's three-year-old abused daughter had recurring nightmares of "black hands coming to get her"—sometimes they would be bear's paws. The child had symbolically expressed a great deal of fear and anger towards "the father" (her own had sexually molested her) in her play therapy, and I had the sense that these dreams were about something else, though I said nothing. In the meantime, Lola, the mother, began talking to me about the arthritis she was experiencing in her hands. It was getting worse; she felt she was developing claws. She talked about the Venus Fly Trap, and imagined her fingers being snapped off by a vicious plant. She sensed that her father had actually stolen her hands long years ago. (A., twelve, sexually abused by her father since age four, also dreamed of her hands freezing off as she lives with a wolf). The doctor had warned Lola that she would probably be completely crippled within five years. In group therapy, Lola watched two films on the life and work of the Canadian west coast artist Emily Carr, and was profoundly touched. She too had lost touch with her creativity in slaving for others to keep a roof over her head. Now Lola started drawing again, and surprisingly felt some relief in her hands. Drawing and painting remain the only "treatment" that prevents her hands from becoming claws.

Six months after her daughter's recurring nightmares, Lola dreamed that a monster cat was waiting to be let into the apartment. When she went to the door and opened it, she saw a tiny kitten looking for a home. Lola told me that when she lay beside her daughter to help her go to sleep, the child had another nightmare. "Evangeline's office is on fire. All her animals are gone." I knew that this little girl liked my small toy animals. I made sure they were readily available the next time she visited me. When she walked into my room she announced, "I am a cat all the time." And she put on my cat headdress that she had just noticed for the first time, and started scratching herself all over. Then she snatched off the cat mask and poured all the little animals onto the floor, stamping on them, hitting them and shouting, "I don't like them any more because they hit." Finding the little cat, she said, "She's mad coz Safeway hit her." It is not uncommon to find hurt children abusing animals just as they have been abused. This is out of their own unexpressed anger and personal powerlessness. Having been subsumed in an elemental world, they try to escape and follow the patriarchal paradigm of attempting to snuff out the animals.

Months later, Lola dreamed of a lion which gave her a warm feeling even though he was so huge. He roared and went on his way—free. Simultaneously, Lola felt free. She told me that she had pushed all the animals away for years, since the time her dog as well as her innocence had been killed. From that point she had not wanted to be hurt and thus had fled, psychologically, into the jungle, paradoxically becoming more hurt all the time, a tradition of victimization culminating in the abuse of her own daughter.

An abused woman who is locked into the pornographized animal life of the patriarchy can, in a sense, only leave her own human child in animal skins. With this image we move into a territory abandoned by the patriarchal church—Pan's territory: which "leads out of the city walls and into open country,"[10] a terrifying Sphinx journey. "Pan himself was abandoned by his wood nymph mother and wrapped in a hare's pelt by his father, Hermes, who took the baby to Olympus where all the gods received him with delight."[11] Pan's ability to preserve and nurture and his ability to destroy through wild, hot panic, appear to be closely linked within the psyche. Hillman suggests that Pan's lechery and fertility are secondary attributes which "arise from the dry longing of nature alone, of one who is ever an abandoned child and who in innumerable pairings is never paired."[12] In our society we can only see Pan as a rogue and the elemental nymph as a witch. Unfortunately for us, "when nymph has become a witch and nature a dead objective field, then we have a natural science without a natural mind."[11] To see Pan as nature, we must "first be grasped by nature, both 'out there' in empty countryside which speaks in sounds not words, and 'in here' in a startled reaction," and thus allow ourselves to experience the "therapeutic way of fear, and the excitation of our imagination by the nymphs."[13]

Jung maintained that God would appear ambivalent as long as we remain *encased* in nature,[14] and therefore unable to see that spirit and instinct are inseparable, forming an "impenetrable mass, a veritable magma springing from the depths of primeval chaos."[15] Without appreciation of the animal nature of the unconscious, we can only flee from it or succumb to it, just as we could never value and respect the violent, destructive or threatening side of spirit.[16] We would somehow be obliged to tame both the unconscious and spirit, not realizing that ". . .when the ego is relaxed the Self masters itself. The body also masters itself."[17]

Aphrodite was the Greek Goddess, possibly of oriental origin, who knew that the animal, the human and the divine worlds merge in our sexuality.[18] In a wonderful image of the goddess as Lady of Beasts and Man, she reflects woman's ability and willingness to love.

Neither sacrifice nor domination over the world of the unconscious is a central concern for the Great Goddess. Over both of these stands the law of transformation, in which she sublimates all life and raises it to a development where, *without losing its bond with the root and foundation*, it achieves the highest forms of psychic reality.[19] [Emphasis added]

As women heal from the effects of sexual abuse, their journey will invariably take them into an uncharted country that belongs to the abandoned goddess of the animals. Premenstrual dreams frequently reflect a Lilith sexuality and consciousness—a pulsating, throbbing, primal, wordless state of being.[20] In these creation myths and dreams, Lilith emerges as an instinctual quality of the feminine emanating from God and the Devil, and connected in a most elemental way with humankind.

Olga is a woman who had been sexually violated as a child and whose daughter is the victim of an incestuous relationship with Olga's husband, Don. Olga dreamed, premenstrually, that she was a deer with secret and unknown powers. She is deeply enmeshed in a deadly power battle with two men, one devilish, one godlike. The latter is trying to help her resume her human form, but she gets stuck halfway and this disgusts her. She had liked being all "animal." Towards the end of the dream, she is a beautiful native woman sitting looking at her reflection in a pond without any male company, and suddenly realizing something of her true heritage from her mother. In her power battles, Olga, the deer woman, can even *will* her antlers to disappear—those protrusions the ancients thought came from the brain and represented the development of the "mind of the body, symbolizing the drive to completion, wholeness, and congruence."[21] It would be easy to assume that Olga has emerged into natural consciousness at this time. In fact much of her development is still based on magic and illusions, with a foundation of extreme, though coerced, willfulness. Deer woman is beginning to realize the paradox that though this fraudulent lover comes from the pit of hell and is, in fact, the Devil, her relationship with him allows for her first glimpse of the fact that she is only part human, and that in such a state she would be unable to be humanly sexual within the sacrament of marriage. Part of her has been encased in the animal. Furthermore, the man from the pit of hell wants her power. The two of them are joined in mutual fascination.

In the dream, the jolt from a hunter's gun leaves her bereft of both the devil and the "other man," to whom she realized she should have paid more attention in the past. The jolting loss of the masculine leaves

her alone for the first time, able to study her own reflection, sensing
the wisdom and power of womanhood still in touch with the wholesome native life. This gives her an inner sense of the goddess and a re-
newed connection with her personal mother.

Yet the scene ends with both a punitive and an aggrandizing response
to the masculine. One can imagine how such a soul will stand at the
judgment door, demanding retribution and payment for past wrongs.

A few days after the "big dream," Olga experienced herself, at home,
going through a horrendous birth process. In struggling to emerge as
human, she found that she had to chew off one of her animal legs. The
pain was excruciating. When next I saw her she was saying that she was
human, paradoxically, "no longer above others." Yet she mourned deeply
for her lost part.

Some months later Olga was still incorporating the human birth process, beginning to have a deeper appreciation of the depth and scope
of her "power issue" first manifested through the deer dream. She found
herself battling inwardly in a totally new way. She writes in her journal:

> What is this devilish pleasure-seeking part of me, that knows no bound-
> aries, that has no limit to satisfaction...this deliciously evil thing that lurks
> inside of me? This bitch, this witch, this hideous whore, that keeps compa-
> ny with rats, spiders, and deadly snakes, and smiles upon everyone's misfor-
> tunes...that watches babies and children suffer, and old people die,
> painfully...and with a smile on my face. The face of this devilish part of
> me, writhing with disgust at their humanness, orders, "Move their dead car-
> casses away, be off with them." There's this part of me that likes to kill beau-
> tiful things, such as pretty flowers, and beautiful relationships, and holds
> hands with death against the living and the beautiful.

This newfound aspect of Olga has so many attributes of the suppressed
and opposed Lilith, who in the third millennium B.C. in Sumer was
Lil, a destructive storm or wind spirit. By the eighth century B.C. in
Syria she was joined with the demonic figure of the child-killing witch.
She became known as "Blood Sucker," "Woman of Harlotry," "End of
all Flesh," "witch," "hag," "snatcher," "enchantress," *and*, the "soul of
every living creature that creepeth."

She was Adam's first counterpart and Lady of the Beasts. She was thus
the first woman created by God from the earth, and was at first cut down
and then lifted up to become the Lash of God...the "bride of Satan,
now the consort of God, ever flaming at the gates of paradise."[22] She
is the one who from the beginning has needed spiritual connections.

She desired to be shaped as the cherubim, but God removed her from them and sent her below.

She is the one who mourns the diminishment of the moon and cries the wounded feminine hurt and rage, being cast out into the place of desolation by the Red Sea, described in the Old Testament as

> a wasteland, drenched with blood, the haunt of pelicans, hedgehogs, owls, ravens, and satyrs; a place of thorns, thistles and nettles, and a lair for jackals and ostriches.[23]

Yet this Lilith is the very one who, with profound healing of consciousness, can become what Jung called the "shamanistic anima" of healing.[24]

Olga writes that she is deathly afraid of this part of her, since it is a wild energy. She described this wild energy as how she would feel with her antlers—charging madly, blindly, through the forest. The wound of this power was like her later image of a green horse riddled with holes which were filled with boiling vinegar, causing the poor beast to tear madly "like a human crazed with pain." Suddenly, as she was writing, Olga's baby began to cry. She continues

> I gently pick him up, and hold him and soothe him. I lovingly admire the life and beauty God gave him, and the voice he has to cry with.
>
> Oh! How do I find a balance between these two parts of me? The destructive part of me seems to have been pinned down for so very long. It is as though it has carried all the hurt and resentment and bitterness all my life. Maybe it's more than that. Maybe it carries a part of all women's hurt and resentment and bitterness.

More integration occurred when Olga decided to have her long hair cut. Her son was frightened because it might bleed. She also found herself crying at "the agony of being in her body." She also allowed herself to "really make love" with her husband "for the first time." Afterwards she cried again because she realized "how empty and alone" she truly felt. What did she need that could not come from even the most intimate times with her husband?

Still later, a neighbor presented Olga with some deer jerky. The idea of eating it, of eating an aspect of herself, was appalling. But she took the dried meat and eventually ate it, relishing its flavor and strengthening substance.

In the *Mysterium Coniunctionis,* Jung refers us to Ripley's *Cantilena,*[25] where new birth emerges from moon consciousness. The round moon mother carries within her pregnant self the symbols of wholeness and redemption. If the willful ego does not interfere, the inner opposites now contained in the pregnant vessel will

> gradually draw together, and what looked like death and destruction will settle down into a latent state of concord, suitably expressed by the symbol of pregnancy.[26]

Jung points out that a subtle feature of the *Cantilena* is that the pregnancy cravings of the mother are stilled with her own flesh and blood, which she must ingest — celebrating, as it were, the Last Supper within herself. She thus experiences otherness within her own Self. Gradually, therefore, the woman becomes more objective. By ingesting herself, the pregnant moon woman learns to endure all aspects of herself, and thus learns to endure others. She learns to "integrate those parts of her personality which are still outside ego consciousness."[27] We can see then that Olga's appalling task of Self-eating is a sacramental profundity which allows her to begin living with a question — what can fill the inner void?

Enter...the Mouse

Some time ago, I gave a presentation at the Canadian Psychiatric Conference, in a large splendid ballroom at a beautiful hotel in the mountains. The curtains were drawn so that we could see the slides of statistics and graphs of previous speakers. As I got up to speak on child sexual abuse, I delightedly commented on a small mouse that had just run across the floor, saying that I could think of no better animal joining this illustrious company in discussion of a topic frequently associated with women's hysteria. There was no response!

Jung gives us some "suggestions about the dream mouse."[28] It is an animal of darkness, of night and of fertility. He tells us of an "old saying that a girl who is not afraid of mice has lost her virginity." We might add that such a woman may be unafraid because she has never *had* her virginity. She cannot welcome the phallus if she cannot rest in her own body, her own truth. Furthermore, the woman's hysterical behavior towards the mouse carries a symbolic truth for the man to inwardly perceive and work on.

Jung continues that the mouse is a symbol of the

> Yin principle in its readiness to conceive...it is a symbol of woman's wish for fecundity...This wish in all women is deeply rooted, because it is only by giving birth to children that woman fulfills her natural task and lives

according to her destiny. And one may not restrict this statement to the material and physical world of woman's body and sex only. It is just as true for the moon-mind of woman, which all the time longs for the seed of the sons of light, in order to bring forth the spiritual children of the moon in dark but fervent creativeness. The wish for physical and spiritual conception is even so closely connected in women, that often they mix up the two and leave it to the discrimination of men to decide what they really want.[29]

About four months after the deer dream, Olga writes

I am small and put down in many ways. I hide like a mouse and when it's dark and no one is suspecting, I run out and do my dirty work. As I think about this, it's like having to swallow my mouse. His fur is stuck in my throat. It's terrible. . .it's terrible. There's something beautiful about evil. . .it's the closest thing to an orgasm. . .I'm a witch. . .I see men with bleeding mouths from my stabbing them with a knife.

A few weeks later, Olga was crying, in her therapy hour, from feeling the effects of "a woman's love." She said, "My tears are wet and warm. Previously I cried only tears of ice. . .Now I have a heart. . .previously I had been a stone cold corpse." She went on to tell me a dream of "screaming in hysteria." A white llama came and explained to her that this was "the hysteria of innocence. . .of naivete." She says that she is terrified of the unknown and has been suppressing this terror all her life. "We women have lost our reason. . .we've become lunatics." And thinking aloud, she imagines that she can cover this up because "pretty Boy George wants a mother." It was a strange paradox for us to contemplate. Finding her mouse, her hidden furtive evil, simultaneously allowed her regressive innocence to come to the fore. It was this coerced, hurt innocence that kept her inwardly screaming in hysteria, disconnected from warm human tears, from her own creativity, and suffocated by inappropriate mothering. She had not been able to swallow and digest the "seed of the soul of light" until she had ingested and digested her mouse. She could not receive her husband's penis because she had no reclaimed and conscious vessel with which to receive it. In the next week, she wrote one hundred and twenty five pages in her journal—an outpouring of herself that had been previously locked away. She tells me that the llama is a beast of burden—just as women are. He has come to help her "become a woman, knowing she has mysteries in her basket to share with her man at the right time."

This began to further affect her perceptions of her husband, Don. She became aware of a constant taste of blood in her mouth. In her

rage at his abusing their daughter, she imagined herself tearing at his
face, eating it, eating his blood. She wanted to "reduce him to babble."
It seems that unless the elemental woman can lay claim to her own "inner babble," she will attempt to coerce a man into being a "babbling
idiot." She will attempt to subvert any power of Logos to which he may
aspire, in a desperate attempt to have another, her own consciousness
appreciated. Although at this time her imaginal interaction with her
husband is violent, its intent is to force him to become aware of the
fact that he does babble. Much has been written about women's loss
of logic when they are caught in their animus complex, talking about
ideas which are not their own, which are not embedded in their own
matter. Very little has been said about the man's "loss of logic" when
his heart is not included in his speech. Jung pointed out that "men can
argue in a very womanish way when they are anima-possessed and have
thus been transformed into the animus of their own anima."[30] It seems
as though the man's anima tries to promote a kind of "togetherness"
and blurs over all distinctions and genuine differences. The woman's animus, on the other hand, tends to draw the sword of power. She can
do this creatively if the man is willing to be the receptive vessel. It is
my experience that the woman has very few opportunities to be received
thus. Very few victims of the patriarchy really want to hear the clear voice
of the feminine, because it will appear monstrous and it will upset the
status quo. The woman's frustration can only mount, and she will find
herself instead falling into a negative complex and becoming destructive. For the truth of the moment to be apprehended, all functions must
be included in the dialogue—thinking, feeling, intuition and sensation.

Months later, Olga's experience deepened further. She was again afraid
of animals in her bed at night. A half-goat, half-man was chasing her:
he had red eyes. Becoming still and calm, I wondered aloud what the
red eyes might be saying. "Be aware of the things deep inside, the blood,
the guts, the humanness of it all." The red goat eyes do not say "be-
ware," but "be aware." And then those eyes of the goat body became
"serene... full of clarity, love and compassion." Their redness was all gone.

I asked Olga what she had learned in the last five minutes. She paused
a few seconds, and replied, "If I don't run away...and if I ask the question the animals become friendly." Asking the question is a new level
of consciousness. We cannot live with a question until we have found
the question, or it has found us.

Of course, if the man in the relationship has a tenuous and yet tight
relationship with Logos, he will be an easy prey to a woman's "stabbings

of his mouth" aimed at reducing him to babble. Such a man is afraid of being devoured by the mother. It is not just his penis he is afraid of losing, but also his phallic tongue. He cannot risk a return to the place of presexual consciousness where infantile reactions are provoked as well as archetypal images that are potentially compensatory and curative. He is unable to return to such a fecund place because of his unwillingness to lose control. An elemental woman relating to him would easily become the carrier of "loss of control" while he sadistically remains in control. Even in sexual response he stays calm, reducing the woman to an infant, humiliated in her desire and and materiality,[31] so that her body and soul live out his repressed madness. Yet in his hidden aspect, he will long for hysteria and the uncontrolled. The only place in which Don can lose control is in relating sexually to his little daughter: there he is completely compulsive. This is not willing descent into the primal place of renewal, a conscious bending the knee to the Great Mother in order to release full masculinity. This is the profane place of the abuse of young Psyche being obliged to carry the offender's craziness.

Now we can see more deeply into the relationships of the intellectual soul period of the Graeco-Roman era, still in full sway in our patriarchal families. The Gaea-Uranus, Rhea-Cronus couples we have already met in Chapter I were modified by the great Phrygean Goddess Cybele, whose cult was introduced to Greece early, so that Rhea and Cybele eventually merged into one persona. Turret-crowned Cybele was the goddess of caverns and caves, yet worshipped on the mountain tops. "She personified the heart in its primitive and savage state and exercised dominion over the wild beasts who habitually form part of her retinue."[33] Her throne was flanked by two lions and she would hold a whip decorated with knuckle bones—a symbol of power. As her cult spread, it was said that she fell in love with a son-lover, Attis. In the early era of Greek culture, still emerging from the Minoan, there seemed to be no fully developed male god to stand beside the goddess. Thus Cybele chose Attis as her priest and demanded from him the vow of chastity, which he broke. As punishment, Cybele struck him with a frenzied delirium, in the course of which he castrated himself. This was ritually reenacted by Cybele's priests as part of spring vegetation rites (March 24) on the Day of Blood,[33] flagellating themselves with whips. At the point of killing himself, Cybele turned Attis into a pine tree, over which she still mourns. Jung suggests that though there are overlapping meanings in the story, the common denominator is the libido. "The son personifies

the longing for the mother," the unconscious, and the "mother personifies the (incestuous) love for the son."[34] For being unfaithful to his
vows to Mother, the son ends up being buried in the Mother, stiffened
in the tree trunk just as Osiris was overgrown by the cedar. The patriarchal soul was obliged to defy mother-love in order to allow new consciousness to emerge, yet does not realize that at some level it remains
encased in that which it sought to escape. The present-day patriarchal
ego, with its loss of mythic roots, seems to oblige the woman to carry
for him his own hysteria in the face of his maddening mother-love: there
is no voluntary castration in the service of devoted chastity to the unconscious, the Mother. There can be no profound fertility because the
unconscious mother-ground must be subjugated, not related to and
cherished. The patriarchal soul cannot sustain sacrifice, so the unconscious mother-ground can only retaliate at her rejection. At this point,
though, the woman remains the carrier of society's suppressed hysteria.

Valuing the Cleft Palate

Beth, a patient of mine, recalls the sensation of being sexually abused
through fondling by a man "friend" at age three. She says that it felt
like "an electric shock . . . (she) knew it was bad." Now she wonders, "was
it arousal or even an orgasm?" During therapy Beth had excruciatingly
connected with repressed memories of abuse by her father, which she
seemed not to want to specifically talk about. I followed her lead. However, she did tell me that as the years passed she had felt increasingly
like "a slut . . . an alley cat." She learned to subdue all physical sensations, despising her materiality, and finally "retreated into marriage for
safety." Her sexuality was not subdued "perfectly," however, until she became a mother. Then she had this special task which demanded "utter
perfection." During therapy Beth had many dreams and waking visions
of a cockroach, a scorpion, and a dragon. She could only orgasm when
they "had hold" of her. Most of her early sessions were full of hysterical
crying and images that could easily have been assumed to be meaning-
less. About six months after we started work, she had a waking vision,
but before telling me about it she informed me that she had taken to
wearing bright pink nail polish, "because it felt right." In her dream,
a black lady turned into a beautiful panther, or maybe a lioness, that
snarled at her and walked away.

Some time later she saw the black lady again. This time she was so
exquisitely beautiful that Beth was drawn to her, mesmerized. It was
then that Beth realized where she was, "on a sacrificial slab. The black

lady was not alone. There were others, many behind her, and a red fire behind them." Beth continues:

> I was terrified suddenly realizing that I was somehow pinned down on a sacrificial slab and they were coming at me with knives. I was trying to get away and then decided to stay and I asked, "Whom does this serve?" The answer was "You...and God." I was still terrified. I asked again and again and kept getting the same answer. Finally I said, "O.K., if it must be that way." And I saw their knives come down and up dripping blood, up and down and up again. I cried but felt no pain, only terror.
>
> Then, somehow above the scene...and the person on the sacrificial slab was a frail girl—very white as if from loss of blood. Her heart was cut out but she was somehow alive...a spark was still there. I was so sad and cried out, "How could this serve any good?" Then all the black ladies turned and walked away, their knives dripping.
>
> The child's body slid off the slab onto the floor and I was in the body again, but it had been transformed into something ancient—at times an old woman, at times a cockroach, at times a snake. Putting my fingernails into the cracks between the cobblestones, pulled myself along with great pain. Then I realized I was among the feet of the black ladies. I must have moved faster than it felt I had moved. Then I was a cockroach again because it can move so fast and no one would ever notice it in such a dark, damp place. Then I was an ancient human again. I had reached my goal. A door, death's door. I knew I would die if I went through.
>
> I watched as the door opened. There was a very handsome young man standing silhouetted against the sun. I thought, "this is not so bad." I stood up and stepped into the sunlight and hit the man on the face with a candied apple on a stick. It made his nose bleed and split his lip like a cleft palate split—very deep. We were both surprised at the action and the result.

Here was a woman who was becoming able to experience the sacrifice of herself in the service of the black ladies and the gods, and it let her see that the acute pain had childhood roots. It also let her see that she was still without a human heart and that her body was numb. In fact, to escape from the frail child, she still alternated between ancient woman and cockroach. She was still in no fit condition to meet with the Sun man. She would be unable to offer him a fruit from the tree of knowledge. What she offered instead was a sugar-coated imitation of the real thing, which caused his nose to bleed and his palate to split in half. It was as if she wanted to inflict on him what the patriarchy has inflicted on women—bleeding noses and cleft palates. It was to be some months before she could truly sacrifice her more whole feminine virginity and "save her daughters" by consummating her relationship with her animus. In her journal Beth wrote:

Every time I think about and truly feel the pain of what happened to me as a child, I have a sort of orgasmic response — the psychic orgasm that I had been afraid of, and that still frightens me. I feel stung by the power of it. As I moan in agony my body arches in orgasm. I do know I am letting out the emotion, the pain and the love that I have trapped there too long, that I have hoarded and protected so that I could not be hurt again.

Again the cockroach visited her, this time in a vision of traveling in a car. It had become copper. Beth was about to put her foot out to crunch it, imaginally, when she realized it was part of her. The insect started chewing on itself and went through some exotic and strange changes. Finally, its legs started to split its body and expose its chest cavity. Then it was working on a hollow at the base of Beth's neck, or her mother's neck. Beth was simultaneously herself, her mother and the cockroach. Beth's mother had been diagnosed as having cancer of the thyroid: she had also told Beth that she had been raped at the age of seventeen. Beth too was suffering all the symptoms of a hyperactive thyroid — heart palpitations, sweating, nervousness, etc.. When the cockroach opened Beth's neck, her heart was where her thyroid should have been. The heart was fibrillating and looking very unhealthy. The insect's legs cleaned the heart, prepared it for removal, and then ate it. As it did so the cockroach became a golden scarab.

It is perhaps significant to know that a swollen throat is the characteristic carriage of the head in Dionysian ecstasy, and which can be seen in vase figures of the Maenads in the British Museum. Dodds comments that the swollen throat and tossing head is at all times and everywhere characteristic of this kind of religious hysteria, which the Greeks associated with the tearing of animals in blood sacrifice. In medicine, the subjective experience of a swelling throat in hysteria is known as *globus hystericus.* Its psychological meaning would be "unspoken words."[35]

Living since childhood with one's unspoken heart in one's throat results in chronic stress to which the thyroid must constantly respond. The word thyroid comes from the Greek word *thyreoedes* formed from two words, *thyreos,* "shield," and *eidos,* "form." It is as though such chronic stress seems to detract from the thyroid's function of shielding the heart, so that its truths can be expressed with form and thus with meaning.

The scarab in Egyptian times was thought to roll the sun over the horizon every day, much as it would roll along balls of dung containing its eggs. Having the heart cleaned and removed and then assimilated allowed for the first possibility of sun-consciousness to enter Beth's damp, cockroach-filled psyche.

By the end of the car journey, Beth's two daughters were feeling nauseous and her husband complained of heartburn. Beth realized that there had been a real "power leak" affecting the whole family. She had "sent it all out" because she "couldn't face it" completely. Beth felt a pain in her sternum, and by bedtime her lips were burning, her breasts tingling and vulva throbbing. She suddenly realized it was an overwhelming sexual energy she was suppressing. She found she was too frozen to reach out to her husband, but neither did she "send the energy away" so that it could crystallize into anger — either at herself or her husband. She saw her dragon, which was now friendly towards her and which she could now ride without being burned up in its fires. She decided to live with the sexual energy until she could "find a way to use it or release it that felt O.K." She described herself at this time as having a black cord running through her — to complement the golden one she felt she had always had, which connected her with heaven. She felt joined to the earth through the black cord. There was more balance and polarity.

From this time on, her dreams became less fantastical and a new quality of reasoning entered them. She would also waken during the night whimpering. . .or was she laughing? She was never quite sure. Then she came to tell me a long dream, at the end of which I spoke to her with a cleft palate which she could understand. I was being warned to stay away from any attempt at linear process in working with this dream. Beth told me that she had always seen her genitals as a "cleft palate." This confusion between hurt women's two sets of lips is one with which I have become familiar. When Freud returned to Vienna from watching trance postures in Charcot's Parisian clinic, he chose the word "libido" for the soul's energy and movement. The word "comes from the Dionysiac-Aphroditic vocabulary referring originally to lips, the downpouring of sexual energy."[36] William Irwing Thompson suggests that:

> . . .in Lilith the symmetry of "as above, so below" is completed, for she has the female lips of the mouth which can pronounce the magic name of God and the female lips of the vulva below which can receive the semen of Adam. . .The revolt of Lilith therefore expresses the rising up from below of all that would be denied by the rational male consciousness. Like the uroboric serpent which bites its own tail, the spinal column brings the mysteries of languages and sexuality, mouth and genitals together.[37]

The brain's limbic ring curves, overlapping the oral genital areas and the bridge of the spinal column, connecting language and sexuality, myth and physiology, and causing us to value the shift from an Apollonian

to Dionysian expression. Lilith can now leave her desert lair, where she
has been an outcast for so long. The return of Lilith to consciousness
allows us to value both the world of spirit and matter, God and Adam.
This "connecting" of the two sets of lips is absolute heresy from the
patriarchal point of view.

I decided to look up the word "cleft" despite its familiarity. It is the
past tense and the past participle of "cleave," meaning "to split," "divide" or "separate." Its root *gleugh* gives rise to some interesting
polarities—"expert in seizing," "skillful," "clever." As I looked, my eyes
happened to wander below to the root *glogh*, which gives rise to "thorn,"
"point," from the Greek word meaning "barb of an arrow," *glotta*,
"tongue," from which we get "glossalalia." I asked Beth if she knew this
word: she started to cry. Yes, she knew about "speaking in tongues. . . it
was forbidden by the church." Her speech often sounded, in fact, as if
she were speaking in tongues, but she had early learned to disown it,
as had the patriarchal church. The Gnostic teacher Marcus would, however, pray to Grace, "She who is before all things, and to Wisdom and
Silence, the feminine element of the divine being."[38] When initiating
a woman into the church, Marcus concluded the initiation prayer with
the words, "Behold Grace has come upon you; open your mouth and
prophesy." Bishop Irenaesus was of course appalled by this, and his shock
has certainly filtered down the ages to Beth.

The term *glossalalia* reflects our own scientific confusion of tongues.
I started to read its definitions: gift of tongues; fabricated non-meaningful
speech especially associated with certain schizophrenic syndromes; talk,
babble. As I read these definitions aloud, Beth started writhing in the
chair, rolling her eyes, not breathing. Taking her dream instructions seriously, the most nonrational thing I could conceive of was to slam shut
my enormous dictionary. She jumped back into her body, as it were,
and I very firmly told her to look at me. The writhing increased with
much crying. She complained of her palate hurting. She wanted to howl
like an animal. And howl she did. She was back as a child of seven in
her bedroom and her father was masturbating in front of her, kissing
her like a woman. Her mother was in the hospital. He wanted more.
The child refused. She went stiff and saw her monsters, the cockroach
and the dragon—but Daddy said they were not real, yet there was never
acknowledgment of the *reality* of what he had done to her. The wedge
was hammered into place. The cleft appeared. What was real was invalidated by Daddy. Fantasy invaded young Psyche at Daddy's behest.

Beth felt a deep measure of gratitude to the cockroach for keeping her alive and not totally lost in craziness. Now she felt very much in her body except for her left arm. It was numb. It wanted to strike at him. She still felt as if she was the one being beaten and whipped, as she did whenever she menstruated.

A month later, Beth recalled watching a contained fire with her friends, just after her father had approached her sexually. They were burning garbage. Beth fainted and fell forward, burning her hands. Long before therapy, Beth had had several prophetic dreams about fires in the city. But we could easily see where her early abuse clouded her perceptions of the details of what was *actually* happening in the city—input from the collective consciousness was distorted by memories of her personal unconscious.

Beth dreamed of fields being drained, of land reclaimed. Between the gushes of water from the draining, she crossed over to where her mother was. She and I, her mother and her daughters sat down to eat a special meal. It was a fish. It had been prepared in two halves which came together as we sat down. A new age seemed to be ushered in. Beth also dreamed of having to look after all the animals in her basement. It had to be done daily, with great ritual, and it was a tremendous amount of work.

There was much steady inner work over the next six months. Beth recalled that at the time of her father's abusing her, not only her mother had been in the hospital, but her grandmother had been put into a sanatorium. No one would visit her except Beth's mother, who insisted that she was not afraid of grandmother's "craziness." The grandmother had kept buying lots of meat, stashing it in freezers, in the garden, or giving it to her family. Once when Beth's mother visited grandmother in the hospital she said, "I see you've been butchering—there's blood dripping out of your truck." Beth thought that this "crazy butchering" was Grandmother's only way to connect with "redness," to balance her milky mothering side. In an attempt to escape from suffocation of motherhood, Grandma was obliged to *act out* Cybele's Day of Blood of annual slaughtering. Beth recalled her own black ladies using the sacrificial knife on the young maiden. We began to wonder what sacred ritual still waited behind the "craziness" for us to appreciate. Beth experienced a further vision after praying one day to "God our father and our mother." She experienced the father picking her up and throwing her down. She knew enough now to crawl into the mother's lap and "snuggle into her breast." The mother welcomed her and told her she was "a dreamer" and that she had "to learn not to twist her visions—

hers or others." Beth did not cease experiencing the visions (as perhaps some therapists might have preferred), but rather their refinement, their release from the distortion of girlhood's trauma and the ensuing confusion of tongues. What had slowly emerged seems to be what Hillman calls "white" maenadism released from its patriarchal connection with the maenadism of Wotan or Christianity's Devil,[39] and secular psychology and psychiatry.

Finally Beth dreamed of lying on a beach—that mythic place where Dionysus found the abandoned Ariadne—with a man. He started to kiss her and her lips burned with passion. She wanted to hurry up the process but he forbade it. In the dream Beth knew that this was her brother, and this coming together was the sacred marriage. He wanted love and passionate speech, not genital engagement. There was no out-of-control fire. She no longer needed to hit him with the sugar-coated apple. The cleft palate was healed. Psyche was connected with heart in soul-making.

In the following dream, Beth was able to allow an insect to enter her, bringing its own sort of healing with the valuing of her own "craziness." I have noticed how frequently women's slips of tongue replace "incest" with "insect." From the previous story it would seem that insects can have an important part to play in redeeming spiritual ecstasy from hysteria. Only they seem insistent and horrid enough to induce the fear and awe necessary for us to value the import of a certain type of intrusion. It is worth noting that the word "insect" is derived from *insecare*—"to cut into." Its root *sek* gives rise to "skin" and "sickle"—words and images that we will meet again in the archetypal field of incest.

In this connection I have found myself pondering the Greek god of marriage, Hymen, who according to some sources is the son of Dionysus and Aphrodite, the personification of the wedding feast, the leader of the nuptial chorus—the "hymeneal" hymn that is sung with funeral overtones before a wedding. We also know the hymen as a "membranous fold of tissue partly or completely occluding the vaginal external orifice." It is derived from the Greek *sumen* and thence *humen*, meaning membrane. Its root *syu* means "to bend," or "sew," and also gives rise to the Sanskrit word *sutra*, meaning "thread," "string," and also the "Kamasutra." The Kamasutra we now can envision as the weavings of love and desire, pain and ecstasy, weddings and funerals. On the lawn of Jung's garden there is still the figure of a little man, about forty inches high, who Jung called Atmavicu, Breath of Life, an allusion to ancient nature gods. The insect-like character, the six arms, is also an allusion to the sympathetic nervous system, which functions unconsciously. The figure marks the grave of Jung's dog, Joggi.[40] So perhaps now we have a deeper appreciation of the gift the insects bring to the mysterious depths of marriage through the offspring of Dionysus and Aphrodite. Indeed it is significant to note that the hymen, as Veil of the Temple, descended from the concept of the vagina as sanctuary of Aphrodite, the virgin goddess presiding over defloration.[41]

Certainly we are drawn into the area of psychophysiology through the sympathetic nervous system. We know that "certain breakdown products of adrenaline can cause hallucinations," that the adrenals stimulate cancer formation, and that during stress the sex glands shrink and become less active in proportion to the enlargement and increase of the adrenals. The pituitary gland is also affected: it seems to be so busy maintaining life that it cuts down on less urgently needed hormones.[42] It has been noted that there is a similarity between mescaline and adrenaline, and that we can inwardly produce chemicals capable of changing consciousness—so women who are sexually traumatized may live with an induced state of consciousness that is profane in its origin (a stress-induced excess of adrenaline) and malignant in its imaginal content. Yet we must also note that there are many sacred occasions when chemicals are taken in order to induce altered states and that these are embedded in a cultural ritual and profound initiatory training. Both "abuse" and "the sacred" seem to beckon to something outside of an ego-bound paradigm. It strikes me as curious that when life itself is threatened, consciousness shifts. To what are we being drawn? And why is there such an emphasis in our society on the use of chemicals to bring about this shift in consciousness? These would seem to be crucial questions necessitating at least the differentiation between black and white maenads and the appreciation of body consciousness, knowing that we have, at present, no festivals of sacred sexuality—no sacred coming together of sexuality and spirituality. We are abusive towards these sacred matters, or we call in the doctors. We perhaps have not asked ourselves which god and goddess are present in hysteria. What is behind the heart flutterings of the hurt woman and her visions?

Hillman tells us that Rabelais has already opened the way for us in addressing these questions. He suggested a connection between the hysterical woman and the maenads, sometimes known as the Bacchae, priestesses of Dionysus.[43] And Hillman urges us to see the myth of analysis opening new horizons, with this evocation, on the contemplation of hysteria—departing from Apollo and Adam, to a witnessing of the "return of the repressed."

I have already alluded to the god Dionysus through his son Hymen. Dionysus is significant in that he is bisexual in the first place; he thus represents no misogyny. The Dionysian *coniunctio* is a given.

> [Androgyny] is not a goal to be sought. . . In fact the seeking of the coniunc-
> tio, as Apollo pursuing Daphne, is self-defeating because it hyperactivates
> the male, driving the psyche into vegetative regression, Daphne into laurel
> tree.[44]

This androgyny has a divine quality rather than being the demonic her-maphrodite we see acted out in patriarchal situations.[45] This given an-drogyny bespeaks natural consciousness. The Dionysian approach to therapy would similarly not attempt to extract consciousness from suffer-ing, since this would be to divide bisexual totality and to favor the male knower at the expense of the female known. A Dionysian approach to therapy would not analyze the internal ambivalence of a complex, since it would value paradox. We can therefore see that a totally new theory and practice would arise out of our valuing hysteria: a cornerstone revalued.

To redeem hysteria from black maenadism, it is necessary to know that our very culture has Wotanized Dionysus. "Psychiatry and classical scholarship rely upon each other's misogyny."[46] The so-called Dionysian "orgies" were, in fact, "acts of devotion," a valuing of a particular kind of religious experience.[47] Women left their homes to celebrate Aphro-dite's chief hermaphroditic festival. Aphrodite's predecessor, Ishtar, the Great Mother, the Sacred Harlot, Queen of Dust and Mistress of the Field, was considered to bring fruitfulness to the earth. Her rites were also orgiastic. In the Vedantic Upanishad, the moon and the moon tree was thought to bring *mana*—a power which induced an ecstasy similar to the Dionysian-Aphroditic mysteries, where a certain kind of conscious-ness was honored, one that could not be controlled by rational laws.[48] We might also note that the women who rejected Dionysus were smit-ten with madness.[49] It seems as if the women did not just run away from domestic life; there was a ritual involved. For instance, once a year in the sanctuary of Demeter and Kore "the women would separate them-selves from their men and enter a bridal chamber deep within the sanc-tuary. [Here] each woman was married in a sacred service to the God Dionysus."[50] We have no such ritual, yet the unconscious seems to force one upon us in one way or the other.

The Dionysian "other" consciousness is also based on the theatrical—music and dance. Even the scientific study of hysterics started with Charcot's Tuesday lessons as "stage performances of the Salpêtrière before the public of Tout Paris." They were held in an amphitheater, and the young patients were always ready to "perform" for the young psychiatric students—enjoying the smell of ammonia if told it was rose water, eating charcoal if it was presented as chocolate, crawling and barking if told she was a dog.[51] Recent research into so-called multiple personalities suggests that a large percentage of the patients revealed both child abuse and incest.[52] It would be easy to assume that we are looking at *only* pathology signifying a weak or absent ego which psychotherapy must strengthen. As with our lack of distinction between black and white maenadism, so we lack the ability to appreciate the complexity of psyche outside the realm of ego. We only condemn polycentricity as schizoid fragmentation[53] which we must congeal into one strong patriarchal ego. When we move into the theater of Dionysus, however, the personality can play the part of many characters, carrying with it "archetypal formations."[54] Certainly the incest victim's ego needs strengthening in order to relate to the victim's inner cast of characters. However, an inner community can be carried by Dionysian consciousness and released into outer community in a free flow rather than merely being coerced into the service of the ego. Once again we see how victims of incest and sexual abuse are pushing at the boundaries of our secular, profane, scientific ideology, and forcing us to expand our conceptual straitjackets.

Though the Maenads left home in the service of ecstasy, in fact they were paradoxically transformed

> not into raving hysterics and rebels but into nurses. They became nurses of the natural, giving such to all life. . . both keeping alive the animal and the child and feeding (both) through the ritual of eating flesh and by letting flow their compassionate milk.[55]

This feeding has an alchemical redness about it, the blood of nourishment generated within one's own imaginal matrix. *This* mother-milk is not the outcome of an unconscious mother complex. Such a woman-turned-nurse is custodian of her own instincts, not those of the patriarchy. And though she is friends with the animals, she is not subsumed into their form. She is in touch with the animals *and* filled with spirit precisely because of her deep connection with soul. She is far from soulless. The man now has to carry his own instinctual life, his own madness and his own ecstasy, involving himself in conscious and willing castration in honor of the Goddess of his Being. In both cases, consciousness is no longer dependent upon the male instigator and propagator.

As with Pan, one of Dionysus' main representations was as child — the Undivided one, the carrier of all potential. In fact his childhood is prominent in myths — more so than that of any other god, including Zeus.[56] Perhaps he will help us reclaim our lost and disappearing children, so that once more we can see the child as "origin and renewal of consciousness rather than as pawn in patriarchal erotic power-struggles."[57]

The central meaning of Dionysus is his relationship to soul. The horror and death involved in his cult activate the emotional and instinctual, the unconscious part of the psyche. Dionysus is at home in the sea. He requires no heroic view of the night sea journey that must be endured simply for a later development of insight.

Kerényi has insisted that Dionysus originated in Crete, proceeding from that place of the high point of feminine consciousness to Greece, whereas the standard view has been that he originated from the barbaric north or the excessive east.[58] To the patriarchal mind, it seems strange that the so-called riotous Dionysus had only one wife, Ariadne. She was the one who

> ...as a princess was the priestess of the cult of the Great Mother, and to bring fertility to her island of Crete must celebrate the sacred Marriage. Perhaps if Theseus did not come from Greece she must submit to her brother — as did the Egyptian queens — but he was the Minotaur, that dark monster bull-engendered on her mother Pasiphaë, the Moon Goddess incarnate, when she put on the trappings of a horned cow made for her by Daedalus.[59]

Theseus had come to Crete from Greece to conquer the Minotaur, which demanded an annual sacrifice of fourteen Greek youths. Ariadne helped Theseus by giving him a thread to follow so that he could retrace his steps, after "victory," back through the labyrinth. Upon his return, he married Ariadne. They escaped the island, but later he abandoned her. Then misfortune set in for him, and his father committed suicide before he could be reunited with his son.[60] Dionysus found his one and only wife, Ariadne, abandoned on a beach on the island of Naxos. Indeed, some authorities maintain that Dionysus was the only Greek god who was faithful to his wife.

I have found it interesting that the Greek Apollonian intrusion into the sacred marriage (the royal brother and sister) was to push past incest at the expense of marriage, the woman, the man's relationship with the bull, and the father-son relationship. The resulting hysteria is the paradigm of an "exteriorized inferior psyche,"[61] that is, everything is merely acted out. In fact, the incest taboo and imaginal life go hand in hand. We are now called to choose whether we will pull our psychic energy inwards to actualize the sacred marriage and thus release the feminine from long ages of hysteria, or whether we will continue to abuse it and destroy our outward marriages and our families because the incest taboo and its profundity have become buried in the unconscious. Certainly the Greek thrust carried a new consciousness for mankind—the Olympian, the male, the ego-dominated thrust out of the formerly matrilinear world. But now we must see that Dionysus held in his arms what the Greek thrust for intellectual soul was eager to leave behind, and which we must now embrace. For while the feminine fled from Apollo, Dionysus attracted the feminine.

And now we come full circle—from craziness to creation, from hysteria to ecstasy. Our daughters can sleep in peace because we no longer need to creep hysterically through the night. Again the mouse appears, unleashing myriad images. Jung tells us that when a woman screams hysterically because of a mouse, and the man doesn't react, then it is very probable that it is actually the man who is the more frightened.[62] The woman is provoking the man to ask a question *to which she can give an answer.* Her answer is an act of creation—it is her child. But the man who is undeveloped on his female side is as ignorant as young Parsifal, unable to ask the right sort of question at the pertinent moment. Usually he is not even aware that the base line is that he is terrified out of his wits. It is easier for him to attempt to shape up "this crazy woman."

Parsifal was granted the vision of the Holy Grail only when he could ask the appropriate question at the appropriate time. Similarly, it is only through man's questions that the woman's soul can be revealed. At such a moment, her thrusting animus can be turned from creating destruction to creating another child: she feels her perspective is valued and honored. She can bring forth with dignity and delight. But the man must be humble enough to feel his fear *and* ask the question of his teacher—the Woman (Woman with a capital W).

Notes

[1]For a history of the study of hysteria, see James Hillman. *Myth of Analysis.* New York: Harper & Row, 1972, pp. 251-298

[2]*Ibid.,* p. 253

[3]*Ibid.,* p. 254

[4]*Ibid.,* p. 255

[5]*Ibid.,* p. 256

[6]*Ibid.,* p. 257

[7]*Ibid.,* pp. 260-261
   Hillman suggests (note 78) that "the vision given by Dionysus to the women who leave their tasks of Athena, their marriages of Hera, is a 'madness,' i.e., it enables them to see the madness of the tasks of the sane world of everyday." Our culture has suppressed the archetype of hysteria so that a healing madness has become distorted (p. 272)

[8]*Ibid.,* p. 138

[9]Reported by Linda Halliday in the *Edmonton Journal,* November 17, 1984

[10]Wilhelm Heinrich Roscher and James Hillman. *Pan and the Nightmare.* Irving: Spring Publications, 1979, pp. xviii, xix and xxxi

[11]*Ibid.,* p. xviii

[12]*Ibid.,* p. xxi

[13]*Ibid.,* p. lii

[14]C.G. Jung, *CW* XII, par. 547
   Jung suggests that the uncompromising Christian interpretation of God as *summum bonum* goes against nature.

[15]C.G. Jung, *CW* XVI, par. 363

[16]C.G. Jung, *CW* XII, par. 547. See also Tom Moore. "The Virgin and the Unicorn." In *Images of the Untouched.* Joanne Stroud and Gail Thomas, eds. Dallas: Spring Publications, 1982, p. 52

[17]Arnold Mindell. *Dreambody.* Boston: Sigo Press, 1982, p. 100

[18]Ginette Paris. Pagan Meditations. Dallas: Spring Publications, 1986, p. 29

[19]Erich Neumann. *The Great Mother.* Princeton: Princeton University Press, 1972, p. 278, 280

[20]Barbara Koltuv Black. "Lilith." In *Quadrant, Spring,* 1983, p. 67
   A Lilith sexuality is the kind women know a few days before menstruation when the female hormones have stopped flowing and the male hormones are

at their raging peak. It is a pulsating, throbbing, primal, wordless state of being.

21Arnold Mindell, *op. cit.*, pp. 108-112

22Barbara Koltuv Black, *op. cit.*

23*Ibid.*, p. 71

24C.G. Jung, *CW* XIII, par. 399

25C.G. Jung, *CW* XIV, pars. 498-513

26*Ibid.*, par. 506

27*Ibid.*, par. 513

28C.G. Jung. *Dream Analysis.* Notes of the Seminar Given in 1928–1930. William McGuire, ed. Princeton: Princeton University Press, 1984, pp. 552-554

29*Ibid.*, p. 553

30C.G. Jung. *CW* IX, II, pars. 29-30
C.G. Jung. *CW* V, par. 458
The man's Logos principle betrays him, as it were, when he is caught in his mother complex.

31Susan Griffin. *Pornography & Silence.* New York: Harper Colophon, 1982, pp. 64-65

32Robert Graves. *New Larousse Dictionary of Mythology.* New York: Hamlyn, 1979, p. 150

33Russell Lockhart. *Words as Eggs: Psyche in Language & Clinic.* Dallas: Spring Publications, 1983, pp. 47-48

34C.G. Jung. *CW* V, par. 659

35Penelope Shuttle and Peter Redgrove. *The Wise Wound: Menstruation and Every Woman.* Middlesex: Penguin Books, Ltd., 1980, p. 252

36James Hillman, *Re-visioning Psychology.* New York: Harper & Row, 1977, p. 185

37William Irwin Thompson. *The Time Falling Bodies Take to Light.* New York: St. Martin's Press, 1981, p. 17

38Elaine Pagels. *The Gnostic Gospels.* New York: Vintage Books, 1981, pp. 70-71

39James Hillman, *op. cit.,* 1972, p. 273

40C.G. Jung. *Word & Image.* Aniela Jaffé, ed. Princeton: Princeton University Press, 1979, p. 140

41Borrowed by Christianity, the veil of the temple was "rent in the midst" (Luke 23: 45) by the passion of the doomed bridegroom at the moment he entered the chthonian womb, and the sun was darkened. H.J. Rose. *Religion* in Greece & Rome. New York: Harper & Bros., 1959, p. 32

[42]Hans Selye. *The Stress of Life.* New York: McGraw-Hill, 1978, pp. 253-272

[43]James Hillman, 1972, p. 258

[44]*Ibid.*, p.259

[45]Stephen Larsen, *The Shaman's Doorway: Opening the Mythic Imagination to Contemporary Consciousness.* New York: Harper & Row, 1977, p. 217

[46]James Hillman, 1972, p. 270

[47]*Ibid.*, p. 274

[48]C.G. Jung. *Dream Analysis,* pp. 370-371

[49]Stephen Larson, *op. cit.,* p. 51

[50]Russell Lockhart, *op. cit.,* p. 142

[51]James Hillman, 1972, p. 260, note 77

[52]D. Schafer (personal communication). See also Chapter Two, note 20.
    The "multiple personality disorder" of incest and rape victims is best understood as a chronic dissociative post-traumatic stress disoreder, with a weakened ego that leaves the individual hopelessly opposed to the polarities of the unconscious, and lost in isolation. This is because consciousness has not been rooted in the body. The regression involved in M.P.D. mainly serves to restore ego balance. A healthy Dionysian consciousness, on the other hand may be considered consciously-sought after life-long exploration, often guided by another, and with deep cultural connections. It is not merely contact with past and infantile experiences, but rather a facilitator in the development of a relationship with the transpersonal realm.

[53]James Hillman, 1977, p. 35

[54]C.G. Jung, *CW* V, par. 388

[55]James Hillman, 1972, p. 276

[56]*Ibid.*, p. 274

[57]*Ibid.*, p. 279

[58]*Ibid.*, p. 275, note 104

[59]Seonaid Robertson. *Rose Garden and Labirynth: A Study in Education.* Dallas: Spring Publications, 1982, p. 121-122

[60]Anthony Hopkins. *Crete: Its Past, Present and People.* London: Faber & Faber,1977, p. 21

[61]James Hillman, 1972, p. 291

[62]C.G. Jung, *Dream Analysis,* pp. 552-554

CHAPTER V

Epilepsy/Fall Down and Kiss the Earth

Stopping the Traffic

In one of my first days at the Child Sexual Abuse Treatment Programme in Edmonton, Alberta, I was asked to see Julie, a young woman in her early twenties. Normally she was too afraid to leave her home. I was told that she had been sexually abused by a much older brother, and that she had been diagnosed a severe epileptic. She was under constant medical supervision. She refused to leave at first, so I volunteered to walk her to the bus stop. I had the very strong impression of walking with a toddler who was either very tired or very willful. I slowed my pace accordingly. As we crossed the busy street, she crumpled completely and lay down on the road. That was my impression of her seizure. Horns were honking madly at this event, which threatened to interrupt the efficient movement of downtown traffic. It seemed to me that the best thing I could do was put my jacket under Julie's head and sit down on the road beside her. Of course a crowd soon gathered, and the young woman opened her eyes and told me that she didn't like everyone looking at her. I didn't like being stared at either, so I suggested that the best thing we could do was to get up and walk away. This we both did, and made it to the bus stop without further mishap. Once there, however, a drunk approached Julie, and I woefully thought the situation was going to happen all over again. Fortunately, her bus arrived and I was able to bundle her into it. She eventually arrived home safely.

Albeit indirectly, epilepsy has already been mentioned in earlier chapters. It is worth recalling that the girl who plunged into icy water was diagnosed as an epileptic, though she claimed she hadn't yet stopped shaking from the cold; and that Beth's recollection of her father abusing her would induce a violently orgasmic response similar to hysterical epileptic seizure. Many women and children complain of dizziness in their therapy sessions. The introduction of relaxation work in these cases sometimes leads to violent shaking.

Pan, the god of epilepsy, and the polar opposite of the shy, hiding nymphs of the hurting feminine, has also been associated with the nightmare. Pan's sexuality seems to be directed towards fostering reflection, for nature longs for conscious union with itself.[1] The ancient writer Soranos believed that in essence every nightmare is identical with an epileptic seizure.[2] Hippocrates thought that "frightful and monstrous things, the confusion of the senses, particularly all kinds of terrifying animal apparitions, [were] signs of epilepsy"—a sacred disease.[3]

A visitation from the goddess Hecate, daughter of Selene, was thought to precipitate an epileptic seizure. James Hillman remarks that the one who reveals Pan's intention is Selene, Goddess of the Moon.

> She was known for her unsurpassing beauty; her eye which saw all things happening below; her rule of menstruation, the orderly rhythm of feminine instinct; her gift of dew, the cooling moisture; her relation with epilepsy and healing; the veil that kept her partly hidden, indirect; the torch she covered and the light-bestowing diadem she wore, the obscure cave from which she rose and in which she set.[4]

She helps us see that feelings and thoughts that remain wispy and flighty, not "incarnated," will draw Pan's raping energy towards the subject. Hillman adds that it seems as if "the lunar state is particularly vulnerable to Pan, just as Pan is particularly attracted to it."

An association of epilepsy with incest is by no means new. Galen, the second century Greek physician, believed that seizures were the result of precocious intercourse; the Navaho thought a seizure meant the girl was a witch, or had experienced incest.[5] In Europe, epileptics were thought to be werewolves[6]; and in many parts of the world, epilepsy is considered to be a visitation of the devil.

Epilepsy is apparently one of the most common neurological disorders[7], yet it is extremely difficult to distinguish a true seizure from a simulated one. It is thought of more as a symptom than a disease. There may be loss of consciousness, excess or loss of muscle tone, disorders of sensation or special senses, or interference with autonomous bodily functions. Although the nature of epilepsy is not yet understood, it is believed that the normal neurological balance of excitation and inhibition is lost. Obviously, inner balance can be affected by birth trauma, tumor, stroke, alcohol and infections, and these types of seizures I am not considering.

The precipitating factors of seizures have to do with the senses — to the activation of body consciousness, which for incest victims is taboo, and which would therefore be likely to elicit excessive excitement. Breathing changes can act as stimuli, as well as visual, tactile, auditory, and vestibular stimuli — where a seizure is brought on when the patient hears a given word or familiar tune. And there are olfactory stimuli, where seizures are brought on by a particular smell. The patient may experience an "abdominal aura" in the stomach, rising to the chest and back. True epilepsy can be difficult to distinguish from "syncope," which can be induced by hunger, the sight of blood, or other stressors.

Goddwin, Simms and Bergman have reported on six young incest victims who experience epileptic seizures. They suggest that the seizure's back-arching and shaking represent movements related to sexual stimulation and orgasm, as well as those related to resisting sexual assault. Sometimes the mouth would be pursed as if in a silent scream. The sense of control described by victims may refer to the "power of the convulsions to control their own tensions, as well as the power to influence and frighten observers," the victim identifying with the original aggressor. The seizure may in fact help to reconcile the mother with the child and reestablish their relationship. Goddwin, Simms and Bergman claim that when the incest victims undergo psychotherapy, their seizures abate.[8]

Certain types of epileptic seizures are called "absence attacks." These manifest as a blank stare, brief upward rotation of the eyes, and interruption of activity. They can be induced by hyperventilation and low blood sugar. Parents will say that in these few seconds the child is *dans la lune* (literally, in the moon) or daydreaming. A related disorder is a breath holding spell, usually precipitated by a painful stimulus or a temper tantrum.

Being in the Moon

The actual translation of Matthew 17:15, is "Lord, have mercy on my son who is moon struck. . .For he falls often into the fire and often into the water." The speakers begged Jesus to help their child, described as epileptic in most translations. David Miller reminds us that "orthodox Judaism and Christianity have been reticent to make too much of the moon, as if they themselves have 'little faith' with regard to this night light."[9] The official Church theology is that Mary is the Moon, circling and reflecting the Sun, who is Christ. Yet Miller points out that the fourteenth and thirteenth hymns of lunar poetry are not so cautious. Here the sun is said to hide in the moon's womb, and also to be Selene's consort and bridegroom. The theme of incest—the son hiding in his mother and the moon woman given over to the urgency of birthing the sun Christ—are ingrained in the Christian tradition.

The moon, however, has not only been celebrated as clothed in and giving forth Divine fire, but also of granting lifegiving moisture, the hidden dew which is the primal source of all birth. Jung quoted Paracelsus saying that "the moon is. . .the fiery water."[10] Both the cold of the moon and the heat of the sun are interlocking and cannot be separated by a Newtonian/Apollonian world view.

Miller suggests that Jesus referred to the disciples as being "of little faith" since they seemed to assume that the child should be *cured* of his lunacy. Jesus, being the unified whole, "the burning fountain," in fact loved the lunacy of the epileptic child enough to speak to him not personally, but rather through the daimon, the archetypal force racing through the child. Jesus spoke to the *daimon* in an intimate way, and the child was cured.

The Call of the "Shamama"

Indeed, shamans all over the world, elected by the spirits, show a recognizable symptomology which includes "epileptoid seizures," nervousness, solitude, being easily frightened, and a proclivity for imitation and obscenities. Certain investigators have suggested that shamanism provides primitive cultures with "a convenient way to accommodate their psychologically ill individuals." Mircea Eliade agrees that there are similarities between certain psychopathological disorders and shamanism, but that this is because both emerge from a common ground in the deep structures of the psyche. According to him,

> . . .the shaman is not only a sick man, he is, above all, a sick man who has been cured, who has succeeded in curing himself. Often when the shaman's or medicine man's vocation is revealed through an illness or epileptoid attack, the initiation of the candidate is equivalent to a cure.[11]

Thus, as with meanadism in the previous chapter, we are called upon to differentiate in a new way—along archetypal polarities contained in the phenomenal complex. The "falling sickness," epilepsy can be activated by either polarity. Healing comes from staying within the complex and "treating like with like," knowing that each polarity speaks to the other. Jung tells us that he has known patients to feel seasick or dizzy because of what seems like a strange wave-like motion, a moon motion when the unconscious is activated.[12] It is as if the archetype seizes the whole personality. Indeed, initiations all over the world have been marked by dizziness (for instance at Eleusis[13]) and by falling. When Black Elk first heard the spirit voices as a nine-year old boy, his thighs began to hurt and his legs buckled.[14] The Senoi would tell children who are terrified of falling dreams that it is a wonderful dream, that they must relax and enjoy the fall. Falling is the quickest way to contact the powers of the spirit world, the powers laid open to us in our dreams.

> The falling spirits love you. They are attracting you to their land, and you have but to relax and remain asleep in order to come to grips with them. When you meet them, you may be frightened of their terrific power, but go on. When you think you are dying in a dream, you are only receiving the powers of the other world, your own spiritual power which has been turned against you, and which now wishes to become one with you if you will accept it.[15]

Dizziness destroys the culture and reality-bound ego. The experience of dismemberment and epileptoid fits are symbolic of the falling apart of the will into

> ...autonomous complexes. One is no longer in control of oneself, and the autonomic nervous system dominates the habitual system identified with the conscious will. One is indeed a victim of unconscious energetic centers, those devilish complexes pulling every which way.[16]

Loss of Legs to the Father

Many incest and rape victims tell me that they feel as if their fathers have stolen their legs. The daughter of an alcoholic told me she lies thinking of her "unfooted father." She has dreamed of her own feet as bleeding, raw and painful. Another patient, Tilly, also encounters legs in a dream. They are floating in the ocean; they have tears of blood oozing from them. A woman, Dolores, is pointing them out to Tilly. "Dolores" comes from the Latin *dolore* meaning "to feel pain," "to grieve." Tilly was being called to actually *feel* the blood, tears and pain of having had her legs cut off and abandoned in the sea. An incest victim, formerly involved in drugs and prostitution, and now trying to "kick" alcoholism, imagines herself kneeling in front of an erupting volcano, the power of the rage coursing through her. She cannot stand because her legs cannot support her. She must remain on her knees in front of the overwhelming volcano until she has reclaimed her womanly legs.

Seizures seem to occur in the absence of genital abuse, or before it takes place. For instance, the girl who dreamed of wanting to take off her pretty dress before the boys raped her told me that her first seizure occurred when she was about eight or nine, playing tag in the field. A boy had caught her and kissed her, and she had fallen down with a seizure. Of course, she was growing up in an incestuous family, though her father had not yet started genitally abusing her. Certainly the Pan/Nymphs archetype had already been constellated in her. It would seem as though it is the archetypal constellation that is the fundamental problem.

Raging at the Mother

Sara was a young woman who had not suffered from incest in a genital sense. However, she was very much a father's daughter. Both Sara's parents were deeply involved in the life of the Evangelical Church. In her family environment there had been little room for the emergence of feminine moon consciousness, just as Sara felt the she had had few opportunities for self-expression. Very little soul-consciousness had been mediated to Sara as she grew up, and she had few opportunities for self-expression. She remembers her adolescence as a time of acute loneliness and alienation. She had been diagnosed as epileptic at the age of eighteen. At twenty-five she came to work with me for depression and an inability to cope. She had dropped out of university and after a while began to work in a dry-cleaning store.

About five months after we started working together, Sara called to say that she had been reading Nancy Friday's book *My Mother: My Self,* and was finding that her seizures were increasing. About six months later, arriving for her appointment, she announced that she was in an absolute rage, wanting to stamp her feet and shout "I won't, I won't." She had already had ten seizures that morning. She began telling me of her previous night's dream, which she felt was somehow connected with epilepsy. She had met a monster-animal. "The professors" and "the child" were trying to corner it in a cave and tame it, but the monster became more and more furious and "crazed." I suggested that she should probably talk with the beast, even if she had to ask it to stay at a distance for a while. She was very frightened and whimpered for a long time. It turned out that it was actually the monster who was afraid — afraid they would "shoot it," would "knife it," and would "take pictures of it," and that "everyone would come looking for it." The monster-animal wanted Sara to come and live with him in his grove of trees. Meanwhile, everyone else in the scenario was riveted into place, as it were, and thus Sara was free to imaginally comply with her inner dictates.

She was very tired by the end of the session, and I suggested that she go home to bed to rest so that she could learn to live with the monster-animal. At the door she cried and whimpered a great deal, and clung to me.

Two months later Sara brought the following dream series to her appointment.

I have been drugged. I know that the men of the Dark Lord and the Lord himself wish to kill me. I tumble out of bed and try desperately to run. As I run in slow motion, using a stick for support, I see the message being passed along that I am going this way and that I am being chased. People of the Dark Side laugh at me and I know it is only a matter of time before I drop completely. Everyone is forbidden to help me. I go down in an elevator to the ground floor. The top floor is a hospital where the Dark Lord keeps people such as me. Below is a department store. I run through the wasteland. Nothing grows here. There is a maze here. I begin to carry a young, short, black man — an employee of the Dark Lord. There is a model up ahead, waist high, the Santa Maria. I hit it with my walking stick and it collapses into a million pieces. I see it's made of paper. I would have liked to hide there but it is not possible. . .

I enter the maze, and a young woman comes out, ignoring me completely.

We round a turn in the maze, a young person falls over, stabbed to death. They'd been hiding in the corner. Blood flows from a wound all over the floor. We went on a bit further and saw some graceful and ornate stairs. At the foot was a large dog going crazy with loneliness. The dog was owned by the fellow who had been killed. The dog refused to go upstairs, but rapidly paced at the bottom of the stairs as if waiting for something to come downstairs.

We could see the dream as showing how Sara did indeed carry the burden of the shadowy, patriarchal Dark Lord inherited from her patriarchal family.

Some healing is taking place in the dream, since the Dark Lord's employee was walking on his own legs by the end of it. There was as yet no inner "Santa Maria" refuge and no inner human woman to help —

no Ariadne's thread to guide Sara through the maze. Yet no male hero emerged from the maze, as Theseus did after killing the Minotaur. Now the young hero is dead. We are left with a dog crazed by loneliness—an apt picture of the shadow of our collective psyche that has abandoned its instinctual nature and rushed into the mode of the eternally conquering hero, who no longer fills the bill in Sara's psyche.

Sara's next dream gives us more insight into the dog. Sara and her mother are taking a walk in the forest when a mutt comes out of nowhere and wants to play. Sara throws sticks for it, which it always retrieves. However, the dream ends with Sara's mother insisting on drowning the dog—"for his own good"—even though Sara wants to keep it and is crying because the dog is going to die. She continues with the dream:

> All through this, I was in agony. I hated myself for allowing mother to talk me into this. I was so intensely angry with myself and sad that I couldn't cry. Instead I went over to the creek where the dog had bounded in, and tried to go swimming. Mother was standing not far away and saying "Now don't go swimming, it's far too cold for that." True, there was snow on the ground but I knew that the waters of the creek would be warm and soothing. I went to do a shallow dive, and I landed above the surface. I was stationary there. If I made swimming strokes, I swam in the air.

Later in the dream, Sara is in the kitchen with her father and mother preparing supper. Dad wants to know why Sara is "choked up." Sara explains that while she and mother had been out walking in the forest, she (Sara) had killed her lover. "It was for his own good," mother interjected several times. Sara was again overcome by loss but unable to cry, and retreated alone to her room.

We began to see how the loss of Sara's inner dog left her swimming in the air, desperately wanting but being unable to reach the soothing moon waters to balance the raging fire. (It is interesting to note that Sara constantly expressed the wish to scuba dive and swim, almost as if she wanted to get under the water to compensate for not being able to imaginally enter it!) She was left groundless, in agony but unable to cry. Somehow her mother's insistence on killing the dog was introjected by Sara as her killing her lover—for his own good, of course. This is an important insight for those of us compelled to kill the instinctual because of the injunctions of the hurt, and probably frightened, mother.

Over the next months, Sara began to see how seizures increased if she didn't live with Matthew, as she—interestingly enough, given the passage from Matthew cited earlier—called her monster-animal. Sometimes she found she had locked him in a closet. It took a massive reorganization of her life to accommodate him—in other words, learning to reduce the amount of stress in her lifestyle. Once during a seizure she found herself crawling, and between seizures she one day had a clear dream of the loss of her animal nature. Coincidentally, she also received a letter from her mother telling her that she (her mother) had absent-mindedly left her dog at the supermarket!

About five months later, Sara was able to articulate for herself that her seizures were "because of a rage at mother for denying (her) feeling." Sara said, "I climb up inside myself. There's a ladder from my chest to my head. When I get to my head I seize."

Finding the Old Woman in the Moon

Then Sara dreamed of having tea in a church, inside a house with a woman who was very low in the church hierarchy. The tea was awful. Then Sara climbed into a hay loft overlooking the church scene, and to her surprise found an old woman sitting on the floor, with lots of cats, some of them drinking milk. The old woman was gently laughing at the hierarchical church scene and saying, "don't take them too seriously." Then Sara left by the back door. By the garbage box she was confronted by the male leader of the church and the woman who had drunk tea with her. The woman chased Sara and told her not to forget to do her homework. Sara grabbed each in turn, by the face, and said, "Don't you ever tell me what to do." Her parents appeared from behind the couple and started their usual attempts at placating. But Sara made a decision to drive her car from the front seat rather than from the back. Of course, in outer life Sara did not have a driver's license because of her epilepsy, but inwardly she was gaining a sense of being able to drive more surely, defining her own boundaries.

The old barn woman and her cats were on many occasions to provide Sara with an inner refuge from which she could continue to gain a new perspective. The old woman asked Sara to describe her mother. So Sara did—"Harsh, critical, and judgmental." The old woman laughed and told Sara to buy a present for her mother, which she did. She also began the slow task of learning to nurture and mother herself.

This dream came immediately after Sara had drawn three "strange" pictures. I say "strange" because they were totally different from Sara's previous drawings. They were a complete about-turn in content, form, color and feeling tone, as was the therapy session. There was more emotional flow from tears to rage, from laughter to sadness, a new warmth and directness. I experienced it as a turning point in our therapy. These pictures had come to Sara out of the blue, about half a day before she began menstruating. She called them tears on the face of the moon, the crying lady madonna (tears of blood) holding tears on the face of the moon, and the broken heart.

Sara had finally found an inner moon sanctum that would not shatter into a thousand pieces like the initial Santa Maria in which she had wanted to hide, giving her a new, releasing and moist lunar perspective of the church and herself. The first suggestions of change in her relationship with her mother developed. Sara was eventually able to perceive her mother as a woman who did the best she could, and whom she could respect. We were by no means out of the maze, but an important corner had been turned that allowed us to pick up some guiding threads.

Sara reached the point, some seven months later, when she was experiencing no seizures, but was incredibly depressed. She was now living alone and feeling that she had in fact been alone all her life. She dreamed that she had been given a bunch of irises — those flowers described as bringers of death to women, as well as bringers of the rainbow.

There were times when Sara was red with rage at me for openly setting my own boundaries — terminating phone calls, ending appointments, and for what she called my "feminine sexuality." This rage became intermingled with rage at her mother for never having had time for her. But this rage is now all expressed: at the time of writing, she has been without a seizure for six months. The neurologist supervising her medication laughed at the idea of seizures being connected to anger, but he has been open and curious enough to call me and ask about our relationship, because he has seen nothing like it before. There had been no hope, on my part, for the termination of seizures — nor was that my intent, though I am sure it was Sara's. But both she and I have tried to listen and respond to the inner figures who had not had a voice for so long.

After another two months, Sara phoned to tell me "a wonderful dream."

I am joining a group of nomadic Indians living on the prairie. They have just pulled up the teepee poles. I am the only white person. I am wearing a beautiful blue skirt covered with white flowers. I love it. A brother and sister are gathering up the children. A little boy has been practicing with his bow and arrow—shooting at grasshoppers.

I suddenly remember the old woman from an earlier dream who lived in a miserable shack, yet who had made for me a beautiful hide dress, for nothing, and which left me speechless. I put on the dress and I have the sudden realization that these people are going to teach me how to live with the land.

Having studied anthropology, Sara was well versed in native culture and its destruction. Though she did not have an idealized view of native peoples, she seemed to have found peace with this inner community who could live with the earth.

Sara now periodically calls me, or makes appointments, sometimes specifically to tell me good things that are happening to her. I find that this is an important step for those of us working from the victim side of the victim/offender complex. It is important for us to learn to tolerate the whole telling of our myth. So many feel they can only tell the therapist when things are going badly. But when we only tell a part of the story, we become stuck. It has also been important for Sara to learn to ask me if I have a few minutes to talk, rather than assuming and crashing willfully through my boundaries if I let her.

Lesbia's Healing

At about this time, Sara dreamed of an intimate relationship with a woman called "Lesbia," and her labia became engorged with blood and moisture. Such an inner relationship is not at all uncommon, and is indeed a necessary step in moving beyond a "primal rage at men,"[17] stemming from not only the abuse of the patriarchy but also from the mother's denial of the truth of the girl's body and her instinctual nature. Lesbos is that island of women in the Aegean Sea whose inhabitants practiced *charis,* "grace," meaning music, art, dancing, poetry, philosophy and romantic Lesbian love, in the service of both Aphrodite and Artemis.[18]

Reconnecting with feminine sexuality and finding the roots of her grace and creativity is essential if a woman is to sustain a relationship with the potent masculine. Miller tells us of a Christmas hymn written by Saint Ambrose, apparently based on Psalm 19:4-6

> He proceeds out of his bridal chamber,
> A royal court of chastity [or modesty],
> The giant of two substances,
> Cheerful to run his course.

When account is taken of the pagan origins of particular words, then
we see that Christ proceeded out of "the inner place of the bride's red
sexuality"—a heretical idea both in that the female is considered the
source of the male, and also in the matter of Mary's eroticism.[19]

All Fall Down: Learning to Dance

Emma Jung says that music can be understood as "an objectification
of the spirit. . . spirit leading into obscure distance beyond the reach of
consciousness."[20] Hence music and dance are an important means of expression for women, so that with unfettered feet they can beat the ground,
descending, and rising again from the mother.[21] In dancing the dance
of life, healing women dance also for death. Their feet rhythm the earth,
shaking the old foundations and formations of the old city to make way
for green shoots to push past the ruins.

The patriarchal seizure, epilepsy, involves a pact with the devil, since
one is seized by willpower[22] and frenzy. The mythic seizure, however,
is a falling down to kiss the earth. The forest clearing is the place that
allows nightmares to become dreams because there is a place for the
beasts and monsters. It allows the swings of enantiodromia to slow down
to a point where both aspects of the polarity, the mythic seizure of kissing the earth and the seizure of willpower as a pact with the devil, can
be appreciated without identifying with either of them.[23]

I am reminded of the knight's initiation. He would first don a white
shirt bearing a red cross over his heart, sewn for him by his lady. And
then alone he would enter the Church and lie prone on his face, his
arms outstretched in the shape of a cross, and spend the night thus—
his lips to the earth mother. Such solitude naturally makes us giddy.[24]
But it is essential that the true knight acknowledge his relationship to
the feminine, with true humility, knowing his heart must be pierced
through devotion to the Beloved. Giddiness becomes the transport of
rapture. As David Miller puts it,

> Mary and Christ can no longer be viewed as symbolizing ego and self. Rath-
> er, both are imaginal figures of a divine drama, a round dance which has
> erotic, incestuous, carnal and mythic dimensions. Sun and moon (Christ
> and Mary) are two aspects of the self, two sides of an archetypal configura-
> tion. Neither is to be integrated into the other. There is no question of imi-
> tation in either direction. It is rather a matter of staying with the round
> dance.[25]

Notes

[1]Wilhelm Heinrich Roschev & James Hillman. *Pan & the Nightmare.* Irving: Spring Publications, 1979, p. xlix. "The other whom Pan chases so compulsively is none other than himself reflected, transposed to another key."

[2]*Ibid.*, p. 20

[3]*Ibid.*, p. 23

[4]*Ibid.*, p. xlviii

[5]Goddwin, Simms, and Bergman, "Hysterical Seizures: A Sequel." In *American Journal of Orthopsychiatry,* Vol. 49, 1979, pp. 698-703

[6]Barry Lopez Holstan, *Of Wolves & Men.* New York: Charles Scribner's Sons, 1978, p. 236

[7]*Epilepsy: A Manual for Health Workers.* U.S. Department of Health & Human Services, p. 1

[8]Goddwin, *et al. op. cit.*

[9]David Miller, "Womb of Gold." In *Images of the Untouched,* Joanne Stroud & Gail Thomas, eds. Dallas: Spring Publications, 1982, p. 86

[10]*Ibid.*, p. 96

[11]Stephen Larsen, *The Shaman's Doorway.* New York: Harper & Row, 1976, p. 60

[12]C.G. Jung. *Dream Analysis.* Notes of the seminar given in 1928-1930. William McGuire, ed. Princeton: Bollingen Series XCIX, 1984, p. 389.

[13]Susan Griffin. *Pornography & Silence.* New York: Harper Colophon Books, 1982, p. 76

[14]Stephen Larsen, *op. cit.*, p. 104

[15]*Ibid.*, p. 98

[16]James Hillman, Comments in *Kundalini: The Evolutionary Energy in Man.* Boulder: Shambhala, 1971, p.203. See also C.G. Jung, *CW* XII, p. 304, note 29.

[17]Florence Wiedemann. "Mother, Father, Teacher, Sister: Transference/Countertransference Issues with Women in the First Stage of Animus Development." In *Chiron,* 1984, p.189. See also Betty Meador, "Transference/Countertransference Between Woman Analyst and the Wounded Girl Child." In *Chiron* 1984, pp. 163-174.

[18]Barbara Walker. *The Woman's Encyclopedia of Myths & Secrets.* San Francisco: Harper & Row, 1983, p. 535

[19]David Miller, *op. cit.*, pp. 87-88

[20]Emma Jung, *Animus & Anima.* New York: Spring Publications, 1972, p. 36

[21]C.G. Jung, *CW* V, pars. 480-481

[22]C.G. Jung, *CW* VII, par. 40,
   Here Jung seems to show his early confusion about Dionysus, not yet having differentiated it from Wotan's blond beast.

[23]John Dourley. *The Illness That We Are: A Jungian Critique of Christianity.* Toronto: Inner City Books, 1984, p. 28

[24]Anne Morrow Lindbergh. *Gift From the Sea.* New York: Random House, 1978, p. 41, quoting from Rilke

[25]David Miller, *op. cit.,* p. 95

CHAPTER VI

The Absence of Masculine Spirit

What defines incest offenders is simply that they do it, and rarely only once. This is the opinion of Dr. Irwin Dreiblatt, a noted clinical psychologist who has evaluated over twelve hundred offenders for the courts.[1] Nicholas Groth agrees. According to him,

> . . . [incest] offenders do not differ significantly from the rest of the population in regard to level of education, occupation, religion, intelligence, mental status, or the like. They are found within all socioeconomic classes. However, they do differ from non-offenders obviously in that, when faced with life-demands they cannot cope with, they seek relief from the resulting stress through sexual activity with children.[2]

I have attempted to show that a psychologically incestuous family is a norm within our patriarchal society, which itself has a faulty relationship with the world-soul, the *anima mundi*. This is not to deny psychopathology, but an attempt to connect syndromes with mythical realities. The absence of a healthy father leaves a child with a sense of depletion that we are only just beginning to take seriously. Our heritage from Margaret Mead and John Bowlby would perhaps lead us to conclude, erroneously, that the father is almost superfluous. We have few ideas of what it really means to father another person's journey.

For the past year I have worked with a seventeen-year old incest victim who initially could tell me nothing about this very abusive relationship except that her father would occasionally wink at her. It was
on this basis that she could describe the relationship as loving. When
she was allowed to phone her father in prison, she would become anxious and aggressive before the call was placed. One day she explained
that she did not know what to talk about—not because she felt uncom-
fortable, but because of something else. She laughed when I suggested
telling her father about schoolwork and what she did on the weekend.
She was simply incredulous that anyone, anywhere, could carry on such
a conversation! She had run away from home several times, taken drugs
and alcohol, joined a fighting street gang, called herself King Tut, but
had no felt experience of an everyday conversation with her father. But
she "knew" he loved her. After all, didn't he wink at her?

Incestuous fathers, "products" of the patriarchy, keep their families
under their iron-willed control, and in particular violate the most ten-
der soul carrier in that situation. Outside the family, the offender's iron
will is often not discernible. The father can appear as a caring, hard working, conscientious churchgoer. Those on the inside of the family wall
experience his rages and abusive behavior with fear and trepidation: they
see the father's dark face. This is, in part, due to the fact that the offenders
tend to be able to "assess their relative power in any situation and vary
their behavior accordingly."[3] Their behavior thus has sociopathic elements
about it. The offender's verbal acuity has a slippery, seductive quality
that disappears completely in the face of any emotional issue. In their
work at the Institute for the Community as Extended Family (spearheaded
by Henry and Anna Giarretto), Brian Abbott and Forrest Rosser have
found that their young offenders groups have a reading ability five levels below norm on the WISC-R, suggestive to me of a profound disturbance in their relationship with Logos.[4]

The Offender's Baby-Face

The two faces of the offender that I have witnessed are that of "baby
face" and the "hairy brute face." Baby-face frequently can cry crocodile
tears which attempt to express that "the dear boy has tried so hard."
These tears flow all too easily, but they are not the tears of conscious
suffering. Young girls have frequently complained to me of their father's
innocent baby face.

One night, before I was to go out to the prison hospital, I dreamed
a single word—"fang." I shared the dream with the first man I had gone

to see—a man who had molested three of his daughters. He responded with surprising emotion. "Fang people," he said, were "bad." They were aggressive and loud and he would definitely avoid them. They represent his archetypal opposite, the hairy brute with no tears. This baby-face had himself lost all his top teeth. He had had most trouble with his incisors—one rotted, one worn down. Now he had none. The prison dentist told him that though he might be seeing "all those doctors and psychologists," it would be his new teeth that would "make him better." The unexplored shadow of this baby-face is hairy and ruthless, with gnashing teeth that always threaten to take him over.

I would like to suggest that certain aspects of masculine initiation provide insightful clues which could strengthen men (and the masculine in women) against falling into foolhardiness in an effort to avoid taunts against their true manhood. Paradoxically, this rite of passage frequently seems to involve the sacrifice of "incisiveness" and "biting through."

Mircea Eliade[5] tells us of tribes where the young boys are snatched away from their mothers by masked men. The women mourn the loss of their sons, whose initiation includes the medicine man "killing them," and removing a tooth before restoring the young men to life. As the incisor is being removed, the bull roarers are sounded. The initiates must swallow the blood of the sacrifice of incisiveness or the wound will not heal. It is as if they must fully ingest the reality of this new level of relatedness, while the roaring in their ears suggests the furor of their Supreme Being. The terror of the boys is religious in nature, for it arises from the fear of being killed by the divinities, who are also responsible for the novices eventual resuscitation.

During the rest of the initiatory experience, the boys are denied speech, can only imitate bird or animal sounds, and can only take food directly with their mouths, unaided by their hands. This is their second babyhood, and it brings with it a kinship with animal nature and with conscious helplessness—so different an experience from unconscious helplessness. They must become one with Mother Nature, and respect her ingenuity and power. Paradoxically, it is this experience of helplessness that simultaneously makes them into responsible men in the community. The missing tooth is from then on a constant reminder that their own incisiveness is forever limited when viewed in the light of their death and rebirth experience, which, for them, recapitulates the sacred history of the world. The regeneration of the initiate is perceived as an occasion for the total regeneration of the cosmos as well as the community.

The initiation of these young men includes an introduction to sexuality which is placed into a much broader context than mere genital sexuality. The regeneration of the initiates is an occasion for total renewal, and thus the emerging men must realize that their chthonic phallic potency is necessary for a deep and wide cultural vitality. And this potency and generativity is the warp of a fabric whose woof is made of the threads of limited incisiveness and death. Without these aspects of masculine initiation, the man is always vulnerable to his fanged, ruthless shadow side, the chthonic mother and father made one, which will constantly threaten to render him helplessly berserk—and furthermore, cause him to ravage Psyche.

Baby-face is nowhere near ready for a second birth into true manhood. He will first have to develop some "bite" before he can relinquish incisiveness to some more profound mode of cognition.

One baby-face I know had a great deal of trouble expressing anger directly. He remained impotent with his wife and had difficulty holding down any steady employment. He lacked needed inner discipline. His wife increasingly became the phallic mother who was obliged to run the show. This mother, with an already weak connection to the feminine, was thus compelled into more and more mothering, and thus became, unconsciously and paradoxically, more phallic. It seemed as though the lack of discipline carried right across the man's life. Judith Herman reports that in her sample not one incestuous situation was terminated by the father.[6] Such a loss of discipline seems to be associated with never having been fathered by a potent and disciplined creative man. The young son has been bullied and ignored, and finally coerced into the bullying ways of his father.

Let us look, very concretely, at the loss of discipline in incestuous families. Shawn (twelve years) is very much overweight, and his stepfather sends him out bike riding to lose weight. But Shawn knows that it is to get him out of the house so that the stepfather can have sexual access to Shawn's younger sister. We should not be surprised that Shawn flies into a rage when the father continually nags him to be more disciplined in his eating habits. Shawn is sent to bed early so that Don has sexual access to Sheri. Sheri is not allowed to sleep when she is tired; she must wait patiently to be abused. We should not be surprised that when Don is removed from the home, difficulties arise around bed time. Sheri wants to stay up for as long as she wants to; this is one of her ways of reconnecting with her truth and independence. She had been coerced away from her body-truth by her father. The mother, Olga, likes to "sleep the day away" because that was the time of the day she used to be abused and withdraw into never-never land to avoid the pain. Another incest victim, Tammy, would be given extra chores if she didn't give in to her father. Most battles in incestuous families center around chores. Lora recalls hitting her father with a frying pan in an attempt to stop him from beating her mother. This was a child trying to discipline a grown man.

All these examples revolve around the feminine—in relationship to matter and our dealings with it, and in relationship to food, and the realm of sleep. How could the abused young woman accept the discipline of Logos now? Sheri's first words, when entering the play therapy room, formed themselves into statements and a question which struck me dumb. "My problem is that I don't know who is stronger—God or the Devil. The Sunday school teacher says God is stronger. But if he is, why did he let this happen to me? What do you think?" Sheri was nine years old at the time.[7]

At a societal level, we need also to see that "discipline" is the word used in pornographic literature to describe a sadomasochistic ritual, not just between man and woman, but between adult and child and between teacher and student. Our projections prevent us from seeing both the true world of nature and the world of images. "Projections change the world into the replica of one's unknown face"—and we become either autoerotic or autistic in a dreamworld whose reality is forever unattainable.[8]

The Offender's Hairy-Brute Face
The other side of baby-face is the "hairy-brute face," and this seems to emerge most markedly under the influence of alcohol and other substances. Offenders will admit that they drink in order to gather courage for the approach.[9] They seem to suffer from a particularly acute loss of spirit.

"Brute-face" also seems to appear in connection with money, over which he is very controlling and punitive. Baby-face often cannot earn it; brute-face does not know how to use it even if baby-face has earned it for him. It is significant that incest victims are beginning to win civil suits against their assailants. One woman won $210,000—"the man's net worth."[10] She explains that he took away a lot of love, he took away her childhood. The only thing she could do to him was take away what he had—his money and possessions.

Brute-face also appears around cars. I have been surprised at how often they are discussed amongst incest offenders. When they talk about working "in the body shop," it is the one time I see much animation on their faces, and in their voices and gestures. Offenders I know tend to be highly stressed workaholics in spite of their difficulty making money, and they spend long hours around cars. This type of hero's thrust is mechanized; there is no instinctual bonding such as occurred between the old hero and his horse. In fact, one offender described himself as always having felt himself to be a man who had lost his horse.

Once the wife in an incestuous family started to complain about her husband's aggressive and reckless driving, Fred, the husband, also noticed this; he had caught himself going through red traffic lights very often. In most incest offenders, the compulsive need to connect with male energy has all the qualities of the lost little boy who turns brute in unacknowledged desperation. Most have experienced little true fathering and many have been child victims[11] who have not felt their own pain, which they must force onto one lower on the patriarchal totem pole.

Father-Son Competition

In the patriarchal home, father and son battle with each other for supremacy. For instance, the son (twelve years) says he will repair a part of the sound system. His father snatches it from his hands and flies into a rage. The young boy disappears and the mother finds him "humping the bed," raging at his father. The father himself has not resolved some of his own little boy issues: certain developmental stages seem never to have been lived. This father oscillates between stealing his son's potency and silently gloating at his son's acting out in school, delighted that he is "bucking authority" in a way that he never has nor ever will be able to. He has never truly taken his own authoritative stand (though he can be an autocrat) because his true phallic potency is still locked in the unconscious and his personal mother.

In a family where sexual abuse of the daughter has occurred, and where the son has been "a side-line-sibling," or been genitally abused as well, mothers tell me that their boys talk a lot about their penises. One boy victim (age six) holds onto his penis much of the time. He tells me that he is afraid it will fly away. Several of the little boys developed an abhorrence of eating mushrooms when the abuse was happening. Brian dreams of his wife Rose with her first husband, Nick. Brian is sure that his own penis is small by comparison. He sees Rose in his own arms but holding onto Nick's penis. It seems to make sense, therefore, that he should thrust so hard that Rose dreams that she cannot remove his penis from herself. The fear of the disappearing penis seems to force males to act out in a futile attempt at convincing themselves that they are in control, that their penile potency is superhuman. Young boy victims are shown by example that masculine potency is judged by "penis power," in its very narrowest sense. What we primarily encounter, literally and symbolically, is the unconscious "devil penis," not the generative phallus. It is hardly surprising, given how largely penis power functions in our society, that the number of adolescent offenders appears to be increasing, and that half of all rapists and incest offenders were nuisance offenders at age twelve.[12]

It is important to see that the bully who is abusive to the feminine, screaming in her ear "you cunt, you slut, you whore," is also the hurt young boy child crumpled in tears, only wanting to nurse at the breast, yet consumed with rage at the breast that never fed him food for the soul. His mother has been suffocating from motherhood, unable to offer soul food and allow the boy to sink into his body instinctual spirit. Because of the abuse she suffered, she cannot do this because her body was stolen from her along with soul, and she had no man willing to stand at her side as potent father to her little son. The vicious circle continues to spiral with the same frenzy as the circus ferris wheel until one person decides to get off. The boy child who emerges from the depths of the unconscious is a gross distortion of a child. His psychological shoulders are so enormous that they leave the little fellow tottering, unable to stand. They had become prematurely large as he struggled to become mother's consort to all her repressed sexuality. Paradoxically, the man who has consciously connected with his inner child no longer is the Mother's slave, nor is he obliged to constantly defy her.

Retarded Moral Development: Poor Symbolic Functioning
From the point of view of moral and ethical development, the incest offender is capable of incredibly harsh black and white judgments, as well as great self-deception and deception of others. Indeed, it is common to find out, from the offender's mouth, details of the abuse months into therapy—details which the child has claimed to be true from the beginning. This eventual honesty of the offender is an absolute requirement for the young child's truth to be honored and for the offender to have the necessary experience of concrete guilt. Offenders frequently have very strong connections with the patriarchal church; indeed clergy of all faiths have been convicted. The Catholic church, recognizing the problem, has added a sex-offender program to its New Mexico treatment center for alcoholic priests.

In general the offender lacks the ability to reflect, to bend back on himself, as it were. Jung describes this as a spiritual act, one of the highest of masculine functions, that runs counter to what we habitually do:

It is an act whereby we stop, call something to mind, form a picture, and take up a relation to and come to terms with what we have seen. It should be understood as an act of becoming conscious.[13]

This reflection is what Jung described as the "cultural instinct *par excellence*," and he proposes that ethical conduct is one of the fruits of this activity.[14]

Society's increasing loss of culture and civility, as we have seen, is paralleled by the individual's loss of the ability to reflect. Jung suggests that it is possible for true human morality to slip down into the unconscious. He says that

...an avowedly biological or coarse-minded attitude to women produces an excessively lofty valuation of femininity in the unconscious, where it is pleased to take the form of Sophia or the Virgin.[15]

This helps me understand some of the very few dreams of offenders that I have come across. In these dreams the underground scene was one of total respect and adoration of the feminine — roses all the way.

The offender's apparent retardation, or incompleteness of moral development, presents the clinician with serious problems. A person who cannot be self-reflective usually does not know that he has done anything wrong unless someone else says so. Thus most experienced clinicians insist that treatment must involve legal intervention: some authority figure has to tell an offender that his behavior is violating. To my knowledge, current approaches do not suggest therapy starting with dreams and other manifestations from the unconscious. The reason for this may include the fact that, in my experience, offenders are singularly alexithymic[16] — they have no symbolic functioning, no true imagination and no words for feelings and emotions. Metaphors usually glide over them or entirely confuse them. They are locked into concreteness, locked into matter. Their tongue's potency is minimal, though they may talk a great deal. Their personal objectivity is minimal. It is initially simply not possible for them to fully experience their incestuous desires at only a *feeling* or *imaginal level*.

In discussing post-war psychic problems, Jung expressed the opinion that redemption lies in a complete admission of guilt, and that it was therefore quite right that the Americans conducted the civilian population through the concentration camps, since it was not ultimately one or two Gestapo who were responsible for the Holocaust. However, Jung insisted that the object-lesson should not be driven home with moral instruction, because repentance must come from within the individuals themselves.

This understanding could well be applied to the treatment of incest offenders. Indeed, offenders are often required to experience the hurt and rage of women's therapy groups. A therapist would have to have come to terms with his or her own "inner offender" if this treatment were to be implemented without moralizing overtones. The male therapist would have to enter into a deep relationship with his Shadow; the female therapist would have to have explored the furthest reaches of her dark animus.

Many aspects of their lives and behavior are, however, deeply symbolic (collecting their daughter's urine, inserting particular objects into her vagina). To understand them would require a great deal of body work and stress-management with a clinician sensitive to the connections between body and psyche, and who could also work therapeutically around the issues of the abuse of power. An offender reported a dream—the only one he could recall. He dreamed it repeatedly about a year before he was apprehended. He dreamed that the police were coming for him—which of course they eventually did. It might have been a possible starting place in his therapy, functioning at his own level of moral reasoning. In fact, he did not persist in therapy.

It is significant that Carol Gilligan's[17] recent work on moral development shows how boys in our society are socialized to make moral decisions through the use of "ideas" and "principles," and girls in context of "relatedness," and "responsibility towards others." In other words, a girl's moral development is likely to remain connected to the murky waters of human, embodied situations. Indeed, it is over this very issue that women's moral development was criticized as retarded by Freud,[18] and recently by Piaget and Kohlberg.[19] We have already seen how our schooling tends to lift ideas away from matter, towards abstraction, and how legal language follows suit. Offenders seem to typify the extreme of what we might call patriarchal morality, which depends on abstracting ideas from matter. Archetypal psychology, however, attempts to look at moralities mythically, since "morality is rooted in psychic images and psychic images are moral powers"[19] deeply embedded in the soul of the body, and only accessible through ego sacrifice. Our choices and decisions always reflect mythic stances, even if we are unaware of them. When we work reflectively with images, we relinquish moral judgments towards them. We do not own the images which spring unbidden into our consciousness. Our task is to learn to relate to them. This immediately gives us a sense of something other than our heroic egos. Giving honor to images as "other" is a more profound level of moral functioning than free floating fantasy, with which the ego simply and unconsciously identifies.

I do not wish to suggest that this is a simple matter, or easy to incorporate into a program of treatment for incestuous families. In fact we are presented with profound considerations which draw us into the deepest and darkest waters possible. We begin to have some inkling that human relationships overcharged with archetypal significance can only break down. If we project our inner figures onto the external other, we in fact end up wanting the impossible, and we become coercive and abusive to get it. We cannot unconsciously carry the gods because we are human,[21] and we cannot expect others to carry a superhuman burden for us. Our inhumanity needs taming by dreaming. To reclaim his dream life would involve an offender establishing his anima internally and releasing the external anima carrier to her own life. Thus he would stop

> ...his monopolization of her time; his restriction of her outside interests, activities and relationships; his sexual preoccupation with her; the role-reversal in their relationship with her being regarded more as a peer than as a child; the identification he forms with his victim, his narcissistic sense of entitlement to her, and his projection of his own needs and desires on her; his preoccupation with fantasies about the victim; and the sense of pleasure, comfort and safety he experiences in the relationship with her.[22]

Languishing or Flourishing Tyrannically in the Arms of Mother

The offenders with whom I am acquainted have not experienced nurturing homes. Several were sent away to orphanages as children, or were in some way deprived of that sort of feminine energy that is in touch with the ecstasies of life and death; nor has anyone ever been able to mediate anima to them. It is significant to note that Abbott and Rosser[23] report that eighty percent of the chief women in the families of young offenders had been molested as children, and were angry at men. Angry women cannot possibly mediate the anima, particularly if relative stability in the home depends upon their suppressing their anger.

Furthermore, three-quarters of the young boys had witnessed the physical abuse of their mothers. Any love the child may have felt for mother would surely be dissipated in his confusion between his mother saying he should not get angry, and yet simultaneously seeing his father beat her. He gets caught in the split between mother trying to pretty him up and father having the right to be abusive to mother. Freud's nineteenth century rendition of the Oedipal complex still helps us understand something important about the present day Cartesian family's patriarchal subjugation of *mater.* Sacrificing the love of his mother allows the boy to submit to his father's authority and gain entry to the privileged male world.

In the words of Freud, the boy's infantile love for his mother is not merely transcended in the resolution of the Oedipal crisis; it is "smashed to pieces." In compensation, the boy learns that as an adult he will inherit many privileges, including sexual rights over women younger and weaker than himself.[24]

Although clinicians are divided on this point (often assuming a political stance and not a psychological one), Groth suggests that

> Incest offenses by mothers may be more frequent than one would be led to believe from a review of the few cases documented in the literature. The socially accepted physical intimacy between mother and child may serve to mask incidents of sexual exploitation and abuse on the part of the mother.[25]

My own experience with women suggests that they may abuse their male children differently than the way men abuse the feminine. At a psychological level, a woman's dependence on her son's spirited animus is equivalent to the father relying on his daughter to bear the burden of *his* soul. Yet women seem to abuse children from their shadow side, totally unknowingly, without premeditation. The young boy is caught both in the mother's web and in his attempts to escape it. He is caught because he has not received what he needs, but he must try to escape in order to become a man. The mother, for her part, feeds on the boy's innocence and psychologically devours him[26]: her own animus remains undeveloped. The boy is encased, feeling himself at once the center of the universe and impotent. He is the wounded king who doesn't know he is wounded. From this dynamic arises possible gender-identity issues. The developing man remains immune to conscious suffering; it is all projected outwards onto the external woman or girl child. To reflect on his wound would take him straight back to mother, and this is intolerable. In his unconscious this tyrannical male flourishes and flounders within the womb of mother. Any external woman in the man's life would be exposed to his abusive behavior, the result of his need to defy the unconscious. In the final analysis this would be impossible, and the man would become increasingly abusive and frantic.

The male offender thus maintains an unconscious relationship with his personal mother, through whom rage all the archetypal energies of the abandoned Great Mother, and little of the mediated anima. His male initiation has only attempted to smash his mother-love in order to align him with patriarchal authority. Although the offender usually maintains a sexual relationship with his spouse, such a man can only have a comfortable relationship when his partner is inexperienced or non-powerful, is unlikely to refuse, resist or reject him — in other words, an animal, a virgin or a child.[27] Such a child-lover will be obliged to become the source of all the man's infantile longing for nurturing. One offender I know was quite convinced that, by introducing his daughter to sex at age six, he was helping her become a "good mother." The un-balanced relationship spirals around the man's issues of competence, self-worth, identity, and recognition: it involves the sexual misuse of pow-er. Extramarital affairs or visits to prostitutes are not typical outlets for the true incest offender. Groth and Birnbaum[28] suggest that this is be-cause they are unable to sustain adult sexual relationships which require negotiation, mutuality, reciprocity and shared commitment (though I have not heard prostitutes describe their relationship with their clients as based on "mutuality, reciprocity and shared commitment.")

The average age of incest offenders (about twenty-nine) tends to be somewhat higher than that of rape offenders.[29] Rapists rape to demean their victims.[30] Their intent is to "fuck the bitch." The incest offender seems, initially at least, to deify the young anima carrier. There is fre-quently much picture taking and present-buying, setting her over against her mother, who is more and more perceived as "the bitch." Could it be that the incest offender is groping towards the inner sacred marriage, where the true virgin and potent masculine unite in a sacred vessel?

As the man's wife assumes more characteristics of his shadow mother, he becomes less and less able to deal with her. I witnessed a graphic example of this in a family therapy session where a man had twice been found guilty of incest with his twelve-year old daughter. Each time the mother started to talk about her anger and resentment toward her hus-band, he would turn right around to the daughter and start winking at her. It had taken the mother a whole year of individual therapy to get to the point of being able to express any of her burning anger, which had inverted to a deep and bitter cynicism and aloofness. The daughter immediately responded to her father's seduction with her well programmed, "stylized"[31] response to "darling daddy." The mother had experienced this sequence very often. Suppressing her rage had in fact been one of her attempts to protect her daughter from incest. Only a superficial glance at this behavior would label it "collusion."

The offender's relationship to his wife is increasingly expressed as "piss on you." But in the minds of young girl victims of sexual assault, contact with semen is frequently viewed as the final straw of humiliation. The assumption is that semen is in fact urine. It is a frequent theme of pornography and rape that the man will turn and urinate on his victim, as a final humiliation. In one family, the only passionate interaction the father had with his son was to take him out into the garden to "piss on the slugs" to kill them. Perhaps significantly, an eighteenth century term for a whore was a "fleshy convenience." The term convenience also meant "outhouse."

The wounded man is unable to ejaculate either his semen or his seminal ideas into the mature vessel. He must dominate and demean it. His sperm becomes confused with urine. He is being drawn to pre-verbal babyhood where the baby boy has an erection as he urinates.[32]

Gradually, patriarchal values impinge downwards on the young soul. She is taught to masturbate by her father, but he never plays with her or reads her a story. Many children abused by incest have been described as "easily aroused, highly motivated and readily orgasmic"[33] and unable to discriminate between erotic and non-erotic relationships. Tina is a little girl (five years) recovering from an incestuous relationship with her father. She has a new stepfather who is afraid of her erotic behavior and withdraws from her. His withdrawal leaves a vacuum into which she must pour more hysteria and erotic behavior—and so he withdraws some more. I asked if he can play with her. No, he doesn't know how to play. I know that Tina likes playdough so I asked him if they could sit at the kitchen table and play with the dough together. No, he doesn't know what to do. And so I suggested that maybe he could let Tina show him. He agreed to try. The next time I saw him he told me he couldn't stop playing quickly enough. The playdough was "yukky"—it stuck to his fingers. He wanted to wash it away in all haste. Such a father cannot allow healing to the young soul because he himself cannot be drawn into matter. He gradually becomes full of injunctions for the child, but rarely does he give her any careful, systematic instruction in anything that *she* might want to find out about. In fact the man has no time or energy to truly relate to her. He shrouds the child in the cloak of his own projections, until by adolescence she has frequently become what, in his fantasy world, he always hated—"an untrustworthy little bitch." She too eventually falls from grace.

If the man has not embarked on the path of individuation and integrated his anima qualities, any relationship with a woman will eventually become a relationship with mother—because he in fact needs to be drawn into the unconscious. Unless the need for mother is understood and deepened, the chance of recidivism is always high. The need for anima cannot be simply suppressed or snuffed out. In the end, mother and daughter must be unified in the man's psyche. Until that time, he will do anything in his power to disrupt the outer mother-daughter dyad.

Paradoxically, a man's incestuous relationship with his daughter can be seen as a maladaptive attempt to avoid having an incestuous relationship with his wife-mother. A return to the mother, the gateway to the unconscious, must initially be avoided at all costs. The incest offender already has a shaky foundation: his ego is so weak that it can be only rigidly imperious. He cannot cope with the burgeoning life and ferocious death aspects of the Great Mother. He has no mediating function. At this point the offender is not able to face his fat inner bitch—the horrendous Sphinx—in order to refine his manliness. He must remain the conquering hero, camouflaging his wound, instead of becoming the seeker, the honorer of the Holy Grail. He must remain outside the potency of the single word, and words that speak singleheartedly. He must continue to erect the tower of Babel with its confusion of tongues. Such an offender will always have the power to hurt a woman.

A Case Study

The following case study gives a picture of a twenty-nine year-old incest offender, Don. He started to molest his stepdaughter Sheri when she was three. The young child complained to her mother that daddy hurt her pee-pee when he bathed her. The mother mentioned this to the psychologist with whom the family was then working because of Don's physically brutalizing their son and breaking his leg. The psychologist initially suggested that it was "nothing, just the child's imagination." The child's hurting was ignored. Five years later, while watching television, the eight-year-old daughter told her mother that "Daddy had sex with me." The mother, Olga, then in the last month of pregnancy with her third child, immediately brought the two children to the center, and I became involved with the family at that point.

Over time, Don was able to tell me that when he first met Olga he had loved her "like a queen." He had adored her little daughter, whom he had looked after a lot. Olga, the only girl in a family of five boys, sexually abused and financially bribed into the abuse by one of them, admitted that she married Don because she could "twist him around her little finger." She complained that for years he had grabbed at her breasts in his sleep, and one night had somehow managed to break one of her teeth. A man's lack of relationship with his actual mother builds up an immense chaos of mother-seeking desire, and when projected outwards, the woman recipient is obliged to carry the image of the rejecting mother who elicits the man's rage. The infant son feels himself to be the lord and mother his slave.

Don recalls always having felt like "a leper." The earliest awareness of this feeling occurred when he was covered by mosquito bites at about ten, when his family had gone on a camping trip. His mother "fussed and fussed," but made *him* deal with the bites. To do this he had to stand outside the trailer, where everyone could see him, bathing the blemishes on his skin. He found this an absolutely traumatic experience.[34] He couldn't let his mother near him because she wanted to "pinch" and "squeeze" the infected spots. She was not able to deal effectively with the results of insect intrusions—she would merely fall into an exaggerated mother complex.

As a result of the bites, Don developed a blood infection that lasted four years. His blood connection to soul had been poisoned. He felt that his "whole blood had gone bad," and he lived in constant terror that his brain would become infected, that he would become permanently "crazy." When I asked if the pimples could speak, Don claimed that they said, "We are going to take you over." He still felt his pimples were alive and as poisonous as ever. Obviously his prison sentence had not addressed the sanity-threatening pimples. Don felt that there was a thick wall under his skin, as though his skin were entirely separate from the rest of him.

Don had made love once before he had married Olga, and it had been a disastrous experience. For some reason, he had taken a young woman to his paternal grandmother's bed. But grandmother and Don's father had returned unexpectedly, and both cursed and swore at the young woman, calling her a "slut" and a "whore." Don never saw her again. Don's father told him to "leave town immediately," and that he "should never use a woman so badly." Don has continued to ponder on this because previously his father had always told him, in relation to women, "to enjoy himself," and "go kill 'em." Don wondered whether this reversal in his father's behavior could have been due to the fact that the father was in front of his own mother. At this, Olga piped up, "And there never was a greater harlot — six husbands and umpteen lovers." Yet it seems that the son had to "shape up" in front of mother.

Don described his father as a "super stud" or "super sport" who constantly "chased skirts" and berated Don for not wanting to join the military. Don had seen his mother beaten and thrown across the room by his father. Don finally talked about his pity for his mother, but this pity quickly revealed itself as the most demeaning contempt, and a deep wish to "kill the bitch." He then went straight into talking about his anger at Olga and the power she had over him: she was also a "fucking bitch." Don was jealous of Olga's former lover, Sheri's father. In role playing, Don saw him as "that fucking bastard...with a Mustang...who is run by his father and mother...such a weasel."

Don's confusion over sexuality seemed to stem from even earlier memories. At the age of twelve he started to hear how great sex was — particularly from a seventeen year-old boy who had failed the fifth grade five times. During the school lunch hour, the boy would go out into his car and "mess around" with his girlfriend. In his own home, Don had only heard sex talked about negatively. At the age of eight he had been found in the bathroom investigating his sister's genitals. Mother gave Don the beating and said that "boys are dirty"; the sister was ignored. In actual fact the sister had told her father that Don kept abusing her, asking him to help her because she was so unhappy about it. The father simply laughed at her.

With Olga, Don had grown to feel impotent. If finances were not right then sex was "cut off" by Olga, whom he would never allow to see the family budget. Olga thought Don "grabbed power" through money. But Don felt he had no power there either. He had worked his way to construction foreman for a large building company. But this was never acknowledged by his father, and gradually Don reverted to unskilled jobs. He said that he saw every intrusion by an authority figure as a threat. If the boss asked him to do something, Don would take it as a reproach. Don felt "that although it was woman's duty" to "perform sexually," society sanctioned woman's being able to say yes or no. Men, on the other hand, were only allowed to say yes: they had to walk around "with a hard-on."

Olga has never allowed Don to explore her body: he was not to see her genitals. There were too many painful memories for her. But Don wanted to find "the fire crackers" that everyone talked about. He turned to Sheri, the little daughter. In this relationship "all anger and fear would disappear." It was an experience of paradise. But gradually he became rougher and rougher. Finally the child would be naked and he would ejaculate over her. His anger started to intrude on paradise, however. The circle became vicious. Each time he would hope for paradise; each time he would be disappointed and made angry, and so he would have to try again, with much premeditation and preparation. In the end he would frantically read the Bible before entering the child's room, in the hope that something would help him. Often he would be crying and the child would be crying, begging him not to do it. He would cry, "I can't help it, I can't help it." He had to persist: he was compulsively driven.

Almost two years after disclosure and the start of therapy, Olga dreamed that

> She was visiting Don, and she suggested that they get married. He lay nonchalantly on his back with his arms behind his head (just as he had when confronted with the reality of disclosure) and B.S.'d. He finally admitted that he didn't love her. The scene changed to a swimming pool. A fat woman came out; Don was in love with her. Next time Olga looked, the woman looked slim and "perfect."

Olga had dreamed this several weeks before Don said that he loved Olga to a point, that he was married to her at eighteen, that he "just hangs on." He really wanted "women, big cars, and travel"—a perfect picture of the eternal boy compelled to fly away from "fat mama," yet unable to leave her and therefore coercing her into being "Miss Perfect." Indeed, Don exerted a great deal of pressure on Olga to lose the weight she had gained while he was in prison. He would constantly say that he would be unable to make love to a fat woman and then they would be in trouble again. Olga, in turn, had seen this period as allowing herself to experience herself for the first time. Certainly the fat woman was part of Olga's shadow, as was her desperate need to be "Miss Perfect," to please the men in her life. The fat woman/Miss Perfect also represented Don's anima. He would never be able to love Olga until he could love his anima—and both sides of it. The dream was telling Olga exactly what the situation was.

A few weeks later Don had the only dream he ever shared with me. He saw Olga and Sheri together. He tried to intervene because he felt that Sheri was mocking him and putting him down.

This most tentative glimpse of a mother-daughter reunion is deeply horrendous to eyes looking through patriarchal spectacles: it threatens the very foundation of the world. The "fat bitch" who needs to be killed and the young anima carrier are in fact two sides of one coin. To see them unified would topple his kingship. Don terminated therapy at this point.

The only other image that Don shared with me was of himself as a weasel, and although Don remembered calling his male rival by that name, I did not see many attempts to digest his own weasel. I have actually been surprised at the number of incest offenders who report an inner weasel. Jay found his inner weasel to be "sly" and "squirming." He "weasels out of discipline." The dictionary says that a human weasel is "a treacherous and sneaky person." "Weaseling" is to "equivocate" or be evasive. To "weasel out" means to "back out of a situation or commitment in a sneaky or cowardly manner."

Significantly, a "weasel word" is a "word of an equivocal nature used to deprive a statement of its force or to evade a direct commitment." This is an allusion to the weasel's ability to suck up the contents of an egg without doing obvious damage to the shell. Such an image aptly describes the unsuspected loss of potency of the words of the offender — eggs devoid of Eros.

In this short review of an offender's experience, we see many of the issues and archetypal dimensions raised in earlier chapters. We see early signs of voyeurism and an emphasis on sexuality linked with the supposed freedom of the fast car. We see the hurt man struggling to emerge from a non-reflective home where women are both aggrandized and abused, where men rival each other, and where the son's needs and skills are never valued. We see the hurt man's need for nurturing, and yet his frantic drive to win his freedom. We see the hurting feminine demean the young boy through her own unrecognized grieving. The offender's wife started as queen, became mother, and eventually "the fat bitch," jealously guarded as male property but never truly related to. The hurt man's instinctual animal has become an invincible machine. He is propelled into verbal monstrosities and frantic articulations to avoid the craziness of his "infected blood." He says he feels leprous. Indeed, Randolph Severson suggests that "skin disease might be simply called the stigmata of the spirit,"[35] a manifestation of the hysteria of spirit. Enormous inflation has been imposed upon the patriarchal penis, but we encounter no generative phallus.

And yet as well as seeing all the difficulties under which the hurt man labors, it is perhaps important to see that his psychopathology reflects a rarely seen mythologem — that is, the physical meeting of Eros and

Psyche. Of course, the offender's Eros spirit is so badly weakened that he must take the young Psyche by force, and so there is no true union and no true healing. We see only the shadow elements of the archetypal situations, because the Mother must still be subjugated, and the Father is absent. It is not enough to say that incest is an abuse of power. This it most certainly is; but it is also a sexual act living out of vast, archetypal mythologems which we must recognize and value if we want to understand the phenomenon of incest.

As we look at and value the offender-against-soul, we see that he barely even functions at the least developed level of animus functioning — the level of power.[36] His power rarely manifests itself as consciously directed will. Moving into the next level — that of deed — frequently presents him with what seems like a superhuman challenge. The next levels of word and then meaning elude him completely; he is a specialist in the weasel-word only. There is little possibility that metaphors can spring to life through dreams. He cannot celebrate the dream's sacrament in flesh and blood. Nor can he bring meaning to psyche hiding under the thick skin of his everyday events.

Don's early skin secretions sent him into hiding. He became a secret person — a leper. His inner barrier seems to be paralleled by the barrier around all incestuous families. Both "secret" and "secrete" come from two Latin words, — se, apart, and cernere, to separate. Paradoxically, leprosy, with its imposition of isolation, also bespeaks the collective. Of course, for all its secretiveness, the incestuous family is absolutely embedded in the collective. There is no sense of the myth being alive, and therefore no individuality can exist within the family. Thus the offender's true tears and his semen, two secretions that do escape his armor, take on particular significance. They emerge only when he is in seclusion with young Psyche. The incredible secrecy with which the offender surrounds his violation of young Psyche takes on other dimensions now that we can see that it is practically only at this time that he displays any manifestations of soul, and that what he is protecting is a most fragile ego-self connection. For the pre-patriarchal man, incest seems to him to be his only hope of life and survival, and he must vehemently protect this secret and profound happening.

As the abused woman heals, she can see that the male model she has swallowed, hook line and sinker, is the offender. This introjected, abusive masculine has become a frighteningly strong and negative part of her own animus, and eventually she must learn to undo his power over her soul. She can only do this when she has reestablished her own connection with the mother. This too is horrendously painful, because she has been so betrayed by her personal mother, and abandoned by her to the ravages of the patriarchal and intellectual offender. Until the connection with the feminine is made, the woman has no other way of confronting the offender, since she had been totally subsumed in patriarchal ways.

To accept a relationship with our own inner offender may sound simple. But Jung reminds us that

> In actual life it requires the greatest art to be simple, and so acceptance of oneself is the essence of the moral problem and the acid test of one's whole outlook on life. That I feed the beggar, that I forgive an insult, that I love my enemy in the name of Christ—all these are undoubtedly great virtues. What I do unto the least of my brethren, that I do unto Christ, but what if I should discover that the least amongst them all, the poorest of all beggars, the most impudent of all offenders, yea the very fiend himself—that these are within me, and that I myself am the enemy who must be loved—what then? Then, as a rule, the whole of Christianity is reversed: there is then no more talk of love and long-suffering; we say to the brother within us "Raca," and condemn and rage against ourselves. We hide him from the world, we deny ever having met this least amongst the lowly in ourselves, and had it been God himself who drew near us in this despicable form, we should have denied him a thousand times before a single cock had crowed.[37]

We all meet these images as we struggle to incarnate the story of Eros and Psyche. Reflecting on the leper, bringing him into our hearts in an imaginal sense, we find that in Hebrew *leper* means "he who is smitten by the Lord." Our word "leprosy" comes from the Greek *lepos,* or "scales"—"perhaps the scaly skin of the fish, the secret sign of the Spirit who rules over Christian Aion."[38] The son's fertile greenness turned leprous can in fact give rise to the most precious gold in the alchemist's retort.[39] The leprosy of skin disease "is the true spirit waiting to be transformed" in the crucible of the alchemical opus. Indeed, Bruegel's famous painting shows the lepers eternally accompanying Christ on the long road to Calvary.

The leprosaria of the European Middle Ages were emptied when leprosy disappeared; they were later to be refilled with "crazy" people—mostly women. "The leper and the mad woman just missed each other" as they marched across history's stage. Randolph Severson suggests that

Had the Leper and the Madwoman bedded down together in some cold, damp tomb, then our age might not find itself with a wounded spirit and an unhappy soul.[40]

Perhaps the woman with a conscious and accepting relationship with death's tomb will be ready to welcome her doomed bridegroom as he descends into the earth mother. Conscious marriages in the underworld may help give the Black Madonna back to the archetypal world, and give her a consort who is worthy and man enough for her.

Notes

[1]Irwin Dreiblatt, quoted in Cheryl McCall's article "The Offenders." In *Life*, December, 1984

[2]Nicholas Groth. "The Incest Offender." In *Handbook of Clinical Intervention in Child Sexual Abuse*. Toronto: Lexington Books, 1983, p. 215

[3]Judith Herman. *Father-Daughter Incest*. Cambridge: Harvard University Press, 1981, p. 74

[4]Brian Abbott and Forrest Rosser. *Adolescent Offenders and Their Families*. Talk presented at Child Sexual Abuse Treatment, P.O.Box 952, San Jose, California, 95108

[5]Mircea Eliade. *Rites and Symbols of Initiation*. New York: Harper & Row, 1975, pp. 1-40.

[6]Judith Herman, *op. cit.*, p. 95

[7]C.G. Jung. *Jung Speaking: Interviews and Encounters*. William McGuire and R. F. C. Hull, eds. Princeton: Princeton University Press, 1977, pp. 228-229

Jung says that for the "awakened" Christian, confrontation with the shadow is a very serious psychic experience. In psychological terms, "one discovers the hidden fear that the devil may be stronger."

The problem is not resolved until "the last trace of blackness is dissolved, in which the devil no longer has an autonomous existence but rejoins the profound unity of the psyche." The inner task of reflection of course is for the adult. No child is developmentally ready for such a horrendous task.

[8]C.G. Jung, *CW* IX, II, par. 17

[9]Judith Herman, op. cit , p.76

Aaron M., Cameron, P., Roizen, J., and Room, R. *Alcohol, Casualties and Crimes*. Berkeley: Social Research Group, 1976

Incest offenders tend to abuse alcohol more than do other types of sex offenders.

Gebard, Gagnon, Pomeroy, and Christenson. *Sex Offenders: An Analysis of Type*. New York: Harper & Row, 1965

The authors found that incest offenders are more anxious and guilt-laden than other types of sex offenders; this in turn could make them more prone to alcohol abuse. It would also suggest a more hopeful prognosis than for those who experience no guilt or repression.

Ken Dixon, 1984 lecture entitled "Characteristics of Offenders and Their Families."

In subsequent research, Dixon has found a significant variation in alcohol abuse in four offender sub-types, although all groups showed some dependence. See Ken Dixon, "Incest Offender Sub-Types," unpublished thesis, The University of Alberta Education Library, 1987

[10]*Edmonton Journal,* January 18, 1984

[11]Brian Abbott & Forrest Rosser, *op. cit*
   In research not yet in print, the authors concluded that thirty to fifty percent of sexual offenders were victims of sexual assault themselves.

[12]Brian Abbott & Forrest Rosser, *op. cit.*

[13]C.G. Jung, *CW* XI, par. 235n.

[14]C.G. Jung, *CW* VIII, par. 243

[15]C.G. Jung, *CW* XIV, par. 221

[16]P.E. Sifneos. "The Prevalence of Alexithymic Characteristics in Psychosomatic Patients." Topics of Psychosomatic Research, 9th European Conference on Psychosomatic Research, Vienna, 1972. In *Psychotherapeutic Psychosomatics,* 22:255-262, 1973

[17]Barbara Roberts, "All Our Lives: Sexual Assault and Other Normal Activities," In *Canadian Woman Studies,* Vol. 4, No. 4, Summer, 1983, p. 8

[18]Sigmund Freud, "Einege psychische Folgen des Anatomischen Geschlechtsunterschiedes." *Ges.Werke,* xiv, p.29. See Wolfgang Lederer, *The Fear of Women.* New York: A Harvest/HBJ Book, p. 93

[19]Carol Gilligan. *In a Different Voice.* Cambridge: Harvard University Press, 1982, p. 18

[20]James Hillman. *Re-visioning Psychology.* New York: Harper & Row, 1975, pp. 179-181

[21]*Ibid.,* p. 187

[22]Nicholas Groth, *op. cit.,* p. 230

[23]Brian Abbott & Forrest Rosser, *op. cit.*

[24]Judith Herman, *op. cit.,* p. 56

[25]Nicholas Groth, *op. cit.,* p. 230
   In a recent NBC television special entitled "Of Men And Macho," Groth—who has worked with male sex offenders for over twenty years—made the startling statement that, in his experience, over twenty percent of them had been sexually violated as children by an older woman.

[26]Barbara Marnett Groth. *The Phenomenology of the Puella Aeterna.* Doctoral thesis submitted to International College, Los Angeles, California; she is quoting von Franz (*Puer Aeternus.* Boston: Sigo Press, 1982, p. 36-39)

[27]Nicholas Groth, *op. cit.,* p. 221

[28]Nicholas Groth & H.J. Birnbaum. "Adult Sexual Orientation and Attraction to Under-Age Persons." In *Archives of Sexual Behaviors,* 7,3:175-181, 1978

29Ken Dixon, (lecture) Forensic Assessment Community Services, Edmonton, Alberta, 1984

30Don Hadlock. "Family Therapy for Incestuous Families." Talk presented at Child Sexual Abuse Treatment Program, P.O.Box 952, San Jose, California, 95108, 1984

31Nicholas Groth suggests that use of the word "stylized" instead of "seductive" to describe the young incest victim's behavior.

32James Hillman. "Salt: A Chapter in Alchemical Psychology." In *Images of the Untouched*. Dallas: Spring Publications, 1982, p.121
"The urine of the boy is one of the many names for the *prima materia*. It refers to the salts in the microcosmic sea before the Fall, that is, the archetypal essence of each particular personality before it has accumulated personal residues: salt not as the result of events, but as prior to events There is potent spirit to be focused in the silly piss of one's little boy (even perhaps in his bed wetting.)"

33Alayne Yates, "Children Eroticized by Incest." In *American Journal of Psychiatry*. 139:4, April, 1982

34Randolph Severson. "Puer's Wounded Wing: Reflections on the Psychology of Skin Disease." In *Puer Papers*. Dallas: Spring Publications, 1983, p. 132
Since Freud, it has become generally accepted that the skin can function as an object of intense libidinal attachment. In 1935, Joseph Klauder remarked "The psyche exerts a greater influence on the skin than any other organ" D.W. Winnicott has said that "the smallest skin lesion concerns the whole personality." p. 151, note 39
In *Madness and Civilization*, Michel Foucault suggests an image of skin disease as the wounded wing of the puer (the boy) who has refused to go about his father's business. It is of note that in the Middle Ages leprosy fell into the domain of Saturn.
The Hebrew ritual cure for the leper was a purification by the priest transferring the pollution to a bird which was carried outside of camp and then released. Severson suggests that "when the spirit bird in the soul is set free and allowed to soar, skin disease can be healed."

35*Ibid.*, p. 136

36Emma Jung. *Animus & Anima*. New York: Spring Publications, 1972, p. 3

37C.G. Jung, *CW* XI, par. 520

38Randolph Severson, *op. cit.*, p. 143

39C.G. Jung, *CW* XII, par. 207

40Randolph Severson, *op. cit.*, p. 144

CHAPTER VII

Little Red Riding Hood Cries Tears of Flowers

The story of Little Red Riding Hood (from here on, Riding Hood) is a story of a little girl's search for flowers. It is also a story of abduction, yet it bears healing possibilities. Though it is one of our culture's most well-known stories, there are few people who have heard of the little girl's active part in her own recovery. Perrault's rationalistic version (in his *Blue Book of Fairy Tales*) makes everything as explicit as possible and renders the tale merely cautionary. Moreover, it lacks the themes of escape, recovery and consolation. Since the wolf's seduction of Riding Hood is so obvious and since she makes no move to escape or fight back, Bruno Bettelheim comments that from Perrault's version it would seem that:

> . . .either [Riding Hood] is stupid or she wants to be seduced. In neither case is she a suitable figure to identify with. With these details, Riding Hood is changed from a naive, attractive young girl, who is induced to neglect Mother's warnings and enjoy herself in what she consciously believes to be innocent ways, into nothing but a fallen woman.[1]

Perrault's eighteenth-century version of the tale underscores the split between innocence and guilt that still haunts contemporary woman.

The Sweet Little Maiden

As the story begins, we learn that Riding Hood is a "sweet little maiden" and that she is "much loved." She is endowed with a special sort of beauty—the sort that as clinicians we have frequently noted, wondering if the beauty of these girl children was their downfall. Hillman tells us that the primary quality of Psyche, the carrier of the soul image, is her beauty. And yet few of us in the realm of psychotherapy have understood or articulated the place of beauty in the soul's health. We have wrongly assumed that beauty is adornment, or something stashed in art galleries, or that it belongs to some symbolic realm, and is "far removed from the soul's desperate concerns."[2] Aphrodite's naked beauty has been pornographized by a patriarchal culture that is spiritually dying and frantically grasping at beauty, as if to snatch some medicine in the hope of reviving. But by snatching at feminine beauty, the patriarchy can dismiss it (not recognizing it as life-giving) because it can be conquered. The beauty of the feminine then becomes objectified.

If the offender could see the essential part of himself as actually residing in himself, instead of in the bearer of his projection, he would surely be less obligated to pornographically "be moved into a social relationship,"[3] but would rather be moved towards a state of reflection, and a valuing of someone else as other, over whom he has no rights. Without being able to surrender to reflection on beauty, the man strives to rid himself of his dread of woman by objectifying feminine beauty. He becomes afraid of the possibility of his transformation, prefaced by the necessary death of his ego.

Grandma's Gift: the Silent Scream
We are told that grandma loves Riding Hood so much that there is nothing she would not give the child; it is because of this that she gives Riding Hood her cap of red velvet, which is "a perfect fit." Out of what indulgence of consciousness did this gift arise? Bettelheim says:

> Whether it is Mother or Grandmother—the mother once removed—it is fatal for the young girl if this older woman abdicates her own attractiveness to males and transfers it to the daughter by giving her a too attractive red cloak.[4]

This, of course, is quite true. But beauty is in the eye of the beholder: the old(er) woman would have to be perceived as attractive, and that is a tall order in a culture whose preoccupation is with slenderized, tenderized, deodorized girls, without a wrinkle or wisp of grayness to leaven the head. Without being perceived, recognized, acknowledged, the

older woman's best intentions to remain in touch with her sexuality tend
to evaporate. But a true Grandma is not one to tangle with lightly. To
acknowledge her would mean being able to value her dark side.

This grandmother lives in the forest, about half an hour away from
the village. She lives under three oak trees and nut bushes, suggesting
that her abode is the place of dynamic movement where heroines and
heroes are forced to unite and bring darkness and light into a healthy
balance. What was it about her that enables or enforces her to live in
a place we enter with dread? Is she a solitary "borderland woman"[5] who
has become dangerous to the patriarchal status quo? Any woman whose
own redness is overlooked and unperceived is in danger of becoming
a little crazy in an effort to have her soul-self loved. The more she is
unloved, the more bizarre and frantic becomes her beckoning, until the
heart of the forest becomes the padded cell of the mental hospital. Of
course such a woman is said to sleep with the devil—she has had no
choice—and we can dismiss her as a witch. Her dreams and visions can
only etch the dark side of her soul, because no one loves her soul-speech
enough to help her send shafts of light into her fertile earth and allow
the light-bearer, the hunter, to emerge from her own depths. And, of
course, this inner dark soul of madness tends to exact a response of violation from the outside world. This is exactly Grandma's situation. She
does not recognize the wolf's voice. In her ill and weakened state, her
ears cease to be able to differentiate the false and seductive voice from
that of the wholesome bearer of light. She allows the devourer to enter
her inner space, and she suffers the consequences. This also results in
some confusion for the child who cannot see through Grandma's clothing and recognize the wolf.

Riding Hood on the path through the forest does attempt to redirect
the wolf's attention from herself onto Grandma by giving instructions
on how to get to Grandma's house. Riding Hood perhaps intuited that
the wolf needs the adult woman, and that she herself (Riding Hood)
needs a mature woman to stand between herself and the wolf. Interestingly, she gives this information without even being asked—thus like
Grandma not perceiving the true nature of the wolf. At this point in
the story both Grandma and Riding Hood are caught in a state of unconscious and hurt innocence, devoid of true sensing, and thus are left
vulnerable.

Recently a woman told me of a dream in which a mysterious and attractive man came to show her the way. Although her instinct dictated
the opposite, she told herself to trust him. The dream ended with her

following the stranger to a castle where she was violently raped. No matter how hard she tried, her scream was silent.

Telling ourselves to trust when our senses suggest otherwise, opening our inner sanctums to fraudulent strangers, casting our pearl words to those unable to value them, wildly swinging between silence and telling too much, are characteristic of the feminine that has had instinctual knowledge stolen away, and has therefore never gone past the stage of immature and hurtful innocence. A woman who has abandoned her instincts is unable to protect herself.

One wonders about the whereabouts of Grandpa. Why isn't he at home making soup for ailing Grandma? Recently a woman told me of her borderland grandmother, whom she now felt she understood for the first time. This Grandmother had always lived outside a prairie town. She became pregnant out of wedlock in the 1930s and had removed herself to an out-of-the-way place to hide her shame and protect the family's honor and reputation. She eventually married the man who had impregnated her, and this was the storyteller's grandfather. As a child, the woman had always had a special bond with Grandma. When she was six or seven, she went to visit her but found that Grandma was still out. Grandpa was there, however, and told her to go in and wait on the hide-a-bed until Grandma came home. The woman explained that she was so naive and felt so helpless that she did just that. Grandfather came in and proceeded to assault her—playing with her genitals and exposing himself with requests that she should play with him. When they heard Grandma return, the child was so horrified at what was going on that she quickly pulled up her pants and pushed past Grandma out of the door, saying that she could not wait.

The child went home and told her mother, who became flustered because she had also been raped as a child and had never dealt with it. There was a fierce family argument over Grandpa, but nothing happened. However, my patient noticed that whenever they visited the grandparents' house and her mother sat on the hide-a-bed, her mother invariably fought with her father.

This family certainly had a hidden bedrock that affected family functioning. Here was a grandmother who isolated herself to protect the good name of others, and by so doing inadvertently gave sanctuary to a wolf who eventually endangered a precious female relationship, affected a later marriage, and would also leave a young woman with suspicious doubts about the good word of grandfather—and not without due cause.

What would happen if grandfather had had no skirts to hide behind?

Would he be forced to test the trustworthiness of his word? How can this generational and inherited problem ever be healed?

Violet was a past incest victim who was presently struggling to "stop being a prostitute," as she put it. Over the previous two years she had made a deep connection with an inner wise old woman, and in so doing had been able to mourn the lack of nurturing in her childhood, and had learned much about nurturing herself. She had in recent months felt the need to leave her husband and two small boys, which was an awesome ordeal for her. It meant becoming alienated from her own family and being the recipient of much reproach, but she needed to stand alone. Violet told me her recent dream:

> I was on the highway and an old tramp-like man offered me a ride. He started to seduce me. In order not to succumb to his advances, I jumped from the moving car and rolled into the ditch. I crawled out and went to the nearest farmhouse. A man and two young boys gave me a ride to the highway and then let me continue alone. I passed by the old man who had just crawled down into the ditch after a piece of foil so that he could look at himself in the mirror. I continued alone pushing in front of me one little cart wheel.

The woman told me that the wheel was all she had, and yet she felt a simple satisfaction at being able to keep this wheel of birth[6] playfully rolling in front of her. I was left with a profound image of a young woman, alone on the highway, content, playful, able to protect herself, and thus providing the old man with no excuse, but rather the necessity of looking in the mirror to become self-aware and see his own face, reflected, for what it is worth. Such a woman will bear within her the possibility of transforming the inner face of the patriarchy into one of light rather than seduction. Such a woman has a hope of being able to filter the plethora of words and images that impinge on her soul, so that the one or two most precious can impregnate her newly reclaimed virginity and allow her true generativity to replace the inherited generational problem besetting the feminine psyche.

The Mother's House
Bettelheim describes Riding Hood's house as one of abundance, which — since she is way beyond oral anxiety — she gladly shares with her grandmother by bringing her sacramental food of cake and wine. At this point we note that the mother in the story has time to bake and is sufficiently concerned about the abandoned grandmother to send her a life-renewing gift. But there is no sign of father in the home, just as we do not hear

of grandfather. And judging from the injunctions that mother gives to
Riding Hood before she undertakes her journey, it would seem that mother is not able to adequately prepare her daughter.[7] She certainly tries,
but it seems that she is not deeply aware of the wolf prowling in the
forest. This does not necessarily indicate that the mother is somehow
in collusion with the wolf, or that she wished the assault on the child.
The child's inadequate preparation is rather an indication of maternal
powerlessness.[8] Such a mother has been forced to over-identify with the
roles of nurturing and hurt naivete. Nor does she have an inner sense
of the masculine, because her feminine foundation is too fragile to be
able to receive the other.

After listening to admonitions and injunctions, Riding Hood takes
her mother's hand and tells her that everything will be all right. Such
a gesture from a young child is absolutely in keeping with what we know
of families where sexual assault occurs. The young victim often displays
precocious nurturing qualities which are in fact a facade covering the
real and underlying craving for feminine nurturing. It is another view
of our society's violent demand for nurturing milk. This is the outcome
of a society that aggrandizes mother, yet blames her for all failures, and
never truly ascribes value to her.

Women grounding themselves in their own insights and strengths
oblige men to become fathers in the fullest sense. This relationship, or
the ill that is produced by the suppression of this relationship, is perfectly expressed in a story told to me by a woman in northern Alberta.

One particular homesteader would hire himself out to others during
the day, but in order to plow his own fields, his wife would come out
at nighttime with him. She would stand at one end of the field and
hold a lantern so that he could plow a straight line. This same woman
had had twelve children. When she was about to give birth to the first
one, someone said to her husband, "Don't you think you should go home
and see your wife?" He declined, saying she would be just fine. That
day the woman had her baby alone, milked their nine cows by hand,
and had the man's supper on the table at the usual time.

Just before Christmas one year, the woman who told me the story
learned that the now-old woman was alone (her husband long since dead)
and had been seen in her home twisting a small piece of cloth into a
hole in one of her old enamel saucepans so that she could heat up some
soup for herself. Her big-time-farmer sons were out frantically trying
to spend $40,000 on large farm equipment so as to avoid income tax.
The old woman died a few weeks after Christmas.

Looking at the rolling prairie, with its occasional homestead returning to dust, I considered this story a painful allegory of the death of
an ancient partnership with the land. The woman brought her light to
her husband's world, but he would not see hers. Indeed she survived,
but she brought forth from her body alone and unseen, unappreciated.
Today her land does not experience the sacred partnership, and large
machines rip at the soil and fertilizers demand higher and higher yield.

The aggrandizing and prostituting of young girls and the rape of the
earth mother go hand in hand. We can no longer afford to be divisive
in how we conceive of the problem. We can no longer afford the anni-
hilation of sacred connections by patriarchal standards. The mother's
house must be newly perceived so that children can go onto life's path
through the forest[9] with useful knowledge from both masculine and feminine streams of unconsciousness.

Mother's Injunctions

Riding Hood's mother obviously went to considerable efforts to prepare
her daughter, giving her four specific suggestions. The first was sound
enough—"go before it gets too hot." Second, she warned Riding Hood
not to stray off the path in case the wine bottle should break and Grandma get nothing. Although mother could not make the journey herself,
she knew grandma was in special need. Riding Hood was also instructed to say "Good Morning" to Grandma when she arrived. "Be nice and
polite, and don't stray away from what is commonly acceptable." This
type of injunction, given wordlessly (and all the more profoundly for
that), sounds familiar to many women today.

As if to sum it up, mother says, "and behave modestly," suggesting
that somewhere in her psyche she knows about being immodest but cannot bring herself to openly talk about seduction and how to handle the
wolf. Being unaware of our vulnerability and seductive abilities leaves
a huge and elemental power bursting through our psyche's seams, and
it is just such energy that we unconsciously hand on to our daughters
(and sons, of course). Because women have been torn between the white
(mother milk) and red (passionate) streams of feminine consciousness
for generations, this becomes a difficult area to work with in therapy.
Mothers often give the message of seeming indifference, casualness and
even blatant exhibitionism regarding sexuality—which can deeply affect
a young child—while at the same time giving instruction to please remain modest at all costs. This comes from the woman intuiting somewhere that she has been obliged to suppress and hide so much of what

is natural to the feminine, that in her frustration she would like to "brandish all."

I recently watched two eleven-year old girls prepare a special meal for the family. It was to be a formal occasion, everyone was told to dress appropriately. The menus were handmade, the candles were lit and an elegant meal served. The two girls had been delicately dipping into mother's cosmetics, and the results were discrete and alluring and all the adults present had the tact to keep back obnoxious and provocative comments. Towards the end of the meal, the phone rang and two boy friends from school were on the line. The mother, in agreement with all family members, invited the boys for dessert. What was most fascinating was that the girls' biggest concern was to rush away and remove their makeup before the boys came — which they did. (Again there were no comments from the adults). The friends' visit was spent eating dessert, laughing and chatting, and the children gradually involved the adults in a game of hunt-the-thimble. Young girls developing healthily do not necessarily wish to have seductive relationships with boys. They prefer the sorts of relationships that young Artemis had as a prepubescent child:

> She has a relationship to the opposite sex which is in a way boyish, and at the same time sisterly, indeed almost brotherly;...she is the dancer and huntress, who takes the bear cub on her lap and runs races with the deer, death-bringing when she bends her bow, strange and unapproachable, like untamed nature, who is yet, like nature, wholly magic living impulse, and sparkling beauty.[10]

Children's initiation into puberty seems to be more and more hurried and, indeed, we have evidence that girls have begun to menstruate earlier and earlier this century. Bettelheim conceived of Riding Hood as being a pubescent child. However, in asking many children and adults how old they think Riding Hood is, the answers range from six to nine — hardly a child the age of puberty. In the clinic, an eight-year old incest victim — sitting on the floor with her legs spread open, playing with building blocks between them — was talking to me about her period, how afraid she was that her temporary stepfather would see blood on the sheet and how embarrassed she was that her older sister teased her. This scene was not a healthy one. This was not a child who was able to become caught up in truly imaginative play. This child's fingers went through some motions, but her feelings and thoughts were disconnected from them. The mind/body connection is a delicately balanced two-way street. Certain stimulation at critical times can elicit increased brain growth, and excessive stimulation—donning a red cloak too early—might result in precocious physical development.

Perhaps mother's last instruction is to the point. She tells Riding Hood that when she gets to Grandma's house, she is not to look in the corners. Bettelheim suggests that this is to remind the child that she must not pry into things that belong to the adult realm and which she has no business knowing about. Recalling that Bettelheim describes this as a puberty-age dream, we should note that if a girl is entering puberty, feeling the support of her family and community, she would not need to pry. She would be appropriately taught. Furthermore, a wise adult would never tell a child not to look in the corners. It would be the first place he or she looked. On the other hand, a young child still in touch with following her interests would be following them whether or not they went into the corner. So it seems as though poor Little Red Riding Hood is in a double bind. She has been sent on an important mission with all sorts of mixed messages to guide her footsteps, and finally she is practically told to look but please don't see too much.

The mother of a two and a half year old incest victim brought in a dream of a woman sitting in a corner and giving birth.[11] She described the woman as "crazed, like the women you see in mental hospital, wild-eyed." I asked if she could talk to this woman. My client was startled, assuming this strange inner woman could not talk. She found out she was lonely and that she could in fact come out of the corner. When the dream-woman did this her pregnancy disappeared. My client commented, "It's a dead fetus of pain. I must let go of it."

The pain that women internalize is what keeps them in the corner forever hanging onto dead fetuses that can only be stillborn. I do not think it possible to merely let go of the pain. Rather, it needs to be understood, reflected upon, and thus transformed. We need to reconnect with all parts of our body and soul to reclaim a feminine virginity.

The Still Birth of Women: What the Wolf Saw

Women's tendencies to internalize hurt and pain is both their strength and their downfall. It allows them to become subjectively involved in situations, bringing in human empathy to them. But it also encourages them to internalize the pain of the world. Women's tendencies towards masochism have been the subject of much speculation. Marie Bonaparte, a Freudian analyst, believed that nature made woman a masochist and man a sadist. What she did not elaborate on, but which Susan Griffin did, is that we are all members of a culture of denial—denial of our corporeal reality.

The culture of denial seems to strike women and girls particularly hard (though of course its ramifications are eventually felt by everyone). Griffin suggests that

> Perhaps here is the clue to why daughters who face the same human condition, and must have the same desire to master nature, move toward self-punishment and self-diminishment rather than to dominance and sadism. For the daughter is taught by culture to identify the "dark and inaccessible" within herself. *She herself is culture's lost self;* she is the power that is both denied and feared. Hers is the nature that must inevitably imperil not only those around her, but even herself.[12] [Emphasis added]

She thus becomes more and more a victim of patriarchal seduction and must suppress her own force, which is only seen as dark and inaccessible.

A woman's negative relationship with her body is of crucial importance in allowing her self-abnegation to continue unhindered. Judith Herman described incest victims as in their own flesh bearing the repeated punishment for the crimes committed against them in childhood.[13] The women I talk with constantly scrub their bodies until they bleed, or chronically douche and help to bring on repeated vaginal infections, or scratch at their breasts and cut at their genitals with pieces of glass—women who, after giving birth to babies out of wedlock, hate their bodies and would push away their babies. These are women for whom sexuality and instinct have become suppressed in favor of sexiness, women in whom the world of the spirit and the world of the body are separated by a bottomless chasm. All the children in this therapeutic setting show symptoms of chronic stress. At the physical level, there is a plethora of tension headaches, stomach aches, chronically cold hands and feet, eating disturbances, enuresis, soiling and constipation, compulsive masturbation and often self-mutilation, sleep disturbances, eczema, asthma, premenstrual difficulties and high incidents of infections. Relaxation work induces epileptoid shaking and collapse.

Psychologically, there are a high number of stress-related perceptual distortions frequently associated with blocking out a reality that is all too painful. Child victims also tend to be given to withdrawal or hyperactivity. There is frequently poor symbolic functioning, so that true playfulness is rare, and the child's learning ability thus severely impaired. In addition, the child is plagued by painful fantasies invading school life and intruding on sleep through repetitive nightmares, as well as an by inability to express feelings. I also see young children with distortions of body understanding which, though normal enough in young children, are particularly confusing to the child who has had attention focused on the body only in a genital sense. For instance, many of my clients between the ages of six and nine believe themselves pregnant as a result of sexual abuse. Ordinary tummy rumblings are interpreted as "now the baby is kicking." Another example is the misconception of having only one hole "down there," which leads to fear of a bowel movement in case the baby would also appear in the toilet bowl. Being weighed down so early with an orientation towards physical pregnancy hardly allows a child to eventually emerge into a young woman pregnant with her creativity in a wide variety of realms, and who will be able to release her creation into the world. Few young incest and sexual assault victims have any hobbies or interests. The families involved often do not have a respectful vocabulary pertaining to woman's anatomy, of either the adult or the child.

Returning again to our story, we find Riding Hood on the road to Grandma's. The wolf has intuited that she can be assaulted through her most vulnerable psychic place, so he walks beside her, pointing out the flowers, asking why she doesn't look about, and commenting that he believes she doesn't hear the birds sing. Senses that are not truly valued, educated and used can lead us astray. The wolf knows this, Riding Hood does not. We are told she does not know the beast is so evil, and so she is not afraid of him. She has lost touch with instinct. Then the wolf describes her to herself as though she is walking to school, even though it is "so merry in the forest." Again he represents the patriarchy that prevents a young child from the playful, healthy and meandering explorations of good sensate and concrete functioning, and that too early coerces young Psyche into linearity.

So Riding Hood was a prime target. Her hurtful innocence became her "seductive power," and the wolf's tool. Indeed, it is disturbing to see how victimization becomes a repeated event. This is borne out statistically in the high incidence of rape among past incest victims.

Red Riding Hood is enticed to leave the straight path and pick flowers for Grandma. We are told she opens her eyes and sees the sunbeams dancing through the trees, and beautiful flowers growing. She immediately thinks of picking flowers for Grandma "to bring her joy." She cannot admire and pick just for the joy of the flowers themselves—again showing us how much she is prematurely identified with caring for others.

When she has picked enough, she remembers Grandma and returns to the path. And this is where the story begins to turn around. Riding

Hood begins to actually see the wolf in which the Great Mother has already been subsumed. Slowly Riding Hood becomes aware that her body too has been taken over and no longer is her own embodiment of the feminine.

Little Red Riding Hood Perceives the Wolf—What Big Eyes You Have!
At Grandma's house, Riding Hood comes face-to-face with the wolf—not as mirrored through the eyes of mother or Grandma. She begins to perceive the wolf's gluttony. Although the patriarchy is greedy for stimulation, Hannah Arendt points out that the masses in fact do not believe in anything visible, in the reality of their own experience, they do not trust their eyes and ears, but only their fantasies.[14] Riding Hood comments "what big eyes you have!" "All the better to see you with," is his reply. Visual gluttony is characteristic of the patriarchy which also predisposes to stressful, selective seeing.

Eyes of gluttony can rape and plunder. So much energy in the last few years has been spent expounding the virtues of making eye contact that we have forgotten the virtue of not making eye contact. The old wise woman described by Anne Cameron in *Daughters of Copper Woman*[15] was one who could listen without making eye contact—concentrating on the word, letting herself conceive through her ears.

Many little girls who have been sexually assaulted are described by confused mothers as the apple of her father's eye or "Daddy's little princess." The shadow side of such adulation is the projection of a whore like Eve who can lead the man astray. Knowing this might alert the vulnerable feminine to the dangers of beguiling flattery.

Winnicott describes our eye contact with our mothers—primary perceiving—as what allows us to be seen.[16] It allows us to accept our simple human bodies so that we feel worthwhile and valuable without the props of all of our achievements. What so often allows our creativity to grow is secondary perceiving—eye contact with someone who knows how to *father* our journey. But if father is blinded by the apple, he will only seduce us and our creativity will be still-born.[17] Father will need to bite into his own inner apple before he will be able to stop projecting his soul life onto young Psyche.

Women healing from being the apple of their father's eye become involved in the reclamation of their own eyes, blinded by patriarchal pointedness, paradoxically coerced into not-seeing. In the patriarchal family, to have truly seen would have involved too much cognitive dissonance, and been too threatening to the existing status quo. Illusions

must reign. The woman learns to keep her face bland and expression-
less to avoid drawing violence toward herself.

But beneath the patriarchal wound to the eyes, there is the victim's
additional wound of never having found herself sufficiently reflected in
her mother's eyes. She has not received enough of that primal looking.
This wound of not having been seen in depth is deep and enduring.
Connecting with the mother's eye is not an easy experience. It means
being confronted with the eye of death that destroys the *participation
mystique* and separates us from those with whom we were unconsciously merged. In a society where primary perceiving is at a minimum, these
eyes of death are

> ...pitiless, not personally caring. To humans who are paralyzed with fear
> and lose sense of process and paradox, they can be the hateful glare that
> freezes life, like a mother's hate-envy that blights her child and makes an
> end of all beginnings—sadism and rage in its archetypal form....
> These eyes of death perceive with an objectivity like that of nature itself
> and our dreams, boring into the soul to find the naked truth, to see reality
> beneath all its myriad forms and the illusions and defenses it displays...
> These eyes...pierce through and get down to the substance of preverbal
> reality itself...
> They mean pain is inevitable, I can't hide.[18]

This kind of exposure strips the ego's ability to run away from such
seeing. Facing hate, feeling it, is what so often allows us to separate ourselves from the *participation mystique,* that unconsciousness of our individuality within relationships.

Little Red Riding Hood Perceives the Wolf—What Big Hands You Have!
One day, while working with six women (several were past incest victims themselves, the others were mothers of incest victims) in a group,
it came to light that I was the only one without eczema of the hands.
The children of several of the women also suffered from this, which appeared to have worsened since the crisis of disclosure of the incest or
sexual assault. There was considerable talk about scratching oneself, particularly one's hands, until they bled. In one woman's case, it was her
feet. This was at the time her husband physically abused their son and
broke the child's arm. Another described a terrible need to scratch her
breasts, particularly the left one, and pubic area, so much so that the
urge would wake her up at night.

At a simple level, none of the women had thought of wearing rubber
gloves to protect herself from harsh cleaning agents. They had lost their

hands to coerced mothering. They were scratching to find soul hidden under their tattered skin. The offender, on the other hand, is separated from his skin by a thick wall. In all cases these were busy women, but they tended to see their hands as useless — even when their actions had been seemingly of a creative nature. Often these doings were really only performed so that the women could become acceptable. But it was never enough. One of these women asked,

> But who am I really, apart from the being who shoulders tasks, does a "good" job, is efficient, competent, direct, hard working, conscientious, helpful, concerned, brilliant, innovative, sincere and *terribly unhappy?* [Emphasis added]

Recovering from numbness is often described in terms of "pins and needles," and there is an interesting French version of Riding Hood that suggests a connection. Riding Hood encounters the wolf at the fork in the road — a place of decisions. In that version, the wolf asks Riding Hood which road she will take, that of pins or needles. She chooses pins because its easier to fasten things together with pins than it is to sew them together.

It sounds to me as though Riding Hood, before her entombment in the wolf's belly, chose the path of least resistance. She would have a quickly made garment that would not bring much consciousness through the stitch-by-stitch process. And yet it is this kind of process which seems to bring so much healing to women.[19] It is not unconscious doing which is most important, but conscious and meditative doing, which may be carried on secretly for a long time.

When Katherine was pregnant with Cecille, her own eczema became so bad that all her fingernails dropped off, so that she had to wear white gloves by the time the baby was born. She asked her older daughter, then three years old, to do most of the caring for her new sister, and this was why they share so much sisterly love, the mother explained. However, in the therapy room, I saw tremendous rage and rivalry between the children. Both children (now ages five and eight) were victims of incest, but the ultimate bedrock of their therapy revolved around this other anger. Mother explained that she could not breastfeed either child because she could not bear them to touch her. This mother had a dream of being held by someone. She didn't know how it felt, she explained, because she had never experienced it. Her thumbnails were still deformed from eczema. Speaking to them one day in therapy, she said:

> I don't want you to get better. You got me all the attention I need. I stuck

out like a sore thumb.

This mother's mother had commented to her:

> Just get over these appointments [her therapy], then forget all about that
> little word s-e-x and then get on with your life.

That mother had never had a mother for her soul life and embodied
sexuality. And that is what is so tragic—generation after generation of
motherless women who have been seduced into a man's world and have
no knowledge of their feminine heritage, and so can never have a sense
of pride in their own being.

   This terrible loss underlies the anger of so many women, anger that
explodes with shattering violence—when we finally can face it. It is what
we find when we stop pulling in our bodies to cover the inner hollow
emptiness. One woman wrote:

> I cry from this desperate hunger that has been in me since the moment
> I was born. It is a hunger with rage. I feel like a saber-tooth tiger who hasn't
> eaten for years. . . I've tried to cover it up but it never changes, I'm still that
> violent, red thing that came into this world with shock and fury. . . I feel
> so aggrieved, so wronged, so vehement, so unjustly accused, I think this festers
> in me and comes out as dermatitis and eczema or whatever. . .a painful itchy
> skin that can't seem to stretch enough to cover my face and neck and
> arms. . .I'm livid and want to kill someone. The power of this rage aston-
> ishes me. . .is it any wonder that I've had asthma and eczema most of my
> life and that the tears and rages that could never be expressed have to be
> expressed through my skin, since energy must go somewhere?

This woman recalled that when she was three years old, her parents beat
her severely for stealing flowers. She wrote:

> I remember masturbating in a violent rage, seeing my mother as a blue fairy
> whom I would punish, beat and from whom I would withhold my love un-
> til she begged for mercy. . .then I would be very kind and loving.

   For years, Olga, the mother of an incest victim, wife of a child beater
and incest offender (see Chapter IV), had had dreams of getting angry
with her husband. But she could never make contact with him. Her hands
and wrists would become weak and ineffectual and soft, and she would
feel overcome by her impotence. After some weeks of working with an
inner Medusa woman, she had the following dream:

> I had been out at some evening class and when I came home again I found

my daughter restless and saying, "Daddy's done it again." I was furious. I found Don [the husband] and in a rage I jumped up on him, as if I were a monkey, clinging onto him and beating him. I smashed the right side of his glasses and made his face bleed. Then I backed off saying, "I'm not a violent person." I told him that I would no longer associate with him. I gathered up the children and left. They are worth more than this.

It was a revelation to this woman that at some level she was a violent person, but that in a sense she needed to be. She was right—our children deserve more than we allow the patriarchy to give them. At the time of this dream, the woman's husband was actually in a hospital prison ward. Because of the necessary separation, the woman had the opportunity to feel the potency of her own anger. She was surprised at how much energy it released. She felt happy for the first time in months, was able to clean her house again, and perhaps most importantly, her four-month old baby once more started to nurse, and the incest victim daughter came home and announced that "it had all stopped now." It turned out to be all the men she had seen looking at her, making advances, etc. This is an example of a parent's bringing to consciousness some element that frees the child. There was still much work to be done with the child and this family, but the expression of healthy anger was opening up a healing path. We do know that our paradigms tend to dictate what we see. Consequently, with restrictive paradigms our seeing is inappropriately limited.

Little Red Riding Hood Perceives the Wolf— What a Horrible Snout You Have!

Riding Hood's last comment is phrased differently than the others— "what a horrible snout you have!" And of course this is when the wolf jumps out of bed and eats her. Riding Hood, making that comment, made an esthetic value judgment which brought her closer to her true nature of Psyche. This type of esthetic awareness is the sort that will often cause a "great stink," because the heart and nose become linked in a way that frequently undermines the status quo. The olfactory system belongs to the old brain—the animal part that civilization attempts to deny. Early in my work I dreamed that I was to ask one of my patients if she ever had nosebleeds. She happened to be sitting in the waiting room the next morning when I arrived at the office. Her response and that of her daughter (King Tut) was so surprising: they both suffered from nosebleeds. "Doesn't everyone?" they asked. I found that this was true of many of my patients, and many of them link the onset of bleeding with the onset of their abuse. (At this time I had heard absolutely nothing of the Freud/Fliess attack on Emma Eckstein's nose that was to come to my attention through Masson's work). So I began taking special interest in noses.

I have been impressed by the tremendous efforts our advertising agencies go through to eliminate smells, or change smells, or create certain smells. One recent television advertisement promoted a cleaning agent with a series of noseless women working in their homes.

In a group session, some women were telling how their husbands liked counting their money while they, the women, felt like servants. We recalled an old nursery rhyme that seems to capture this theme:

> The King was in his counting house
> counting out his money.
> The queen was in the parlour,
> Eating bread and honey,
> The maid was in the garden,
> Hanging out the clothes,
> When down came a blackbird
> And pecked off her nose.

During therapy Rose had visited her doctor because of sinus headaches and a stuffed nose. He had taken the trouble to explain that "nasal tissue swells just like the penis." That night Rose dreamed that her clitoris turned into a nose-penis. A hurt woman is very susceptible to introjecting patriarchal explanations, and ends up with a phantom penis. The doctor could have used the analogy of the labia and clitoris swelling with sexual arousal. It is significant to note that Jones said that Freud maintained that the female child's libido is more male than female because her auto-erotic activity concerns predominantly the clitoris. He goes on to make the obscure suggestion that perhaps all libido is essentially male.[20]

The suppression of the feminine nose is by no means new. When Ezekiel was railing against the religion of the goddess, one of the "filthy" things he accused the worshipers of was "facing to the east, bowing to the sun and raising a branch to their nostrils."[21] Merlin Stone suggests that this was probably a branch of the sacred tree known as *asherah*. Ezekiel continued, bemoaning the fact that the women were sitting weeping for Tammuz. And so we see women at the time of the death of sentient soul—or matriarchal times—condemned for valuing the sense of smell that was somehow connected with the yearly sacrifice of their son-lover.

Still later, in about the fifth century A.D., directions were given in the *Abodah Zarah,* a book of the Hebrew Talmud, on how to destroy the power of the idol. This could be done by knocking off the tip of its nose or ear. Stone suggests that this injunction may account for the missing noses of so many statues of the goddess.[22]

One of the patriarchal traditions around Lilith is that she would steal babies at nighttime. She would tickle their feet first, since she liked her victims smiling, and then would strangle them. If mothers heard their children laugh in dreams, or saw them smiling in their sleep, they were to hit the baby's nose three times, crying out "Away Lilith, you have no place here."[23] Some clinical examples of this are Jade, a past incest victim and prostitute who dreamed of punching her witch-child's nose, and Olga, who in some sessions described herself as "a bloody bitch," and noticed that on these days her sons had nosebleeds. Women cast out into the wilderness like Lilith are not in a position to mourn the loss of Tammuz or Adonis, their son-lovers. Thus the young boy is caught up in mother's frenzy of hurt. These women need much healing time in which to reclaim their noses and ritually mourn the death of their son-lovers, so that the boys can be released into their own ways.

It is no surprise, then, that in their healing process sexually assaulted women usually encounter, quite early in therapy, their "witch-child," identified with supernatural powers. It is an image that wields tremendous and devastating power, and is often first recognized in the women's own biological children, who frequently are sexually assaulted themselves, who often are very undisciplined children, difficult to handle, and naturally most contemptuous of the mother-bond. One woman's inner witch-child could threaten to blow up a huge building just by pressing the elevator button, but he fell downstairs instead and had his nose pushed sideways.

If we let the nose lead us, it eventually takes us to the realm of the mothers and to death.[24] The mother's organic odors have always caused men to react with hostile apprehension as well as longing. When Peter started to talk about an inner dog he began, absentmindedly, pulling at his nose. When I mentioned this to him he laughed and said his nose was probably a symbol of his penis. Later in our conversation I asked him if he could remember the smell of his mother. The question provoked a great deal of feeling. The memory was partially pleasant and partially unpleasant. What he suddenly felt overwhelmed by was "the smell of death." He felt that in some ways his mother had denied him his life, for Peter had always had to protect her from his brutal and alcoholic father.

Women and men reclaiming their noses, their instinctual, intuitive natures, learn to live with the stench of death in their nostrils. It takes the sort of courage and passionate commitment to the wound shown by Dr. Densen-Gerber in her emotional legal testimonies aimed at protecting children from prostitution and pornography. She told one law maker:

> Coming from my medical training you cannot clean a gangrenous wound by remote control. You have to get in there...you have to *smell* the tissue to see what is diseased and what is not.[25] [Emphasis added]

Before women can appreciate their noses, their sense of smell and of themselves, they will frequently talk of hating organic smells. Jenny cried a great deal over her "hatred of the smell of semen...which [she] had to carry around." I have talked with other clinicians who say that their patients complain of olfactory hallucinations—menses, semen, genitalia in general.

Breastfeeding also has an important connection with the development of the olfactory system. In our society it can be a tumultuous and problematic experience for a woman. In the 1940's Harry Stack Sullivan discovered that even though its survival depends on nursing, the infant will actually reject the nipple offered by a severely anxiety-ridden mother.[26]

When there are particular conditions of upheaval in society, breast-feeding pairs (mother and child) appear to suffer sooner that bottle-feeding pairs; what is healthy and normal can be violated very easily. Josephine Elkes has reported two incidents of this nature to me. First, the acute suffering of breastfeeding pairs is a well known phenomenon in concentration camps. The second example came from Professor Mannheim of the London School of Economics during World War II, though it was not reported in the journals because of the wartime conditions. These were the days before penicillin and sulfonamide. Because of the fear of infant meningitis, mothers with babies of a year or less were asked not to go down into the very congested London air-raid shelters. The breastfeeding pairs were most upset by this dictate, and it was because of their distress that the rule had to be relaxed. It seems that the breastfed babies refused to nurse and screamed constantly, which further upset their already-terrified mothers. In personal communication to me, Josephine Elkes makes sense of this phenomenon:

The air raid sirens triggered the alarm response in Mum —"flight or fight." Since one cannot fight a bomber and London was very, very short on antiair-craft, Mum's only alternative was "flight." If this was denied her, in the presence of real and immediate threat to herself and her infant, she developed a state of acute anxiety which seems to have been sensed by the preverbal infant. Mrs. Mannheim speculated that perhaps this was due to changes in the chemistry of the mother's sweat glands, since the breastfed baby's nose is very close to the underarm area of the mother.

Since then, pheromones have been identified as olfactory cues to the limbic system involved in the flight-or-fight response. Furthermore, the olfactory/limbic system is relatively active even in newborns, and in fact appears to be one of the delicate interfaces between mother and child. Bonding with mother at such a primal level is essential for the later development of grounded body acceptance and creativity. Without it the child becomes more and more a victim of erotic frenzy.

The death of the seductive, witchy prostitute, a product of the patriarchy, is a necessary inner transformation, healing bleeding noses of the feminine, and leading to the release not only of the perceived, non-coerced mother, but also of the sacred harlot. The following dream marked the beginning of this transition for another patient, Jenny.

My daughter Kate (five years old) is having her friend Bea sleep over. Their sleeping bags are in the kitchen with a lot of other sleeping bags. I am anxious for them to fall asleep for my man is over and I love him something fierce. It's uncontrollable what I feel for him. He is tall and slender, muscular and just delicious. His face is so beautiful. I have never met such a beautiful face; it's angelic in a manner that is masculine. He is a priest who is married and we discuss all the taboos we face in our relationship.

My whole body quivers to be near this man. I am on the verge of exploding. We go to the bedroom. We are caressing each other: kisses are electric. Just when I feel I can explode, there is a knock at the bedroom and Bea's mother is there with a nosebleed. She has come to check on Bea. Both girls are fine and the mother leaves. We resume lovemaking, but again Bea's mother comes and we have to help her stop the nosebleed . . .

By morning we still have not had intercourse. I walk with him out of the door and his wife is waiting. There doesn't seem to be any jealousy.

Then a crowd of people came carrying a dead woman. Her head is falling back and her arms also. They drop her on a pile of leaves on my lawn. She has very red lipstick and thick makeup especially around her eyes. The minister and his wife look content and happy and walk away. No one seems shattered at this dead woman. I'm not either. She is supposed to be dead.

It is as though Jenny were being drawn to see that part of her that was ready to die, and of which she could let go. She called it her "prostitute." Her initial response to the man was almost uncontrollably sexual. Yet, in a manner reminiscent of Lilith, she wanted closeness to an angelic aspect of the masculine. The mother with nosebleeds, constantly and compulsively concerned about her child, kept interrupting the consummation of this relationship. This seemed important. We had to learn more about the bleeding. In fact Jenny and her two children all suffered from nosebleeds; Jeni's used to start about eight hours before her period, though since she has gradually come to accept her own femininity this is no longer the case.

Following this was a series of dreams relating to putting a more healthy distance between Jenny and her children in order to consummate the relationship with the priest. Whatever the current controversies raging over priestly celibacy, it appears to be an important archetype in allowing women, whose shadows are coerced, manipulated, and manipulating prostitutes, to imaginally learn new ways of relating to the masculine *outside* the realm of compulsive sexuality and coerced and coercive mothering. Sacred celibacy allows the possibility of relating in greater depth to the other. Of course where the outer priest has a poor anima connection, he can only deny woman her body or steal it. Many women in therapy report this phenomenon. However, it is important for women to get their true motivation to the surface because,

> By maintaining a passive attitude with an ulterior purpose, she helps the man to realize his ends and in that way holds him. At the same time she is caught in her own toils, for whoever digs a pit for others falls into it himself.[27]

The dead woman in Jeni's dream was a prostitute. It is as though the night's happenings culminated in her timely and appropriate death. Being able to withdraw from compulsive mothering and the compulsive shadow-sexuality of the prostitute descending into the true feminine, so that bleeding noses heal, is exactly what is needed for the emergence of the sacred harlot—the archetype of profound heart consciousness so deeply repressed in our society. We learn that alchemy referred to two smells—the stench of graves and the perfume of flowers, the latter being a symbol of resurgent life, attesting to the rebirth of the King.[28] The spiral of transformation revolves through the stench of death and decay, through to Aphrodite's fragrant emergence with a red-rose-covered body, buoyantly poised on her muscle shell, arising from the ocean depths.

Descent Into the Belly of the Beast

At the last moment, Riding Hood comes closer to her true self—
identifying with esthetic awareness and a recognition of animal nature,
with some increase in consciousness, albeit a sense of horror. At this moment she becomes the wolf's tasty morsel. Having first swallowed Grandma, the wolf gobbles up Riding Hood. This is a repeat performance of
Zeus greedily swallowing mother wisdom (Metis) and her potential child,
later to be born as the father's daughter, Athena. Riding Hood must
come to her senses by truly realizing that her encasement in the wolf,
as she is swallowed, is symbolic of where she has actually been all the
time. Becoming conscious is always tinged with both horror and appeal.
Entering the inner space of transformation has never been an easily chosen
step—it is usually one life nudges us into. We may sense the horror of
relinquishing who we were for what life compels us to become. However, this descent into the reddened, interior blackness is what offers the
possibility of true healing—if we can tolerate the temporary blinding
of our outward eyes and the illumination of the inner.

Being swallowed alive is not a rare image in the transformation process. Knowing that meaning can arise out of such a descent can make
it bearable, or we will never allow the necessary death/release process
to actually happen. This is particularly true if we have felt ourselves to
be living in a coffin for most of our lives. We will only be able to conceive of it as a total disappearance of any form of reality: an ultimate
abduction. Resting in the belly of the beast is what allows for a reunion
with Grandmother, which is well understood and valued in all shamanistic healing processes.

In willingly descending into the black cave, women find their own
womb caves. During their healing, women frequently begin to menstruate regularly, and several have commented that they bleed less at
menstruation. One past incest victim explained that, now more ready
to express her anger, she no longer needs to bleed so much from her
womb. Indeed it is this precious part of her body that seems most vulnerable to the hurt woman. Olga explained to me that she now knows
when she is feeling something but is unable to express it: her uterus
begins to ache, and this ceases as soon as she expresses her feeling. She
also recalled giving birth to her last child. The placenta would not separate, and so the attending physicians began to pull on the umbilical
cord. The result was that Olga has a memory of seeing her uterus, a
vibrant, pulsing redness lying on the table with the hands of two men
on it trying to push it back into place. She cried at this memory, and

in spite of her hard life, it was this memory that hurt her more than anything. She felt more deeply violated than ever before. Rediscovering our own womb, listening to its pulsing messages, can allow our womb wounds to be transformed into womb words significant because they are deeply embedded in feeling and the soul of body. Such a release is important for those who have had no words for feelings, and whose symbolic functioning has been curtailed through chronic stress.

Slowly, as hurt women become conscious of their true needs, they will dream of their husbands dressed in women's clothing, or they will find themselves holding up an item of woman's clothing in front of their husband to "see how he would look in it." The woman comes to realize that she is searching for her mother. At this point in her development, without an inner mother she can only sustain rape and violation from the realm of the patriarchy, and maintain a relationship with a hermaphroditic man locked in mother.

The hurt woman frequently has an icy aspect to her. She is like a delicious chocolate with a stone inside: she hopes her lovers crack their teeth on her, as one woman put it, not knowing the ritual initiation of the sacred surrender of incisiveness — so essential to man's growth, but so rarely enacted. The hurt woman seems to maintain a shell of self-sufficiency. To be truly touched by sexual yearnings would be to rupture this shell. No emotional demands must made of her; in fact, there have been too many already. She seems to threaten, "how dare you love me," which is really, "I dare you to love me. . .you see I am rotten, disgusting, unworthy." To avoid the rupture, she must keep herself on ice. Indeed, a frequent dream theme of the healing process is of the freezer defrosting to reveal meat — some of which may be rotting. Death must be felt and experienced rather that kept hidden in the ice of what seems like the weight of interminable ice ages. Some of the meat found is a total surprise — the freezer owner didn't know it was there before. So it is for traumatized women, who begin to find the bodies they never knew they had. Their shell of self-sufficiency has been a protection, and it speaks much more of hurt innocence than of hypocritical innocence. It is the innocence of a girl who in fear has run to hide like a fairy among the roots of a big tree, or who becomes a shy deer hiding in the forest. The woman becomes an elemental being, lost to her human body and human connection.

The girl/woman takes on all the guilt of her own abuse. She must have caused it — the smell of her fingers from masturbating, the way her hair was, the fact that she ended up *going to him,* which is a common behavior in victims. In assuming the guilt, she identified with enormous power — a little girl can do this to a grown man — and so she represses her knowledge, her intelligence, her gifts, in order to appear innocent. Her sense of survival depends upon it. The girl/woman herself is lost in the split between the mother and the whore, ever more open to exploitation. Her very hurt innocence draws the plundering patriarchal soul towards her.

The Loss of Creativity in Incest Victims

Where the incest has remained at an unconscious level and not been genitally acted out, there can also result the woman's loss of body reality and creativity. Marion Woodman[29] writes of many creative women who have prospered through a close relationship with their fathers and benefited from his bright, spiritual and creative side. The dark side of the relationship can be psychological incest, if the father's anima binds and represses his sexuality. This can deeply interfere with the woman's developing sexuality: the creative woman can no longer repress her sexuality, since "sexuality is the spirit of our age." Such a daughter's budding sexuality at puberty may become split off from the ground of her being — she cannot direct it at her father, who has been, until this time, the object of her love. And so she becomes cut off from her creativity and may even experience it as a sort of rape.

A young girl of fifteen, a victim of incest who would bring her dolls for therapy, shared the following dream with me. She was at school. The boys were lining up to rape her. She begged them to wait until she could remove her pretty dress, which had already become a little torn and soiled. Somehow she found herself putting a leather motorbike outfit over the delicate and torn dress. She became the leader of the motorbike gang.

A male psychologist who commented on the dream was thrilled by it. He said, with a thrust of his arm and clenched fist. "There is so much power in the girl... if only we could capitalize on it."

He did not see the girl's torn dress and the faces of her dolls that could so easily be swept away, and the convulsive shaking that was the result of her relaxation work during her therapy. Any power here certainly had no body and no soul.

For the suffering soul of incest to heal, she must be joined with the Great Mother, in those deep dark places of silent and excruciating transformation. The woman on her underworld healing journey must meet the wise woman who teaches her to listen to her own heart and to connect with the center point of Self — her inner priceless pearl.

Of such learning, Violet writes:

> I call to your memory my dream in which there was an old woman who
> is digging out handfuls of red soil and eggs, asking me to look at them.
> My reaction at the time was to ignore her and be suspicious. You've planted
> little seeds, I like to think, about eggs and what they mean to me, as well
> as references to my very fertile womb. Those, too, I chose to ignore or be
> suspicious of. But the symbols have persisted and at last I see them for what
> they hold for me as far as wisdom and guidance.
>
> The old woman I see, most importantly, as my positive mother image,
> the healer. The eggs in the red soil I see as eggs of possibility in a very fertile
> womb. But alas my womb is sad, for it thought the eggs would never be
> fertilized. Who would notice the eggs and offer the seed of inspiration? Partly
> my positive animus—he is the one who provides the seed for my lonely, hun-
> gry womb. A womb that cries out to express itself and create a vision. The
> child of possibility and inspiration. Now I feel very pregnant and one day
> I'll be blessed with the child, and what joy that day holds. So now I bide
> my time waiting and helping, however I can, to nourish and protect the
> child within me, my vision . . .
>
> The chicken was called to her nest to warm her eggs lest they should die
> from neglect. For they had been fertilized, she just never noticed. So now
> she sits on the nest and takes good care of her charges. She no longer stomps
> around the chicken yard pecking at other chickens' eggs and creating trou-
> ble for them.

This woman—and others like her—had the courage to make a deep
connection with Grandmother in that dark place of silent transformation. These women have ceased being compelled victims with a patriarchal mind-set, constantly enraged and invalidated, and being coerced
into very doubtful positions of pseudopower that regularly terminated
in rape of their soul. They have become free to make some choices. They
have become conscious of their bodies in a new way, and have learned
to differentiate passivity from receptivity. Thus they can embrace within themselves what culture has decreed is only dark and inaccessible,
and which formerly would draw them towards self-punishment and self-
diminishment. They now have some option to move into a state of vibrant repose, of quickened senses, receptive to the promptings of the
heart. Thus for the first time they are capable of encountering a co-
operative loving relationship with their inner lover Eros, and thus of
releasing their visions, their children, into the light of day.

The Dark Feminine
Women tell me that they have pushed their daughters away from them-

selves in the hope that this would ensure that they will not have to suffer as their mothers did. They push them away because of the hurtful competition between themselves and their daughters, set up by patriarchal norms that pornographizes the image of women unified and links it with male pleasure, at the expense of the women, who are conceived of as incapable of self-love.

Such a wounded daughter has no inner home, and her sexuality has become disembodied. Marion Woodman describes such sexuality as going into the negative mother:

> It is sexuality against the woman, against the receptive, against herself. If this negative sexuality is reinforced by a drive for revenge, the woman can be enormously destructive in almost every area of her life.[30]

The negative and witchy inner mother helps to steal away the daughter's leanings and soul-quality. Rose writes:

> I see more and more of this demon old woman in me. I hear her in my screeching voice, my harshness, and the gruff and relentless way I treat the children when I'm angry—like a shark, cutting to shreds. I see the pain on their faces and I stop. Sometimes I can't. She keeps on raging and raging. Sometimes their hurt faces make me more and more angry. Then I feel sick, crazy, out of control. As she rages outwardly, this old woman must be cold on the inside also—flogging relentlessly, harsh, always shredding and cutting down to size, just in case I feel too good, or things get "too good." Too good? Life is harsh and bitter, what else can you expect?

Rose kept permitting both the inner raging old-witch-mother and the hurt little girl to have their voices. Of the hurt inner child she writes:

> I think I can't forgive myself; I still reject her, the little girl who should have known better. I cannot forgive myself that I wasn't in control, couldn't make it right, and couldn't make me have a mother who loved me. The little girl brings me flowers. She gives them to me, her dark eyes look searchingly. She sees nothing and so leaves. Sometimes, she sobs violent shaking sobs, when she is alone. She comes again, waits and leaves.
>
> She is not very pretty. Maybe she would be if she was looked after. Her shoes are scuffed, funny shoes, high brown boy's shoes with laces that are much too long and trail. Her sweater is too small. It barely covers her chest, and the sleeves are near the elbow. Her grey dress is too short.
>
> She wants to cry but she is too proud. She is so ugly and different. She has a shell around herself. It is hard to hug her, she has a defiance, and is proud too soon, I turn away. I don't like her.

Rose's external eight-year old daughter was also dealing with the same issue at the same time. She wrote her mother a note:

I had a special dream, that my mom was an angel and that she turned into a star and I had a magical heart that turned into a real-shaped heart. It felt that it was thumping so hard and it felt like my heart wanted to find a place in my mother's heart.

The child wants her mother to reflect on her, and wants to see her own reflection in her mother's eye. Until this soul need is satisfied, the child is obliged to resort to seeing a disembodied, angelic mom.

After many months of relating to all of these inner female figures during her therapy sessions, to her actual daughter, and to a woman in the group who reminded Rose of her witchy mother, Rose dreamed that she was "persevering through a stormy sea...and a salt island emerged for me to stand upon...I had survived the storm." It was as though Rose had done so much crying and weeping that her salt had been brought out of its "interior, underground mines."[31] What had been "cruel, corrosive salt"—which could destroy both the children and *him*— was now softened so that the inner hurt child could finally find a place to stand. Jung tells us that

In the child, consciousness rises out of the depths of unconscious psychic life, at first like separate islands, which gradually unite to form a "continent," a continuous land mass of consciousness.[32]

A woman working with both poles of the hurt witch-child and the tirading wounded mother slowly becomes able to value the mother's discipline: she no longer needs to goad the mother into disagreement, or to reenact childish temper tantrums or defiant adolescence. She can also talk with the daughter without being caustic. She can see the daughter as needing her protection, yet without perceiving her as seductive. She can reclaim the child's hurt innocence from beneath the coerced cute seductiveness of the patriarchal eye. Thus she no longer needs to project a red cloak and hood onto actual girl-children.

When I work with mothers and daughters, I have frequently found it useful to start with the child in the playroom, meeting with the child in an environment that is developmentally appropriate in terms of size, layout, and content. When the child has settled into contented play (and this may take quite some time), I will invite the mother to watch and listen through a one way system. The mother invariably sees a child she does not know, and we will talk later about her responses. I invite her to join in the playroom activities, which of course immediately alters the child's play. Any adult in such a setting—either patient or therapist—will immediately reveal the degree to which they themselves are sons and daughters of the patriarchy through their need to constantly stimulate the child into activity, through their need for up times and the frenzied buzz that so many adults think belongs to childhood. My work involves the process of reexperiencing and valuing the down times.

The first task is to learn to see the child, just as Rose learned to do. This is an extremely difficult journey at any time. What are the child's eyes saying as her hands play with the clay? Does she drool when she snuggles up for a story? What feelings does the drooling awake? Adults can accept their children aimlessly rocking in the chair when they know how to take a tea-break themselves; they can let the child enjoy the warmth of cuddling when they can let their own bodies be comfortable; they can allow a child to explore when they are at home in their own bodies and can live comfortably with the fear of novelty; they can allow the child's unfolding sense of humor when they themselves are open to deep belly laughter; they can let the child play when they have let the animals into their own lives. They can listen carefully to the child when they feel themselves to have been listened to; they can tell a story when they have heard stories. Some of the most poignant silences follow story-telling to groups of hurting women. Often this is the first time many of them have experienced quiet, imaginative story-telling. Such an adult has begun the task of recovering something of her own uniqueness and integrity, and can thus allow the child hers. Such an adult, knowing the importance of being seen, would appreciate the Ukrainian tradition which encourages the children to say, "Put your eyes on me, I wish to speak."

For those emerging from victimization, a change of world-view with an inner positive mother to balance the negative tyrant can actually be terrifying. Love has its element of terror. Love says that I am worthy of love, that it is all right to simply be what I am at this moment in time. It means that I can be a loving woman. To accept love in my life is terrifying because it says that I am responsible. I can respond to the situation as I see it. I no longer simply react to whatever is dished out by the other.

An example of this emergence is a girl of eleven years who dreamed that her cookie box was empty. She awoke on the Friday morning, feeling not very well, and so her mother suggested that the child stay home from school—a rare occurrence. The mother also took a day off work, and during their healing time together she gave her daughter a massage before bed time, after which her daughter said sleepily, "I have two cookies in the box now." After a restful weekend the child happily informed her mother that her "cookie box was again full" and that she was looking forward to returning to school. What the child had obviously needed was a much more profound reconnection with the mother.

Allowing the mother and daughter to heal not only allows the return of the daughter-bud to the tree, but also the reclaiming of the Mother Tree—and this, paradoxically, redeems womanliness.

Violet experienced becoming the "Mother Tree" towards the end of her third pregnancy, with three and a half years of hard inner work accomplished. This pregnancy was different from the other two, which had been "a breeze." She had risen above them, so to speak. The rest of herself and her life had remained virtually untouched by the mystery taking place within her. From the beginning of this pregnancy she felt invaded, taken over. She was not sure she wanted the baby. In dreams she would find herself floating out in space—half way between the earth and the moon. Towards the end of the pregnancy, she dreamed of tree branches coming out of her legs. She felt afraid—she was unable to fly away any more as she was so used to doing. After the birth, Violet's husband was afraid because Violet kept "disappearing"—she would talk "nonsense" and be pale and distant. He feared for her sanity. At this time it was impossible for him to look at his own hidden hysteria. But Violet was found by a wonderful inner mother and an old ailing grandmother on these inner journeys. She also found herself dancing in a circle with other dream women. She found that there were many times when all she wanted to do was rock and sing to her baby. This was all very new and potentially terrifying for a woman with a previously hard-driving animus.

Then Violet dreamed of walking through the forest with her husband. As they came to the edge she could see a pile of old greying lumber. As they got closer, Violet was terrified at discovering that this was not cut lumber but disconnected parts of women's bodies. Violet was so frightened that she left that place and went, with her husband, back to a cottage in the middle of the forest. There she became a tree—great roots connected her to the earth, its moisture, its stability. Her branches stretched to the airy sky and became a house for birds. She was safe. She had finally come to that centering place where the triune face of the feminine can be reunited—where grandmother, mother and child can be united. Here the Mother Tree can flourish and grow.

The Hunter Arrives

When the hunter passes by Grandmother's house, he hears loud snoring, and such loud snoring could not come from Grandma. He enters the scene and says to the wolf, "Oh, I find you here too, do I?"

In Grandma's house the hunter becomes alive to his shadow side, recognizing the rapacious, patriarchal devourer that is within him also, and so is not caught unawares. He does not blast at the wolf with his gun, but, surprisingly, takes out his scissors to release the united feminine elements. He cuts open the wolf and releases first Riding Hood then Grandma. This second birth of Riding Hood allows the hunter to recognize his shadow. He also facilitates the birth of his more conscious anima. By contrast, Athena never experienced a second birth that allowed the patriarchy to become conscious of its shadowy rapacious nature. Riding Hood has learned a lot. She recounts how frightened she was and how dark it had been. Grandma (although barely breathing) is alive too, and she recuperates by eating the cake and drinking the wine. The sacramental feast that drew three generations of women together now brings new life to the Grandmother.

Riding Hood bends down and puts stones in the wolf's belly, so that when he wants to spring away, he instead sinks to the earth and dies. It is as though he, too, must experience death so that the hunter can take this skin home with him and be truly joined to his profound animal nature. There is to be no more springing away from earth's grounding reality. In this place of happenings, deep in the heart of the forest, we see new life and transformation. Generational rifts between the feminine elements disappear and man is reunited with animal life, giving rise to a more stable interaction of four energies.

There are some striking similarities and differences between the figures of Riding Hood and Athena. Riding Hood shows the young feminine as more conscious and ready to appreciate the feminine. Athena, who was swallowed by the father while still in Metis' womb, brought us out of our encasement in both the mother and father. Our heritage from intellectual soul is not all negative.

Athena's gift is our potential to become conscious of our process of individuation. The shadow side of her gift is that because her birth was an armored, phallic eruption from her father's head, we have inherited the intellectual component that kept her tied to the father and unable to bring the sacrament to the ailing grandmother. We see this often in aggressive men and women who have not learned to support the feminine in their relationships and life styles.

The belly birthplace of Riding Hood can be seen as the mediating place between earth and sky, mother and father. Riding Hood goes through a second birth when she emerges from the wolf. She seems to have had a more conscious incubation with the wise old woman.

Riding Hood's gift is a deepening of Athena's journey, for she carries for Athena her abandoned sexuality and instinctual spirituality. Unfortunately this was projected too soon onto the young child, who was forced into having to don Aphrodite's red cloak, since the patriarchy cannot afford to allow this vital shadow to disappear completely into the unconscious.

The journey resulting in her second birth carries us into the Medusan territory of blood and guts. This is the territory that Athena abandoned by refusing to deal with her own sexuality and banishing that part of herself (Medusa) to the unconscious.

The woman who has incubated with her wise old woman is open to the arrival of the inner hunter. Because the hunter recognizes his wolf potential, he does not have to play superman on the scene and blast off his gun. The hunter's arrival occurs mysteriously within the heart of the woman. A mature relationship between the feminine and masculine poles — inner and outer — is now possible. This involves being open to mystery and having a fair amount of personal objectivity. No longer dominated by the father-animus or wolf within, today's woman can speak with a tongue that does not blast with a bitter, vindictive and hurtful ego-based language. During communication she does not lose touch with the inner eye which keeps her related to the imagination of her own heart's truth. This is possible when the inner negative father has been transformed. The loud, dogmatic inner voice that once dominated *the woman* is mediated because she is now able to use her imagination and live creativity. A duality has been transcended: yin and yang are now a sacred connection. The ego has a mother and father who are positive, and who no longer beguile, chain or seduce the soul.

A New End for Our Beginnings

The story of Little Red Riding Hood does not seem complete. The four elements are only brought together for a very short time. In fact, we hear that only three of them are "very happy." The fourth element, the wolf, is dead. The last vision of the story is disquieting: the hunter walking away from the three nut trees, the wolf-pelt across his shoulders. What will animal nature have to teach him?[33] Will he allow himself to be penetrated in his most vulnerable place?

Norbert Glas's version of the tale ends with moralizing boredom — never will Riding Hood again disobey mother and enter the forest and stray from the path. Such a sad conclusion. The child is being condemned to a life of non-individuation — no fear, no growth, no disobedience, no retrieving of psyche's truth. There is little thought that the child is condemned to such a life because her cultural milieu has projected her too soon, and too unprepared, onto a path more befitting her later years.

Notes

Much of the material in this chapter is based upon the version of "Little Red Riding Hood" found in *Once Upon a Fairy Tale,* by Norbert Glas. Spring Valley: St George Publications, 1977

[1]Bruno Bettelheim. *The Uses of Enchantment: The Meaning and Importance of Fairy Tales.* New York: Random House Inc., Vintage Books Edition, 1976, p. 169

[2]James Hillman. "The Thought of the Heart." In *Eranos* 1979, pp. 156-181

[3]Joseph Campbell. *The Way of Beauty* (Cassette Tape)

[4]Bruno Bettelheim. *op. cit.*, p. 173

[5]Marie-Louise von Franz. *The Feminine in Fairy Tales.* Zürich: Spring Publications, 1972, p. 191

[6]A symbol of the Self might be a horoscope viewed as the wheel of birth.

[7]Judith Herman. *Father-Daughter Incest.* Cambridge: Harvard University Press, 1981, p. 48
What distinguishes the mother in an incestuous family is that she seems to have been deprived of self-fulfillment even within the family. Such a mother would be incapable of soul nurturing.

[8]*Ibid.*, p. 49

[9]Entering the forest is often an image of the soul awakening to inner perceptions in order to deepen consciousness — i.e., Hansel and Gretel, Snow White, The Maiden Without Hands, etc.

[10]Karl Kerényi, "A Mythological Image of Girlhood." In *Facing the Gods,* James Hillman, ed. Dallas: Spring Publications, 1980, pp. 43-44

[11]Russell Lockhart. *Words As Eggs.* Dallas: Spring Publications, 1983, pp. 113-114
Lockhart tells us of Angerona hidden in the Roman sanctuary of pleasure: her mouth is bound and sealed. An uplifted finger touching her lips points to her silence and her suffering.

[12]Susan Griffin. *Pornography and Silence.* New York: Harper & Row, 1981, p. 148

[13]Judith Herman, *op. cit.*, p. 108

[14]Susan Griffin, *op. cit.*, p. 186
I have used the word "fantasy" rather than "imagination" (which Arendt uses) in order not to confuse the reader with my use of the terms (see Chapter II)

[15]Anne Cameron. *Daughters of Copper Woman.* Vancouver: Press Gang Publications, 1981, p. 85

[16]Donald Winnicott. *Playing and Reality.* London: Penguin, 1971, p. 131

[17]Recall Pinkerton in Puccini's opera *Madame Butterfly*, singing to the woman
he loves:
"Child from whose eyes the witchery is shining
Now you are all my own."
Later he abandons her, a tragic example of projecting "witchery" onto a wom-
an from the man's own so-called "love space."

[18]Sylvia Perera. *Descent to the Goddess.* Toronto: Inner City Books, 1981, pp.
30-34

[19]von Franz. *op. cit.*, pp. 127-128

[20]James Hillman. *The Myth of Analysis.* New York: Harper & Row, 1978, p. 240

[21]Merlin Stone. *When God Was A Woman.* New York: A Harvest/HBJ Book,
1976, p. 186

[22]*Ibid.*, p. 193

[23]Patricia Monaghan. *The Book of Goddesses & Heroines.* New York: A Dutton Paperback, 1981, p. 180

[24]C.G. Jung, *CW* V, par. 299

[25]Clifford Linedecker. *Children in Chains.* New York: Everest House Publications, 1981, p. 279

[26]Harry Stack Sullivan. *The Interpersonal Theory of Psychiatry.* New York: W.
W. Norton, 1953; Joseph Chilton Pearce. *Magical Child.* New York: Bantam Books, 1977 (see Chapters 6 and 10.)

[27]C. G. Jung. *CW* X, par. 240

[28]C G. Jung. *CW* XIV, par. 432

[39]Marion Woodman. *Addiction to Perfection.* Toronto: Inner City Books, 1982,
pp. 168-169

[30]*Ibid.*, p. 169

[31]James Hillman. "Salt: A Chapter in Alchemical Psychology." In *Images of the
Untouched,* Joanne Stroud and Gail Thomas, eds. Dallas: Spring Publications, 1982, pp. 117, 119

[32]C.G. Jung. *CW* XVII, par. 102

[33]Norbert Glas, *op. cit.*, p. 135
  Glas points out that the wolf had laughed at Riding Hood for keeping so
exactly to Mother's instructions. Glas sees the story as "a wonderful victory of
the human soul over the wild and tempting forces over which the wolf would
prevent it from treading the true path into the future" (p.144). I consider this
to be an excellent example of spiritual growth being conceived as "set against"
the instinctual and spiritual animal world.

CHAPTER VIII

Embracing the Good News of the Fish Tail

Coerced Mother/Prostitute

When a woman has journeyed to the center of the forest through her process of healing and individuation, she is then able to reclaim her body. A woman's reclaiming of her body from a numb, suppressed erotic frenzy enables her to release her daughter to experience an appropriate childhood. The mother, in turn, reclaims her embodied sexuality, and can thus sustain a relationship with Aphrodite.

We have seen how woman's numbness and terror has been called frigidity or witchiness, how her rage has been called madness and imbalance, her ecstasy turned into hysteria, and her dance into the seizure of will. Judith Herman summarizes that the patriarchy produces the adult woman who

> ...may deeply resent her feminine identity...who seeks confirmation of her importance in sexual relations with men who are more powerful than herself, and in the care of others who are younger and smaller and weaker than herself. Her capacity for full erotic expression may be considerably blunted, but her ability to nurture, to sympathize with others, and to express affection is highly developed.[1]

These women have never been ritually and sacredly called away to the Dionysian marriage, and thus they and their children remain condemned — reduced to flesh, but a flesh denied. Such a woman remains locked into mothering, and her suppressed whore tends to be projected onto her daughter.

Abused teenagers tell me that they find themselves wondering constantly about prostitution. Adult women abused as children explain that their motto had become "If all else fails, then fuck." Well publicized figures certainly link child sexual abuse with prostitution. For instance, Mimi Silbert reports on a study of two hundred juvenile and adult street prostitutes.[2] Sixty percent of the subjects had been previously sexually exploited by an average of two people each over an average period of twenty months. Two-thirds were sexually abused by father figures. Seventy percent of the women reported that their early sexual exploitation definitely affected their decision to become prostitutes.

After King Tut came back to earth from "outer space," she dreamed of buying a "club" where there were lots of pinball machines and video games, and "rooms" upstairs. It took her a long time to tell me that the rooms were for "hookers," but that she, King Tut, would never be going upstairs. She had decided that she was going to be "a virgin" forever. The next week the topic came up again. She was worried because she thought that her boyfriend wouldn't stick around much longer if she didn't have sex with him. Then she wondered aloud why she shouldn't just be a hooker, anyway. After all, she had already been one. Her father used to give her "twenty bucks a shot," and her brother "five bucks." They would "do it" in every room of the house, except the kitchen. That was where she was beaten for stealing food when she was hungry. King Tut had already experienced the life of a prostitute as described by Jeanne Cordelier:

> Being a prostitute is like living through an interminable winter, at first it seems impossible. Then, as time passes, you start to think that sun is nothing more than a word thought up by men.[3]

The word *sun* becomes fictional just as do other words, because the words for one's own experience, one's own self and one's own soul have been false. The potency of words rooted in the earth is lost, because the earth of the body is lost. King Tut has imbibed little soul food and her inner life presents the nuts and bolts of the patriarchy — much beer swilling, games that both dull and titillate the senses, gambling and prostitution. And somewhere in the frenzy there is an almost forgotten image of a little girl looking for food in the refrigerator.

The prostitute's loss of and preoccupation with the mother was reported by Tony, a practicing physician in his mid-thirties who was paying his first visit to a prostitute because of his "incredible horniness." He was appalled to find himself impotent at what he described as the "absence of relationship." The woman would not let him kiss her because "that was how you get diseases." Her only comments were about being three months pregnant and becoming a mother. Ironically, Tony's external success was very much tied up in performing for his over-solicitous mother—carrying her undeveloped animus. Paradoxically, he had come to this prostitute to escape "mother" and pregnant women and concerns about "germs," but these were the very shadow issues the prostitute was struggling with in her inability to allow both sets of lips to be used in relationship with him.

The Victim's Numbness Redeemed

About eighteen months into therapy, Beth dreamed of a dirty old man—like the one who had abused both herself as a child, and her daughter—coming along and sucking off her penis with a vacuum cleaner. She reported being unable to make love to her husband since the dream. When we started to work with the dream, I asked her to imaginally look at her body and see what she had left. There were no genitals at all. The penis had been of the phantom variety; there had been no divine androgyny, only the unconscious hermaphrodite. She had been left a Barbie doll. She told me that she had lost her genitals the night her father had eroticized and violated her, when she had seen the monsters on the ceiling. She reminded me that a very early dream in therapy had been of a man throwing a marble statue of Venus (or Aphrodite) at her. But she had thrown it back because in the dream she had only been a child. Her body had indeed become statuelike, numb as a Barbie doll, passions subsumed to coerced mothering. Yet, paradoxically, in her dream life of early therapy her daughter's bedroom was cluttered with a fast food store. Beth complained of masturbating compulsively but of feeling nothing.

In the next dream she saw herself lying in bed in a sexual relationship with a man who resembled her husband. But, frozen with emotion, she saw that she kept switching to a witch/black panther, lost in sensuousness, bent on destroying him because he somehow triggered this change in her. I suggested that, privately, Beth might like to look at her vulva in a mirror, and even to draw it, to look at Judy Chicago's work and let herself truly experience the journey through the flower. These were all rather shocking and new ideas for Beth. I suggested that she recall her previous dream where a man had thrust a flame tipped sword into her vulva, bringing her body to life. She had found that masculine energy vivifying, compared with the phantom penis she had carried for so long. The sword needed the Grail vessel, and the vessel needed more reclamation. A month later the dirty old dream man came again — this time he was drunk. Beth offered him soap and coins to get cleaned up in the wash-house. But he immediately grabbed her and started kissing her. Beth was shocked and repulsed but could only "squirm ineffectually" until she felt the presence of three young men behind her. Then she freed her mouth, demanded to be let go, and stood back in the half circle of young men. She smoothed down her dress and said:

> "Did you even think to ask if I wanted to?" At this he shriveled and became young and whiny and very insecure saying "But you were concerned for me, no one ever wanted me to be clean before. . .they just sent me away."

Then he ran away. Beth was upset not just because of the kiss, but because she had hurt him, he had run away, and more importantly, he still didn't understand her perspective. Then she was imaginally listening to a group talking about a really quiet boy who was going to commit suicide, and she knew the victim was the dirty old man/insecure boy. The scene changed, and Beth was looking after the register at a motel, when there was a knock at the door. There was a brawl going on between large, rowdy drunk men who threatened to kidnap her. Beth still felt supported by her bodyguard. She stepped forward because in the rowdy group she had seen the "quiet fellow" who seemed to "have gathered the noisy fellows along to get up his nerve." She insisted that he must start at the beginning, asking her for a date and making direct eye contact. The friends were shocked at her decision "after all he had done to her." But Beth remained true to her Self, and though she felt like swooning, she placed her hands in his and stepped into the darkness.

As they did this, he became the "Prince of Darkness." In a glass-enclosed space, surrounded by their supporters, together they sat on a couch talking earnestly. He took her pain and, in return, gave her a box. She opened it to find a beautiful flower. Crying, she realized the Prince of Darkness had given her back her flower genitals and her body.

In the "glassy sepulcher,"[4] Beth was learning that she could easily be hooked into mothering the man (the undifferentiated little boy baby-face/brute-face), who actually needed educating in order to realize that there was a perspective other than his. In imaginally educating this inner man, she was finding her upper mouth, articulating her boundaries, and stepping outside of group consciousness towards a reconnection with her embodied Self. She was in fact living important aspects of the educative value of courtly love, to which we will return later.

Just before the dirty old man dreams, there had been another dream of special significance for Beth. She and her husband had been driving, looking for a friend's new house. They discovered that some of the walls were missing — those around their daughter's bedroom. Then Beth was combing her hair, standing by the bed she and her husband had slept in. Their daughter was lying with the husband. Beth asked if she was frightened of Mummy and Daddy making love. The child replied, no, she wanted to see more, to have a closer look. At this the dream husband lowered the sheet and ejaculated into the child's face. Beth wiped the child, tasting the semen in her own mouth, and led the child away explaining that the child was not strong enough to cope with a man's sexuality. Beth awoke feeling afraid that her husband might really abuse their daughters.

When she went back to the dream in her therapy session, Beth entered it at a point where the husband was lifting the bedclothes. Beth found herself raging with the butcher's knife in hand, chopping up the child. Then she cried out, dropped the knife, and with her hands molded the child back together again, telling her she loved her and that it was not her fault. Again Beth picked up the knife and whacked off her husband's penis and threw it out of the window. As it flew away she again cried out and the penis came back and she molded it back into place. At this point she became conscious that she had a mermaid's fish tail, and in that moment of awareness it split to the knees and she could stand up on proper feet. The rest of the active imagination revolved around removing the child from the parental bedroom.

In seeing to the establishment of appropriate boundaries between herself and her daughter, Beth was able to take responsibility for some of her previously unrecognized destructiveness. On the one hand the child had not been separated enough from the parental bed (as had been the case in Beth's own childhood) and on the other hand was too enmeshed in the mother's rage. Where there should have been walls and boundaries there were none. We see again Gaea castrating Uranus for his inappropriate parenting. The splitting of her fish tail also recalls this myth, for Uranus's genitals fell into the sea, and from them arose Aphrodite. But for Aphrodite to emerge in her muscle shell, with flowers erupting from her body, instead of being the marble, prostituted Aphrodite, it is first necessary to descend to the bottom of the sea in order to find its treasures. It is worth noting that it was Aphrodite who turned Pygmalion's beautifully sculptured woman into a flesh and blood reality at his request, and after he had been to worship at her temple.

The Mermaid

Aphrodite's predecessor, Ishtar, was said to be covered with scales like a snake and to be half fish, perhaps the forerunner of the mermaid. Esther Harding says that the unconscious mermaid woman, playing the role of the anima for men, can live erotically and remain as cold as an iceberg, getting what she wants through manipulation.

> If the man is immature in his own emotional development, his feelings remain sentimental, and he will be flattered by this apparent interest in his intimate and personal life. He will feel that his woman has a peculiar connection with him in things which are ordinarily secret, which *only a mother knows* or cares about. It gives him a curious feeling of warmth and closeness, almost a sense of body contact which is well nigh irresistible...he is lulled to sleep by the narcotic of the animal-like instinctive contact.[5] [Emphasis added]

Harding explains that fish women are auto-erotic, conquering men to gain power over them, but remaining themselves outside of their own passions.[6] Their sexuality has been pressed into the service of their egos and functions as part of their desire for power.[7] All this is certainly true, but it is essential to see the roots of the passionless fish woman as lying in the patriarchal abuse of the child and of nature, and in the coercion of the child to dissociate from her body into the world of the power-oriented animus ego.

Lynne, a past incest victim, dreams of a little fish caught in a tree. It reminds her of catching a fish as a child and feeling excited. But her father threw it away because it was "so small." She explained to me that she didn't like making love: she didn't like her own fishy smell. Without any suggestions from me, Lynne gleefully retrieved her small fish and a few days later found that she no longer had a "swamp fish" but a beautiful fish named Brandy who took Lynne on underwater journeys to the bottom of the ocean. In connecting consciously with the fish woman, Lynne found her body tingling in an ecstatic union with "a man."

Arnold Mindell suggests that the fish symbolizes:

...pulsatile, somatic sensations which are potential allies and aids to consciousness. [Stranded fish] refer to subliminal impulses which will dry out if not properly propagated or amplified by consciousness.[8]

As Lynne was connecting with her body's pulsing, she was in fact connecting with aspects of the Great Mother. For instance, Mother Kali was the virgin keeper of life and death, whose real name was "truth" but who was called "fishy smell." Indeed the common yonic symbol (or symbol of the vulva) was the *Vesica Piscis*—vessel of the fish; Aphrodite's principal rites at Paphos took place under this sign. Aphrodite, Isis and Frigga appear, in their sexual aspects, under fish-net veils.

Anne's armored dream-fish was caught in a fish-net and drawn to the surface. This was after she had dreamed of a prostitute being overdosed by her pimp for seeing too much. Anne explained that her inner prostitute was like the virgin Anne Frank—locked away to hide from the Nazis. Of her fish she wrote

> This fish comes from the bottom of the sea where it is very dark and very cold. It got caught up in some fish nets and discovered by some fishermen. It was believed that this fish was extinct. It has armor plates which it needed for protection because of the great water pressure at the depths at which it lived.
> This poor fish must have been really stunned when it was hauled to the surface. So much light, so much movement. It must have been overwhelming.

Learning to see in the underwater depths is like working with sparks in the darkness. Jung tells us that

> ...those laboring in the darkness must try to accomplish an opus that will cause the "fishes' eyes" to shine in the depths of the sea, or to catch the "refracted rays of divine majesty" even though this produces a light which the darkness, as usual, does not comprehend.[9]

This is quite different from dragging everything into consciousness, becoming overdosed from too much seeing.

So we are beginning to have a deeper appreciation of why the patriarchal father does not want to hear the news of the fish tail. It would mean the undoing of his world, bringing light to the deep-sea fish eyes in order to perceive both the depths to which the patriarchal father's cut-off genitals have disappeared, and the birth place of Aphrodite struggling out of her phallic straitjacket.

Even the colors of the sacred harlot are images from the deeps. In his alchemical studies, Jung tells us that

> Red and rose-red are the colour of blood, a synonym for the *aqua perma-nens* and the soul, which are extracted from the *prima materia* and bring "dead" bodies to life.[10]

Descending into the darkness, we find an area feminine in nature, an *anima mundi,* the mercurial anima, the feminine part of the her-maphroditic Mercurius, a woman with a serpent tail or a fish tail faith-lessly abandoned by the second form of God. We call her the mermaid, maiden of the sea. She longs for the embrace of the One, the monad, the good and perfect.[11] Such a one will wail interminably for her demon lover, giving herself over to his dark embrace out of sheer desperation for the Spirit. This mercurial anima is the "divine soul imprisoned in the elements,"[12] whom it is the task of alchemy to redeem and release from captivity.

Looking at a picture of the mercurial anima, a woman commented with astonishment that she was not svelte like her own "banished mer-maid." The Mercurial Anima has a muscular torso, and a strange rounded belly, looking almost as though it bears the full moon. She carries a vessel and a snake—suggestive of transformation and reclaimed femi-nine strength. Her wings show that she is at home in the air as well as in the water. The patriarchal mermaid indeed springs from both the old man Uranus' wound of rejected fathering, of non-sacred castration, and the wound to young Psyche eroticized so that she can only either remain submerged in the watery depths or make a pseudo emergence as a secular whore or coerced mother. Her flesh and soul remain sub-dued and therefore assume gigantic proportions in the unconscious. The mercurial anima, on the other hand, knows and loves her rounded body and is not condemned to submersion in the unconscious. She has some choices.

The Exaggeration of the Victim's Body

Don once admitted that making love with Olga was frought with difficul-ties because he was afraid of "getting lost in a dissatisfied fat bitch." For her part, Olga explained that she had had a secret fantasy ever since her brother had bribed and sexually abused her. She imagined her vul-va was a large city in which one could get lost; she also imagined it as a cave with a treasure in it. She herself had never explored either city or cave. The wound, swollen to city size, is the inevitable outcome of the hurt woman's denied essence.

While discussing the image of Jerusalem in his *Symbols of Transformation*, Jung suggests that a man's crippling attachment to the mother fosters civic virtue and enables him to live a useful life in the community. But the city that allows for this is not the city of the Whore of Babylon; this city must be transformed into a new Jerusalem, bringing us from the lower half of the mother to the upper, where everything that incest would have made impossible now becomes possible.

Living in the unconscious patriarchal "whore's city," Olga had a dream in which she found a man whom she wanted to "just fuck off." What came out instead was "just flirt off." In active imagination, Olga found that she could kneel in front of him, and at that moment also felt the tension around her ears abating. The man had come to teach her about mutual respect and understanding, but she would laugh at him and kick him because men had been so unkind to her; she "fights" or "flirts" with him. As she stayed still, she felt her face begin to peel and her eyes became those of a child. Looking through them,

> Little flowers became as important as getting to my appointment in time. There is a whole world in a flower. It is a world where everything is important, every gesture carries its own magical significance, everything is breathed in, every pore of my body opens up. There is total mind body experience. They become one. . .to enjoy.

Then Olga saw two colors, red and white. With urgency she exclaimed:

> I can't feel the red. . .my doors close. . .I fly into space. I don't like red, it's blood, life's substance. . .a woman, and I don't want to be a woman. I want to be a child.

At this point Olga paused,

> I have to stop. I want to feed you a bunch of crap. I don't want to look.

Another pause.

> A tiny seed, a blob of red. It grows and overpowers me. It takes me in. . .I don't want to live. I want to stand on the side and watch.

Becoming able to "suffer the redness" instead of falling into fragmentation is what can eventually release the hurt feminine from being a patriarchal pawn; it can thrust one into true life, where each gesture and word is filled with meaning.

Change in Relationship with the Masculine Principle

Moving from the secular hurt prostitute to sacred harlot, the woman's relationship to the masculine principle undergoes some profound changes. There is initially much castrating revenge intermingled with unrealistic idealism and sentimentality.[13] Lola dreams of a magical battle with underground men, one of whom she eventually burns as punishment for raping her, though she first assumed that she had wanted to help him *away* from the flames. Tilly dreams of meeting a man among "fecal people" in a hospital for the criminally insane. He has greasy hair and is deceitful, "a weasel-man." Suddenly she is flooded with rage: this is the man who had abused her as a child. She wants to choke and castrate him, and she finds him telling her that he only abused her because he was so dead. Olga dreams of being shut naked in coffin with Don, before they were married. Don's penis was shoved into her by a "schizophrenic man" who refused to take his medication. Someone rescued the two naked people from what felt like a very black *coniunctio*, and Olga was left feeling embarrassed and outraged. She connected it with the recurring childhood dream, during the time she was sexually violated, of falling down the church steps to the devil while rolling her tongue into "baloney." Such a schizophrenic animus cropped up months later when Olga dreamed of asking a man about to rape her to leave her house. Her words were, "Please leave so that you can come back later." They seemed like strange words to her. We might say that these are the words of a woman at least able to talk with a potential assailant, protecting herself until a more potent union might be possible. But it is also essential to realize that to ask a man with psychopathic tendencies to leave cannot be done simply and straightforwardly. Women in relationships with such men since childhood have had to learn all sorts of wily maneuvers in order to avoid further hurt and abuse. It is all part of the confusion of tongues, the "baloney," that pervades patriarchal homes. And in this sense women become addicted to abusive relationships.

Many hurt women tell me that they hate and fear their sons because they will grow up to be men who hurt women. Dreaming of having intercourse with a son-lover is the opposite side of the same issue. The abused woman must have her sexual needs met or make the object of her love serve her maternal instinct. Esther Harding suggests that the woman who has not "sacrificed the son" usually does not suspect that she cannot say no to him because she cannot say no to herself, or deny on a deeper level her own softness and selfishness.[14] Having seen, in the patriarchal family, the loss of discipline through abuse and the inherent confusion in our society between the red (sexual) and the white (maternal) streams of women's consciousness, we can see why it is such an incredibly difficult sacrifice for women to make, involving not only their relationship with their physical children, but their children of creativity.

Jeni's relationship with the penis shifted dramatically in therapy. In an early dream she sees boys with cages strapped to themselves. Inside the cages are mice or hamsters which turn into wiggling penises. The watching women cackled and laughed at the boys. Jeni told me this was actually because the women were afraid of their *own* sexual powers. Because they had been so repressed, they were sensed as gigantic and elemental and threatened to take over the entire personality.

Jeni had the following dream, which she described as "mindblowing."

> There is a man, my husband but not my husband. He is lying on the chesterfield with this long erect penis, his arms are beside him. He is distressed, calling me. I am busy with my doings—children are needing me for help, and this man is calling. [impatiently] No, I will not go to him. I see he is curled up and sucking his penis. The children have gone and I go over to see if he needs help. He looks like he is in such pain and despair. I can see he is ready to ejaculate. I ask if I can help. He nods "yes." I hold his penis while he thrusts. Soon there is semen spurting all over his face and chest. He seems more in distress as he doesn't know what to do now that he has ejaculated all over himself. I get a face cloth and towel and tell him he can begin by wiping the semen up. His arms are still by his side. He is looking at me to do this work. I don't. I walk away. After he has wiped himself off he comes to me a very confused and humble man, which delights me. He has no words and neither do I.

This dream is reminiscent of the man who wanted his wife and children to witness him sucking his penis, and who reverted to abusing his wife and shooting the animals. He was attempting to connect with the phallus, but couldn't because he had only profane ritual at his disposal. At this time, still "hating semen and penises," Jeni was beginning to learn how to set her own boundaries, though she was unable to support a self-fertilizing action on the part of the dream-man. She is locked into mothering and anger, with little true compassion for his male struggle. Thus she confuses some of the issues. For instance, wiping his face with a cloth feels too much like mothering him. The husband is still not in a position of energetic release,[15] but masturbates more like a timid boy. In waking life, the man cannot give himself permission to masturbate anyway. He is still a child waiting for mother's permission to become a man.

Seven months later, Jeni met a dream priest down in the "red light district." They both sat on apple boxes and talked. She also dreamed of making love to a woman, an experience which brought her body amazingly to life; she did not have to cope with the fear of being prematurely penetrated. Such a dream allows a woman to begin to accept her instinctual sexuality through relating to the feminine. This is important for women whose mothers had never supported this process. Eventually, Jeni dreams of camping with her children and meeting a strange man. They move their trailer away from the children and start to make love. Jeni is amazed because this man does not have an erection. He makes love to her whole body. He values her. Just seeing his penis become erect is orgasmic for her and entirely new. In outer life, her husband only touches her genitally and he gets angry with her for undressing in front of him because it gives him an erection. Jeni and other women with whom I have worked claim never to have seen a flaccid penis, only erect or partially erect ones. Their men certainly seemed to be burdened by the patriarchal ever-ready machine missile that would help them feel invulnerable.[16]

This dream opened up a whole new inner area of experience for Jeni. In separating her sexual relationship with a man away from the sleeping children, she was truly touched, and for the first time experienced a sense of awe at the male penis—now more easily perceived as a phallus through which life and death, tumescence and flaccidity, can flow. Experiencing such a transformation from the inside allows us to value the history of the red light of the whorehouse. It descended from the houses of the Roman *venerii* who displayed the sign of an erect phallus, painted red,[17] the phallus that had been blessed by the sacred menstrum.

About six months later, Jeni had the following experience, which I report just as she had written it.

During the night I had this pain flood me with rage at the patriarchal God we worship, and it seems to make sense. Here we praise and worship and give thanks to a God that is torturing, unjust and dishonest. He himself is an offender. I wailed at how dare He take my two daughters, torture me and Kate; we are always subjected to his torture. He claims to have a plan—a just and honest God would be up front and honest with his people. He would not keep them in a constant state of confused agony. I screamed out, what have I done or what has Kate done to be put through this pain. We have done nothing wrong—yet you play with us and torture us and somehow I'm to be grateful to you for this—no way—I don't buy secrets and plans. I want to know what is real and here. How can a just God allow such injustice to go on? I relinquish my faith in the Patriarchal God. He is not for me. He is for pain, torture, destruction and sadism. As I was shaking, freezing and crying, I felt a horn of some animal penetrate my vagina. I couldn't stop it—it just happened. I felt confused. Why when I am denouncing the masculine am I being penetrated? Yet this penetration was different. There was no sexual excitement involved. It was not hurtful or painful. First I felt the horn on my upper thigh and gave myself permission to allow whatever was to happen. Then it was the hardness and the roughness of the horn that penetrated my vagina. I felt I was taking in something very sacred and gentle. Then it was gone and I lay very still.

This woman had traveled through a profoundly healing, imaginal journey with a transformation of how she regarded the male organ. From a wriggling rodent worthy only of ridicule, it became an agent of something that was both numinous and completely beyond her comprehension at this time. This woman was like Job—railing at God and intuiting that God remains unconscious, as it were, until received within a single, completely receptive soul. This horn was fierce and hard, yet engendered amazing tenderness at the moment of penetration, bringing with it some new awareness of spirit and instinct bound together in a way incomprehensible to the patriarchal paradigm. But it is a mystery that can now slowly unfold as the woman lives within the image. She can receive the monad, the One.

Dying in the Rubedo: the Emergent Sacred Harlot

Elsa arrived for one of her sessions with a large cold sore on her lips. She immediately said that this herpes sore spoke of "love and hate." It began to tingle as she spoke to it. She told a long dream that ended with a passionate embrace with a man on fire. Elsa had not consummated the relationship because she had had to tell him that she was an Anglican priest. She had awakened from the dream with a sore clitoris. In talking of it, she found the "pain of the maiden" congealed into "hate from sorrow, grief and care." She found herself painfully recalling two maiden occasions that she had never mourned and should have. The first was as a teenager telling her father she had been sexually violated. All he did was blame her. She found this astonishing because he had always maintained that he would "kill anyone who touched her."

The second was that she had felt so sad after she and her husband had first made love. He had insisted in having his way and she was afraid. Afterwards she was afraid again because he would think she was "a slut."

She had never dealt with it because she was sure it would simply be labeled "guilt over sexuality." Somewhere in her being she knew indeed that she was living in a society that had forgotten that hymeneal hymns reverberate with funereal overtones. There had been no wise woman to talk with about the sadness of the marriage night. She had not heard words of understanding and comfort.

In asking how the image of the clitoris was connected with the herpes sore, Elsa was suddenly intruded upon by "whiteness"—a startling image of a "nun's habit and wimple"—the word "cloister," and the phrase "violated by love." Elsa had not ovulated for four days, though the signs of a fertile mucus were present. This had never happened before. She suddenly felt it would be safe to ovulate because she had decided to remain "cloistered," even in the post-ovulatory time (in fact, this happened). She still needed to don the veil and complete the mourning for her enforced loss of the maiden. She would not be able to make a voluntary sacrifice and allow her hymen to be newly penetrated until the mourning was complete.

Elsa also claimed that she did not want to use her mouth to speak the truth as it seemed to her. Her truth was different from so much of what she saw around her and certainly different from the priest's truth with which she has been previously aligned. Robert Sardello suggests that herpes is a "disease of surface sexuality"; its victims are "like oracles—bearers of something we need to hear." Herpes,

> ...far from being an evil of promiscuousness, is in fact the puritan ethic raging within those who have bright ideas about sexuality but have restricted its experience to personal relationships and have identified sexuality with intercourse.[18]

Some time later, Elsa dreamed of going to an underworld cavern where there were many "women's things," like jewels and perfume, which Elsa considered "decadent." The dog with her kept tugging her in that direction, but Elsa kept escaping to find refuge with a man. An oriental Buddha-like man appeared suddenly, accusing Elsa of being "a harlot," telling her that she should wear particular clothes and put perfume down both sides of her body.

Elsa spent an hour and a half dressing herself "meticulously" before coming for her appointment, absolutely omitting any perfume or jewelry. She said there was no way she wanted to meet the accuser again. However, after settling into the cave with her dog, who contentedly lay beside her, the oriental man appeared again. Elsa's face became very red, her vulva throbbed, and there was a strange stirring in her stomach. Her vulva said one word—"love"—the sort Elsa said she knew absolutely nothing about. Soon she was recalling her "perfection" about diet, vitamins, natural family planning, home births, mothering in general—all important ideals, but all done in secret judgment of others. The new love came close to reminding Elsa of the experience of having her first baby— but not quite. This was different, and she felt somewhat overwhelmed and frightened. She wondered where this new love would lead her.

In redeeming her lips from the unmourned sorrow of the hurt maiden, Elsa began the task of reclaiming her virginity through which could begin to pour a new love—the love of the sacred virgin harlot. Like Isis, her dog had led her to the place of husband Osiris encased in matter, the place of mourning and ritual that would release the new god to life once more. And we must note that the sacredness of Isis was recognized by the Queen through her maidens. Isis had curled their hair and scented them with the perfume of her own body.[19]

The release of this new love is no easy romantic transition. The passage is excruciating. Entering their own clay, discovering that their bodies are in fact different from men's, women, no matter how liberated, invariably howl with shame, horror and disgust. In fact, the more conscious women are, the more horrified they can be by the reality of the feminine. One writes, at such a transition time:

> He can be so calm and quiet, and I cry, sob, bleed and ooze. It would be so nice to be clean and compartmentalized like him instead of oozing and being worked through. . .I am disgusting. . .with my insides always coming to the outside. I have internalized the horror, disgust, and shame that is centuries old, instead of respect for and love of my own "beingness" and life flowing through me.

Dying in the Rubedo: Gertrude's Story

Gertrude came to see me because of severe anxiety attacks which would occur in the darkest of night. She had been on prescribed medication for fourteen years. She was a woman completely devoted to her family of three sons and her second husband. The two oldest sons were in their teens and the other was a preschooler.

Gertrude showed immediate talent for working with her hands. Her first sculptures were of family scenes epitomizing the blissfully happy family. When I first saw her work it was unpainted and the people

reminded me of the Pillsbury Dough people. Her first dream in therapy, however, was of her sprouting penises all over her body. She was in
fact an extremely controlling but hysterically sad mother—a true phallic mother through her very devotedness to her family. Such an unconscious hermaphrodite mother appears perfect and superhuman. Her
castration allows her son to see her as only human and he, paradoxically,
no longer feels himself to be constantly threatened by castration.

Her eldest son, having difficulty with drugs and with his peers as well
as his mother, felt the need to leave home and go to live with his father
in another city. Shortly after this, Gertrude dreamed of raping her youngest son. The first summer of therapy was a summer of raging and an
agony of "moving upstairs," as one dream put it.

As she was able to quiet down her external life, particularly around
menstruation, she began to see more of her inner dynamic and of her
relationship with her family. She dreamed of her eldest son in a grave-
yard, giving psychedelic drugs to Nazis to "get rid of them by driving
them crazy." The dead began to rise from their tombs, but only bones
arose. This was a scene where there was again no true meeting with the
soul of death, only a perversion into *fantastica* and a violation of the
senses through threat of "Nazi invasion."

At this time Gertrude began to talk about her first marriage, realizing that it had in fact been continual psychological rape. After intercourse, her husband would list all of her inadequacies. She still became
nervous at these times in her life, and was seeing how this was connected with her anxiety attacks. She told me that she had recently made
love with her husband during menstruation and that, though she had
always been orgasmic, this had been a completely new experience. It
was very puzzling to her. She had no conscious knowledge of the healing power of the sacred harlot's menstruation.

Some five months later, Gertrude had the following dream:

I am meeting an old school chum (who I actually don't recognize). She is
a prostitute but she looks mousy with her hair straight and a camel coat
buttoned to the neck. She invites me to her downtown apartment and I
want to go because I have to ask her about being a prostitute. But I have
to get a babysitter first. When I arrived, it was actually the prostitute who
had the questions to ask. Firstly, how is it to be a mother? I explained that
having a baby is wonderful. I am surprised at my answer because I had recently been feeling that having children had been a big mistake. The prostitute's second question was, how is it to be a wife? I don't know how to answer:
I don't know how to be a wife.

With this surprising situation we entered the dream imaginally, noting that Gertrude had never asked the prostitute the question she had prepared. Her question was about what the prostitute offers the man. "A non-relationship," replied the prostitute. Gertrude found herself recalling a Norman Mailer quote about Marilyn Monroe, a figure who had held a compelling fascination over Gertrude for years:

> She would ask no price. She was not the dark contract of those passionate brunette depths that speak of blood, vows taken for life, and the furies of vengeance if you are untrue to the depths of passion. No, Marilyn suggested sex might be difficult and dangerous with others, but ice cream with her.[20]

It seemed as though between them Gertrude and the prostitute knew about having babies and having non-relationships with men, but neither of them knew anything about marriage to a man, about being a wife.

Gertrude's next dream found her leaving behind a mothering woman and walking up a hill, with her youngest son, to where some primitive people are gathered. There is to be some sort of sacrifice. First of all everyone must kiss the breasts of Kali. Then everyone must cut off a lock of one's hair and put it in an envelope on the altar. Gertrude was terrified and ran away with her little son.

Wondering aloud what might have happened had she not run away, Gertrude saw herself go up in flames, turned to ashes, leaving her little son pathetically alone. But strangely, her hair didn't burn at all. She felt as though the sacrifice had not been accepted. She suddenly saw that this hair that didn't burn was black; it was not her own hair. It was a wig. She pulled it off, and the primitive people cheered. Then she cut off a lock of her own blond hair. Suddenly the fire descended and consumed every hair on her head, leaving her completely bald, but still with her little son, who seemed to remain totally unaffected by all this high drama going on above his head. I asked how she would live if she was bald. "Not beautifully" she replied, "And my husband wouldn't like it . . . my being beautiful has been part of the deal we have had together." At this time Gertrude made some masks. One was of the untouched beauty her husband wanted. The other was of Pusturia, the hideous woman Gertrude felt she herself was becoming.

Gertrude made some distinct changes in her life at this point, moving into an even deeper aloneness, letting herself be unmade, and refraining from compulsive daily showering. She sent her little son to day-care. She was writing a lot of short stories and found, to her surprise, that her older son wanted to come home. Interestingly, he was also gifted in writing. Some months later her son attempted suicide. Gertrude somehow managed to stay centered throughout the experience. She said that she had come to the point where she knew she could go on living— even if he died. Slowly, the family members began to talk with each other in a new way. It gradually became evident that the son had been carrying some of his father's abusive Nazi-like behavior that had so affected Gertrude, but which the son knew nothing about at a conscious level. Yet he had been attempting to protect his mother and keep at bay the Nazis that he had inherited.

Gertrude brought a beautifully sculpted Black Madonna and Child to our next meeting. Recalling the Pillsbury Happy Family, she explained that it would be easy to assume she had come back to the same place. But in fact she hadn't. *She* was now the child in the mother's arms, and the color had changed from white to black.

Gertrude complained that her eyes wanted to look at men, to ogle them, to inspect them. She had also met an inner priest who, with sadness, would not consummate their relationship physically. She also began to see just what power she had over men. She found that just by looking at them she could draw them to her.

It is hard to express just how much Gertrude suffered in releasing her sons and reclaiming her sexuality: the experience felt excruciatingly suicidal. She developed an ovarian cyst which had to be surgically removed. She indeed felt she truly died through this terrifying experience. During this time she dreamed of punching obnoxious neighbors on the nose. She also dreamed of having to lay aside three manuscripts to squat down on the floor and howl for having allowed her oldest son his psychological freedom. She needed to develop her own healing ritual of release, such as is practiced in other cultures. The Aztec mother, releasing her son and reestablishing her virginity, speaks these words as she cuts the umbilical cord:

> I cut from your middle the navel string; know you, understand that your birthplace is not your home. This house where you are born is but a nest. It is a way station to which you have come. It is your point of entrance to this world. Here you sprout, here you flower, here you are severed from your mother, as the chip is struck from the stone.[21]

Just before entering hospital, Gertrude wrote a poem in which the following lines appeared:

I feel the approach of The Beast
Cold, black, monstrous and implacable.

Gertrude felt this black beast wanted to absorb her. She was in a panic.
I asked if there was any feminine image she knew that would balance him.

There is one, something like Marilyn Monroe, but not her. She emotes
from the pelvis; she is mammoth compared with him and he is like a tiny
speck beside her. I am more like him than her. Both he and I have to bend
to her. Her mammothness just IS. When we both kneel in front of her he
stops engulfing me. She is smothering yet I must live within her. She is less
personal than my Black Madonna. I don't have a human connection with
her. She is pregnant with the earth but it is all on the inside — it must come
to the outside. She is moaning and pushing. There is blood between her legs.

Not surprisingly, Gertrude still experienced some difficulties with the
great black, male beast that threatened to overwhelm her. But she was
developing an awareness, for the first time, of an impersonal, enormous
and virginal feminine entity through whom the whole of creation poured,
such as is suggested by the Sphinx. It is this impersonal feminine who
holds masculine/feminine relationship in her embrace. Without a conscious relationship with her, that is, without respecting the incest taboo, we are held captive in Her elemental power.[22] Such an insight seems
to be essential for any woman in allowing otherness to flow through her
being, and to release her children from her own suffocating embrace.
In such a way we are also released from seeing creation as essentially
and only masculine.

Gertrude found herself recalling a dream that she had had prior to
entering the therapeutic process, and of which she had never told me.

I am on a sailing clipper in northern seas. All the animals are dead. The
moment I see this terrible thing I am flying above the water.

Gertrude turned to me and said she finally understood this dream.

NOW I HAVE DIED
I NO LONGER HAVE A GRIP ON LIFE

Rather, life could now flow through her as she disengaged from identification with either pole of the Great Mother.

Now Gertrude imagined herself enwombed within a ferocious male
dragon, like Metis must have been when swallowed by Zeus. Gertrude
was bent double in her now familiar feminine agony. This was how she

had felt all her life; but now she could see the scene imaginally and therefore more objectively. Her father then appeared to her in a dream, telling her she could no longer have ecstatic out-of-body experiences. She was to stay with embodied ecstasy. This was somewhat puzzling because in outer life Gertrude's father had done everything humanly possible to deny his daughter's body and sexuality. This was some new father image much more in keeping with a Dionysian figure.

Her next picture burst through Gertrude with tremendous passion. "I am in the very jaws of death," she explained to me, "Yet I am giving birth. I am the fetus and I carry it also." After painting the picture, Gertrude synchronously found herself reading about Ariadne and was amazed by what she read. This story mirrored Gertrude's own story and seemed to imbue it with deeper meaning. Christine Downing tells us that, left stranded on the beach, Ariadne suffered death in many ways. Yet on the island of Crete there was no abrupt and final demarcation between life and death as there was for the Greeks. Crete was close to the older matriarchal values. According to one tradition, Ariadne dies just before she gives birth. In fact

> Ariadne enters the realm of death with the unborn child still within her, and gives birth in the underworld. This is the only account in Greek mythology of a birth in the world of the dead.[23]

Obviously something profound must have happened. Downing states that when Dionysus is fully present in intercourse, "the result issues in a birth unto death, into the imaginal, a birth in the soul, a birth of soul. Ariadne is the one through whom such birth is possible." Incest is redeemed through the birth of soul in the realm of death. Returning to what was left behind by the Greek intrusion into the sacred marriage, we find Ariadne, mistress of the Labyrinth, embraced by Dionysus. What she gave birth to did not spring like the fully-armed Athena from Zeus' forehead. What is so significant is that the offspring of this union has the qualities pertaining to "working with sparks in the darkness," of "bringing light to the fishes' eyes" and of the *filius regis,* the royal son of the sacred harlot.[24] What emerges from her is the redeemed Dark Son, at once an Earth Father and a creativity that has its root in primal blackness.

The emerging noble harlot, Venus, is clothed in abounding colors of reds, scarlet, and purples, and associated with rubies, garnets and amethysts that glow like coals in the transformation process.[25] The deep red rose, with its five-fold form, was the flower of Venus and the emblem of the sacred harlots. The Virgin Mary was Queen of the most Holy Rose Garden, and the rosary was a flower wreath to encircle the head of the phallic god in sacred marriage.[26] Kali's rosary of skulls was alternately red and white, symbolizing her dual aspects. The early Christians originally rejected the rosary on this account, though eventually they adopted it, with some of the early rosaries being carved from bone or ivory into tiny skulls.[27] Today the rosary is frequently used to implore Mary to be present at death, just as the Tantric sage implored Kali Shakti[28] to cut through his illusions and decapitate him with her sword.

In Britain there was the traditional five-pointed Mummers Dance, known as the Rose, in which five dancers formed a five-pointed star of swords over the victim, called the Fool, who was symbolically slain and resurrected with a mysterious elixir, the Golden Frosty Drop, or Dew Drop in the Rose. This is a western version of the Jewel in the Lotus, a seminal drop in the female flower. The dance originated as "ring around the rose wreath" (German) and "ring around a rosy" (English). The nursery rhyme instruction of "all fall down" was a request to Morgana, the Grim Reaper, Mother of Death, to bring to an end the fertility season.[29] This was known to be essential for the dance of Life to continue.

Thus we arrive at what I imagine as an alternative ending to the story of Little Red Riding Hood—a forest dance, ring around a Rosy, unified by the one in the center of the circle—the emergent Aphrodite. Now her heart is redeemed from the beat of frenzy, and her eyes are redeemed through inward seeing. The Dance and Logos are released because in reclaiming our legs we have learned to bend our knees to the Great Mother, through whom pours death and life in never-ending profusion.

As we gaze into the rose, perhaps we can fleetingly appreciate its constantly changing and unstable form which reminds us to center ourselves in the present. The promise of the bud, the pungent openness, the fading of petals to release seed life—all are delicate and interlocking unfoldings that come about in their true order. We cannot chisel open a rose. The joy of beholding the rose does not push us on to mighty deeds, but rather to a vibrant repose of quickened senses.

The Archetype of the Sacred Harlot

In reclaiming her body, in giving value to her experience, the wounded woman can indeed release the heart-sore prostitute from her patriarchal entrapments into the sacred virgin/harlot portrayed by Ishtar, Isis, and Aphrodite/Venus. We can now appreciate some of the confusion in terminology under which we have previously suffered. For instance, the Greek word *parthenos,* applied to Athena and Artemis, commonly translated as "virgin," means no more than "unmarried woman." Artemis was not worshiped as chaste, but was concerned with the loss of virginity and with childbearing. The Hebrew word rendered *virgin* in Isaiah actually means no more than "young woman." The virgin Ishtar referred to herself as "a compassionate prostitute," and Aphrodite herself was a virgin. The Chinese Holy Virgin Shing Moo bore a son while still a virgin. Her conception has also been deemed immaculate, yet she was the patroness of prostitutes.[30] Even within the Christian church, to this day in Europe there are certain highly revered shrines of Mary, Mother of God, Moon of the Church, in which Mary is black. For instance, Chartres Cathedral has the ancient Black Virgin in the crypt beside a deep dark well. To visit this holy place, one must get the key from two old ladies who keep a candle store nearby. It has been said that the Mary of this church did not hesitate to admit Mary Magdalene and Mary the gypsy, both black in hue. Layard describes the sacred harlot as the

> ...archetype of the free woman, the woman untrammeled by man's laws...she is in fact the ultimate anima, the temple priestess who marries the god and bestows her favors upon devout men, thus raising them also to a semi-divine status.[31]

Layard sees it significant that in the St. Matthew genealogy of Christ's birth there should be listed four women (Tamar, Rahab, Ruth, and Bathsheba) with connections to sacred prostitution, which distinguishes them from all "the respectable married ancestry like Sarah."

Christianity does not provide us with many viable models of sacred sexuality, and it thus perpetuates a sacred/secular split. In fact, one of the striking differences between heretical and orthodox branches of Christianity is that the former use sexual symbolism to describe God.[32] The Gospel of Philip, discovered in 1945 in Upper Egypt, suggests attributes to Christ quite unheard of to most of us:

> The companion of [the Saviour] is Mary Magdalene. [But Christ loved] her more than [all] the disciples, and used to kiss her [often] on her [mouth]. The rest [of the disciples] were offended...They said to him, "why do you love her more than the rest of us?" The Saviour answered and said to them, "Why do I not love you as I love her?"[33]

In fact, here Mary Magdalene is described not only as one of the three disciples chosen to receive special teaching, but was also praised above the other two, Thomas and Matthew. Other secret texts use the figure of Mary Magdalene to suggest that women's activities challenged the leaders of the orthodox community. Peter complained that Mary Magdalene dominated the conversation with Jesus, displacing the rightful priority of himself and his brother. And later Mary admitted to Jesus that she hardly dared speak with him freely because "Peter makes me hesitate; I am afraid of him, because he hates the female race." Jesus replied that "whoever the Spirit inspires is divinely ordained to speak, whether man or woman." Most of us, however, have only a dim recollection of Mary Magdalene as being a common prostitute out of whom Jesus cast seven devils, and who fades into insignificance beside his mother Mary.

Piercing the Heart

In Middle Eastern tradition, it was not unusual "for every woman of the land once in her life to sit in the temple of love and have intercourse with some stranger."[34] That is, every woman ritually enacted the role of the sacred harlot. In the Babylonian tradition, once the woman had taken her seat she was not allowed to return home till one of the strangers threw a silver coin into her lap, saying, "I summon you by the Goddess Mylitta" (the Assyrian Aphrodite). No matter the size of coin it could not be refused. Those were times when coins where still imbued with the rich symbolism of the ores,[35] as well as believed to emanate from the goddess (as we saw in Chapter I). Returning them to her through the individual woman had therefore a quite different meaning than present-day prostitution, where neither the feminine nor the coins of psychological change are valued. Once the woman had intercourse with the stranger *to satisfy the goddess,* she could go home and from that time on was unbribable.[36] She had dedicated the impersonality of instinct to the service of the Goddess, and thus had the power to sustain herself in remaining her own person. In later times women were allowed to sacrifice their hair (instead of their vaginal virginity[37]), as was requested imaginally of Gertrude.

But perhaps the most vital of sacrifices now is to sustain receiving a golden coin into the well of the heart—to indicate acknowledging and receiving the value both of heart truth and the sacred marriage redeemed from unconscious incest. Until the heart has been pierced by such a happening, images remain locked away and cannot serve their purpose of personal and communal enrichment.

When the full harvest moon lit the sky, a woman dreamed of a golden, blood-tinged coin landing between her breasts. The sensation of its arrival was so startling that she awoke trying to find the coin in the bed clothes, while incessant words throbbed in her ear—"the release of Charity...the release of Charity." Starting with the word *charity,* we see that the root *ka* means "to like," or "to desire." It is associated with the Germanic *horas,* meaning "one who desires" and "adulterer," and the Old English *hore,* meaning "whore." The Latin *carua* means "dear," "caress," "cherish," as well as "charity." Further back still, we find the Sanskrit word *Kama,* meaning "love" and "desire," from which developed *Kamasutra.* Joseph Campbell describes Sanskrit as the most spiritual of languages,[38] but for one raised only with the Charity of Paul's first letter to the early Church in Corinth—and not the Kamasutra—this can all be very confusing. Awakening to the confusion can feel like a heart piercing.

We learn further that Charity was the name of a young woman who had been abducted for ransom from her house by a band of brigands at the very moment when hymeneal hymns were being sung for her wedding. We read of this story in *The Golden Ass* of Apuleius—one of the three great works of imaginative prose narrative bequeathed to us from the ancient world. It is reputedly an autobiographical account of initiation into the mysteries of Isis,[39] with a language that "embodies the organic harmonies of the medieval world"[40] in an anticipation of the future's poetry—heart language, language that expands our vision and releases from our encapsulated hearts a new wisdom.

The one journeying towards initiation was Lucius, who, along with his friend Socrates, thought he could ignore the power of the harlot queen of tavern keepers. She had the reputation of powerfully turning against those who did not value her—for instance, an unfriendly lawyer was condemned to spend his life as a horned ram, butting and rebutting; the scandalized wife of one of her lovers was doomed to perpetual pregnancy. Indeed the whole city had turned against her, intent on stopping her. But through her "witch-like" powers, she had blocked everyone into their homes so that no one could break through any barriers. The chief instigator and his household, even his house and foundations, were banished to the top of a waterless, rocky mountain top.

This old woman and her friend burst into Lucius's thought-safe room. He was reduced to the hysterical laughter of terror. The old woman doomed him to a fate "worse than having his penis cut off." He was obliged to deal with his friend's dead body and bury it. As if to seal his fate, both old women straddle his body and empty their bladders all over him, then leave the room, which miraculously returns to an untouched state. The only difference was that Lucius still lay flat upon the floor, nerveless, naked, chilled and wrung-wet with urine, like a child just discharged from the mother's womb—gasping indeed as if in death-throes, yet (as it were) surviving and soliloquizing posthumously—at the very least like a candidate for crucifixion.[41]

Further trials rendered Lucius mute, turned into an ass. It was not easy for him to learn that a dead man's speech is brutal and devoid of heart. He had to silently witness Life in order to become self-aware and fully human. This was all part of his initiation into the mysteries of the goddess.

In this asinine, silent state, Lucius was in the cave with captured Charity, demented by grief, tearing at patches of her hair and clothes. The old woman who cared for the brigands did not give a damn for Charity's tears. Somehow this toughness seemed to change the young lady. She kissed the old woman's hand, called her "dear mother," recognizing the milk of humanity in her, and the wisdom and holiness her gray hair suggested. Charity's response to the fierce old woman differed markedly from that of Lucius, and it was Charity's intuitive knowledge that constellated a change in the old woman. To comfort the girl she told Charity "some pretty fablings and old wife's tales," as she called them.[42] She went on to tell the wonderful stories of Psyche and Eros, and it was these that sustained the girl as she was obliged to survive suspense-in-nothingness, at the very moment when joy and ecstasy had so cruelly been stolen from her. She *did* survive the ordeal and was eventually released from captivity; indeed, we learn her name only at her release. Thus Charity and her courageous husband (who enacted a mythic drama to bring about her release) seem to offer an important counterbalance to the Eros-Psyche story—in this case there is no etherealization of the anima figure.

Courtly Love
Courtly love did not advocate unfleshly love, but was rather a discipline of eroticism that united life and death, like the Hindu Tantra, with the lady enacting the truth of the Goddess. Here Eros and Psyche, Charity and Courage, can be united on a human level—disappearing neither into the upper world nor the underworld. According to Whitmont, in courtly love

...the woman herself sets the date of the single night that is to serve as a test, and invites the man to come to her if he so pleases, on condition that he will do "everything I should like," as Beatrix de Die put it. In fact, it is she who takes the initiative and gives all the orders. It is she who embraces, caresses, and asks for caresses and intimate embraces in return. The lover must be able at once to contain himself—for it would be unseemly for his sexual impatience to show—to give her pleasure, and to gain her confidence. This custom of the first night of tenderness and respect, entirely devoted to caresses and declarations of love, *preparing the heart for the act of love,* is attested to by more than one writer.[43] [Emphasis added]

The story of Gawain's initiation wonderfully exemplifies the knightly quest for courtly love. King Arthur himself, in a year and a day, had been given the task of finding out what women most want in the world. After a year he still had not found the answer, but finally met a hideous woman called Lady Ragnell who knew the answer and would reveal it to him on the condition that Arthur find her a knight to marry. Though Arthur refused, Gawain—the first knight of the land—submitted to the loathsome sacrifice; he (at first) thought that what women most desire is to have sovereignty over men. In marrying this Lady Ragnell, Gawain indeed encounters no less than a Sphinx-like creature, for

...her face is red in the sinking sun. Long yellow teeth show between weak, weak lips. Her head is set upon a great thick neck; she is fat and unshapely as a bell. Yet the horror of her lies is something more than the hideousness of her looks, for in her great, *squinting red-ringed eyes there lurks a strange and terrifying shadow of fear and suffering.*[44] [Emphasis added]

On the wedding night she demanded a kiss. Again Gawain submitted with grace, and Lady Ragnell was transfigured into the most beautiful maiden Gawain had ever seen. But she is only partially freed. She is to remain hideous for half of the time. She told Gawain that he could choose to endure either shame in court or revulsion in bed. Again Gawain submitted, saying he would abide by *her* decision. By this surrender to the fearsome Sphinx-life feminine, the enchantment was broken completely, and Lady Ragnell now was allowed to appear beautiful by day and night.

Gawain now understood that the terrible and fearsome Sphinx does not *ultimately* want power over man, only choice and recognition. But she will not be content with a shallow surrender; she would have the knight at his highest form of manliness. Only that can bring mutual satisfaction and joy. Gawain's real challenge was not to reject her and all her temptations by withdrawing or by becoming aggressive. While maintaining his own integrity, he was able to truly respond to her and to her needs. He is embracing the archetypal patterns of enacting "the jewel in the heart of the Lotus."[45]

If the woman is aimlessly lost in her own wounded city, bewitched by her own animus ego, embittered and crusty, having never moved to an impersonal connection with both poles of the Great Mother, she cannot enter with empathy into the male's journey of initiation. She can only contain him or despise him. She will not be able to act the part of the initiator because she will not empathetically comprehend that the male's "relation with the anima is a test of courage, an ordeal by fire for the spiritual and moral forces of man."[46]

Meeting the sacred harlot, the male initiate is in fact meeting with the emissary of the Lady of the Animals, as the virgin harlot goddesses were called. This is the shamanistic anima. Such a goddess indeed gives birth to everything—the hunter and the hunted, the eater and the eaten alike. The woman is not the goddess, but an emissary. She allows a feminine truth to come through her and she allows soul to unfold in her partner so that he becomes conscious. She does not need to *make* this happen. Indeed she learns that her insistent efforts usually come between soul and her man. A woman lost in her hurt cannot do this. She will instead cling to the hope that he will need her mothering, thus preventing his descent to the fearsome bipolar Great Mother. The healed virgin harlot, however, can see the godhead embodied in her human partner. Thus she can portray her abundant fertility and allow the male to make his own descent. She is releasing the son.

One woman related the following dream:

> I am just about to make love to a beautiful young man. Suddenly I find myself in his mother's bathroom. I am having my period, peeing and shitting all at the same time. Suddenly, his mother comes in and screams at me, "You are a disgusting monster." Then I see a young woman looking in the mirror. She *is* terrible.

In active imagination, the dreamer discovered that this terrible young woman was named Ellen. She was fat, with dyed blond hair. She was very lonely and very miserable. The woman recalled being so when she was pregnant, and she cried at the memory. She explained that she had actually felt beautiful; it was the most profound time of her life. But her husband hated it with a passion and would refuse to make love with her. During her second pregnancy, he fell in love with a prostitute named, ironically, Madonna, telling his wife that she was fat and ugly, and that he could not take her anywhere. Interestingly, the woman's nose had become numb during that time of terrible suffering, and remains so today. The woman had met Madonna and described her as only wanting to use her husband; he was really nothing to her. But he was drawn to her like a moth to a flame.

Of course, the man, still patriarchal at heart, must eschew the pregnant woman because behind her lies an archetype that speaks of the most profound secrets of life and death, and which certainly does not support the status quo. Such a man has only enough strength to relate to a child psyche, or to one whom he could subjugate. In addition, few women have enough roots in the depths of their own ensouled spiritual tradition to withstand his raging escape. Mostly they themselves still have to face the raging mother-in-law who actually values the female monster, the sphinx of initiation. This is so in Aphrodite's initial relationship with her daughter-in-law, Psyche.

But to deny a woman the beauty of her pregnancy (both physical and spiritual) is to inflict one of the deepest wounds possible on the female psyche. The depth of this frequent wounding is almost never articulated, because as a society we have not traced it to its very profound roots. We have not seen that pregnancy is the very archetype that stands behind all imagination, the key to ensouled living. To deny a woman pregnancy is to deny her life. To deny woman her life is to deny our society the most profound symbol behind all symbols — the most fertile womb of the Great Mother, the storehouse of all possible imaginings. Without this we are doomed to collective hysteria.

The sacred harlot, having been redeemed from memories of a coerced death, has bent her knee to the impersonal sphinx. She has been through the process of dying in the *rubedo,* of becoming red, of being so destroyed she cannot run away. She has not only reclaimed her wound and her passion, but also her own visions, her own imaginations. She needs these inner children to sustain her as she continues the path of releasing her husband and children to their own destiny, and releasing herself from negative flashbacks of sexual abuse.

The pregnant imagination of the sacred harlot is reminiscent of the results of Psyche's fourth task. She is prepared for this journey; the other tasks have had an effect upon her. She comes to this task with bread in hand to appease Cerberus, the three-headed dog guarding the entrance to the underworld. She has coins in her mouth: she has the wherewithal to pay her dues to Charon, who steers the ferry across the river Styx. She is told not to stop to help the lame ass driver or dead man floating by who will beg for help. Nor is she to become involved with the old women weaving fate. These are all traps set by Aphrodite for which Psyche must not fall.[47] It is in completing the task of retrieving the beauty ointment for Aphrodite that Psyche is finally released from being her puppet. She is no longer compelled by an archetypal mythologem. She has recovered her own myth from the great ocean of the unconscious. It is as though Aphrodite is keeping Psyche away from Eros until she is sure that her future daughter-in-law has enough stamina to complete the mission. Psyche does not swoon during the mission. That is, she has developed a pointedness that has absolutely nothing to do with the animus-bound addiction to perfection that can *only* press forward. Psyche has learned about *diffuse* seeing in her previous tasks; now she can develop focused flowing through a feminized ego.

Yet a final yielding is still required of Psyche so that Eros can be drawn to her side. In the second part of the fourth task, we read that Psyche "emerged from hell, brimming over with new life" and bearing within her hand a box of Proserpine's beauty ointment. She worshiped the Sun for its tide of light, and then was overcome by one of her traits—curiosity. She murmured to herself:

> What a foolish carrier of divine beauty am I, who do not cull the tiniest little smudge for myself, so that I may please my beautiful lover.[48]

And then she opened the box, and what it contained was no beauty-recipe, but a terrible sleep of death which penetrated Psyche's whole body until she collapsed on the ground as a sleeping corpse. Of course, there can be no recipe for beauty—no pat formulas. But Psyche seems not to have known this. However her seeming failure was exactly what was needed to bring Eros to her side. At this point he left the high room of his mother's house, where the wound on his wing had healed to a scar, and where his wings had become stronger than ever. Unable to bear the separation any longer, Eros came to Psyche's side, rousing her with a prick of his arrow and purging her of sleep. It was this same weapon that Psyche had handled earlier in the story, when her curiosity got the better of her. And although at that time it caused her to fall in love with Eros, it also caused her to spill tiny drops of rose-red blood from her hand, which condemned her to Aphrodite's tasks.

Perhaps it was Psyche's sincere wish to be the bearer of beauty to a relationship that redeemed her curiosity this time. Perhaps her sleep of the innermost darkness, so reminiscent of her recent descent into hell, is what allowed her to commune with and summon Eros, because of the sharing of mind that can occur at these depths. Certainly her final release seemed to have demanded deathly stillness, *so that* something else could be released, drawn magnetically, and seemingly magically, to that virgin soil. Then Eros and Psyche each terminated their personal

tasks of healing, which culminated in their receiving the blessings of
Zeus (who acknowledged fathering Eros) and in Aphrodite dancing at
their wedding. Eventually Psyche (who had been pregnant all during
her trials) bore Eros a daughter whom they called Joy.

When she was first in love with Eros, Psyche had been spellbound,
stirred by an extreme of agonized love, and unable to rise in the air with
Eros had when he had to leave her. She had been left behind, with arms,
eyes and voice straining after her vanishing husband. This time, because
of Eros's blessing, Hermes himself lifted Psyche to heaven, where Eros
presented her with a cup of ambrosia whose draught would make her
immortal. He told her that Eros would embrace her in eternal wedlock,
having already made sure that Eros' "youthful sportiveness" had been
"hampered with nuptial fetters." In other words, Eros has learned the
joy of bondage because he was yoked, through Psyche, to heart-beauty,
and it is this that brings relief and quiet, serene joy. It is this yoking
that bears an eternal truth.

This stillness demanded of Psyche is a very fertile image. Patricia Berry maintains that this type of tension is exactly what is required for the
recovery of the worked gold of the virgin. It is "the purity of the virgin's
resistance that is crucial to this intensity." This is because the virgin Psyche truly has something to protect—"a dedication to the impersonal and
its values."[49] Something beyond us intervenes.

The Virgins

The virgin masculine in both men and women is truly phallic. He
has descended into the belly of the beast, and through willing and conscious sacrifice becomes aware of his entrapment in the patriarchy, and
thus becomes conscious of his inner polarity of baby-face and hairy brute-
face, which have been brought into dialogue through the dark side of
God. The patriarchal skin has been penetrated by the fresh instinctual
blood of the pelt. He knows a language that is rooted in the earth. He
does not speak the weasel-word. He is no longer concerned about his
penis power, because he trusts the ebbs and flows of both soul and spirit. Thus he is no longer goaded by an inner sense of inadequacy. He
has been drawn down into a Dionysian passion which draws forth the
feminine. He is no longer goaded into violating young Psyche, nor raging against Mother. Indeed, he knows that his only true partner must
be the reddened and sacred virgin-harlot. He is ready to die in her arms,
and not merely to please her or gain gratification for himself. He knows
the dance is more than the sum of them both. He too is at home in

the vessel of creation. Indeed he has been touched by the Christ arche-type, as St. Augustine describes it:

> Like a bridegroom Christ went forth from his chamber, he went out with a presage of his nuptials into the field of the world. . .he came to the marriage bed of the cross, and there, in mounting it, he consummated his marriage. And when he perceived the signs of the creature, he lovingly gave himself up to the torment in place of his bride, and he joined himself to the woman forever.[50]

Seeing Christ able and *willing* to take on the wound of the feminine, to feel the wound through and through, has touching and profoundly numinous significance for the hurt woman.

The sacred and virgin harlot is the archetype through which the healing woman can wear both the veil of virginity and the veil of mourning. She can be sustained by her own imaginal life. She has slowly reclaimed her body and her precious wound to find release into ecstasy and sacred dance, becoming an initiator rather than one to be seduced. Such a woman no longer requires pseudopimp-protection. She can be loved by one who loves her for her blackness. She can be loved by one who is a stranger, one who is other, one whom she no longer has to subsume in her own likeness.

Having imaginally traveled the spiral path of Mary Magdalene, we can now appreciate Robert Graves's comment that

> The Black Goddess is so far hardly more than a word of hope whispered among the few who have served their apprenticeship to the White Goddess. She promises a new pacific bond between men and women, corresponding to a final reality of love, in which the patriarchal marriage bond will fade away. . .she will lead men back to that sure instinct of love which he long ago forfeited by intellectual pride.[51]

This Black Madonna is, of course, none other than Aphrodite now released from the Father's unconsciousness of his phallic potency, and arisen from primal depths. She was born from violence and was un-mothered. The great ocean became her mother as she journeyed through it to embrace the sun.[52] She did not stay underwater: to do so would have been to remain identified with the Great Mother. This Aphrodite emerges, yet still she is connected with death and with the tomb. She does not fly away from the womb's tomb. She teaches us the acceptance of the inevitable.[53]

The woman who has emerged through the Aphrodite mythologem has connected with her sensate function and thus differentiated her imagination from fantasy. She values polarities and paradoxes: she lives within them. Her passion is intense but she is not overwhelmed by it. She cannot be seduced and she does not seduce. She has reclaimed her red moon truth, the truth of heart. She can appear naive because she is open to wonder.

She knows Aphrodite's valuing of divine madness, just as she knows the unity of beasts and God, and culture rooted in the sensuousness of matter. Jung suggests that

> Women are increasingly aware that love alone can give them their full stature, just as men are beginning to divine that only the spirit can give life its highest meaning. Both seek psychic relationship, because love needs the spirit, and the spirit love, for its completion.[54]

The Marriage

The alchemists tell us that sustaining a marriage between male and female virgins, redeeming demonic invasion and negative fertility, requires the love-fire of the divine Venus. That of Mars is "too choleric, too sharp, too fierce, and would burn the material." Both Mars and Venus must have reclaimed their own virginity in order to live together in sweet harmony.

> Then the virgin Venus will bring forth her pearl, her water spirit in you . . . to soften the fiery spirit of Mars, and the wrathful fire of Mars will sink quite willingly, in mildness and love, into the love fire of Venus, and thus both qualities, *as fire and water,* will mingle together, agree, and flow into one another.[55]

Epilogue

The transitional place[56] of therapy, deep in the forest's heart, is the walled garden of the sacred virgin harlot. This is the place where *fantastica* is transformed into imagination, where mother's breast, the birthplace of concrete symbolism, becomes the birthplace of the purely symbolic, without concrete superstructures. In this garden, the senses, the body, death and disintegration are allowed their places. The garden becomes the place where the naked truth may be seen stripped of illusions, *and* where the virgin cloaks herself in robes of scarlet and moon purple. Here flowers slowly unfold and die, cats bask in the sunshine or leave their paw-prints in the snow. This is a place of vibrant repose and quickened senses where mother and daughter have been reunited into the wisdom of the feminine, which knows and can practice the art of sacred surrender through the experience of charity and wonder.

Redeemed from the lustful patriarchal sniffing, the perfume of the place draws the Beast, crashing through the forest undergrowth, half crazed, berserk, searching frantically for relief from itself through an objective relationship with the other. Nothing in the garden seems perturbed by the sound of its thunderous hoofs and snorting, groaning roars. Only the virgin harlot can stay centered. The forest and its inner sanctum, the *temenos,* remain in paradoxical interdependence.

Emerging from the smell of decay and death of the jungle, the Beast leaps the fence with arching and rippling brute strength. This is not the leap of him who uses compulsive and abusive sexuality as a grappling hook into life, and who remains at the level of the hunter and wolf congealed into unconscious oneness. Neither is it the staggering and arrogant, stumbling strut of him whose only tool is the weasel-word that sucks life out of Logos. This is faith's leap.

The quiet garden receives the rush of savage, bristling potency that is at once profound light and utter blackness. This is the place where mother's milk is transformed into the milk of Sophia and Isis, which nourishes the earth and mankind. The natural order of things remains undisturbed. There has been no violation. Instead, the individual has been enlivened by a mighty, erotic and spiritual mythic drama that carries her (and him) deeply and passionately into the fully human life of imagination. Such a person will be able to carry the secret of the forest's heart deep into the city—into prostituted matter—and thus be able to remain in relationship, both to the wound and the phallus, for the ultimate enrichment of self and community.

Notes

[1]Judith Herman. *Father-Daughter Incest.* Cambridge: Harvard University Press, 1981, p. 58

[2]Mimi Silbert. "Sexual Child Abuse as an Antecedent to Prostitution." In *Child Abuse and Neglect,* Vol. 4, 1981, pp. 407-411

[3]Susan Griffin. *Pornography and Silence.* New York: Harper-Colophon Books, 1981, p. 248

[4]C. G. Jung. *CW* XIV, par. 355, note 26
A paraphrase for the retort as the place of rebirth

[5]Esther Harding. *Woman's Mysteries Ancient and Modern.* New York: Harper & Row, 1971, p. 119

[6]*Ibid.*, p. 118

[7]*Ibid.*, p. 120

[8]Arnold Mindell. *Dreambody: The Body's Role in Revealing the Self.* Boston: Sigo Press, 1982, p. 150

[9]C. G. Jung. *CW* XIV, par. 345

[10]*Ibid.*, par. 420

[11]*C.W.* Vol. XII, par. 413

[12]*Ibid.* For a representation of the Mercurial Anima, see Jung, C.G., *CW* XII, p. 305

[13]Bradley Te Paske. *Rape & Ritual: A Psychological Study.* Toronto: Inner City Books, 1982
Te Paske elaborates on how Diane Russell (in *The Politics of Rape*) and Susan Brownmiller (in *Against Our Will*) swing between these poles, disregarding psychological realities (pp. 19-21)

[14]Esther Harding, *op. cit.*, pp. 193-194

[15]It is interesting and significant to compare this dream image with one reported by Edward Edinger in his *Ego & Archetype.* Baltimore: Penguin Books Inc., 1974, pp. 70-76
"Here the inner man, burdened by his erect phallus, is 'an athlete of both body and spirit,' associated with sun-consciousness and supported by a group of men. The woman has compassion and admiration for his burden, and is able to join with him in a now. . .ecstatic union, releasing not only the woman's sensate function to consciousness, but also her creativity."

[16]Robert Stein. *Incest and Human Love.* Dallas: Spring Publications, 1973, p. 93

[17]Barbara Walker, *The Woman's Encyclopedia of Myths & Secrets.* San Francisco: Harper & Row, 1983, p. 822

[18]Robert Sardello. "The Suffering Body of the City: Cancer, Heart Attack & Herpes." In *Spring 1983,* p. 158

[19]Esther Harding, *op. cit.,* p. 174

[20]Norman Mailer. *Marilyn: A Biography.* New York: Grosset & Dunlap, 1973

[21]Nor Hall. *The Moon and The Virgin: Reflections on the Archetypal Feminine.* New York: Harper & Row, 1980, p. 104

[22]Charles Taylor. "Sexual Intimacy Between Patient and Analyst." In *Quadrant,* Spring, 1982, pp. 47-54

[23]Christine Downing. *The Goddess: Mythological Images of the Feminine.* New York: Crossroad Publishing, 1984, Chapter 3

[24]C. G. Jung. *CW* XIV, par. 420

[25]C. G. Jung. *CW* IX, I, par. 537

[26]Barbara Walker, *op. cit.,* p. 865

[27]*Ibid.,* pp. 865-866

[28]*Ibid.*

[29]*Ibid.,* p. 868

[30]Esther Harding, *op. cit.,* pp. 101-103

[31]John Layard. "The Incest Taboo and the Virgin Archetype." In *Images of the Untouched,* Joanne Stroud and Gail Thomas, eds. Dallas: Spring Publications, 1982, p. 178

[32]Elaine Pagels. *The Gnostic Gospels.* New York: Vintage Books, 1981, p. 58

[33]*Ibid.,* p. 77

[34]Esther Harding, *op. cit.,* p. 135

[35]Mircea Eliade. *The Forge and the Crucible.* Watford: Rider & Co., 1962, Chapters 5-7

[36]Esther Harding, *op. cit.,* p. 135

[37]*Ibid.,* p. 136

[38]Joseph Campbell. *Public Television Program: The Power of Myth.*

[39]Apuleius. *The Golden Ass.* Jack Lindsay, trans. Bloomington: Indiana University Press, 1962, p. 6

[40]*Ibid.,* p. 19

[41]*Ibid.,* p. 39

I have heard several women express their incomprehension at their partners' request to urinate over them. Such a request would suggest that the man is groping to connect with the deepest and most terrifying side of the dark Goddess. See Chapter I p. 21

[42]*Ibid.*, p. 104

[43]Edward Whitmont. *Return of the Goddess.* New York: Crossroad Publishing, 1984, p. 176

[44]*Ibid.*, p. 170

[45]Barbara Walker, *op. cit.*, pp. 550, 973

[46]C. G. Jung. *CW* IX, I, par. 61

[47]Apuleius, *The Golden Ass*, p. 138

[48]*Ibid.*, pp. 139-140

[49]Patricia Berry. "Virginities of Image." In *Images of the Untouched*, Joanne Stroud and Gail Thomas, eds. Dallas: Spring Publications, 1982, p. 33

[50]C. G. Jung. *CW* V, par. 411
Also, the tree as Mother Goddess has always had bipolar attributes. In par. 661ff, Jung quotes an old poem which says that the Christian cross has been looked upon as being the terrible stepmother who killed Christ.

[51]Robert Graves. *Mammon and the Black Goddess.* New York: Doubleday & Co., 1965, p. 164

[52]Christine Downing, *op. cit.*, p. 204
In discussing Aphrodite's love of the sun, Downing states that the Greeks perceived in Aphrodite a "joy-creating sun-like magic" and in the sun "a mysterious femininity, that sisterly helpfulness and goldenness of young women," so different than the prostitute's relationship to the sun.

[53]*Ibid.*, p. 211

[54]C. G. Jung. *CW* X, par. 269

[55]C. G. Jung. *CW* XVI, pars. 506-509

[56]Donald Winnicott. *Playing and Reality.* London: Penguin, 1971
My use of the phrase "transitional place" is taken from Winnicott's work on the emergence of symbolic thinking in the young child.
Jung also writes about the feminine soul as Ariadne; his discussion is centered around Leonardo da Vinci's painting Virgin on the Rocks.
See Van der Post, L. Jung and the *Story of our Time.* London: Penguin, 1976, p. 158
"There is the eternally feminine soul of man where it belongs in the dark feminine earth. See how tenderly and confidently the Virgin holds in her arms the child—our greater future self. She is the feminine soul of man,

the everlasting Ariadne. She is content, confident and unresentful because she is also the love that endureth and beareth all things even beyond faith and hope. She knows that, in the end, the child will grow and all shall be well."

BIBLIOGRAPHY

Etymological information has been drawn from *The American Heritage Dictionary of the English Language.* Boston: Houghton-Mifflin Co., Inc., 1981 edition.

Aaron, M., Cameron, T., Roizen, J., and Room, R. *Alcohol Casualties and Crime.* Berkeley: Social Research Group, 1978

Abbot, Brian, and Rosser, Forrest. "Adolescent Offenders and Their Families." Talk presented at the Child Sexual Abuse Treatment Center, P.O. Box 952, San Jose, CA 95108

Alper, Harvey. "Regression Toward the Real." In *Parabola,* VIII, 3:72-81. Summer 1983

Andrews, Lynn. *Medicine Woman.* San Francisco: Harper & Row, 1981

Apuleius. *The Golden Ass.* Jack Lindsay, trans. Bloomington: Indiana University Press, 1962

Arguelles, José, and Arguelles, Miriam. *The Feminine: Spacious as the Sky.* Boulder: Shambhala Publications, Inc., 1977

Aries, Philippe. *Centuries of Childhood: A Social History of Family Life.*

New York: Vintage Books, 1962

Armstrong, Louise. *Kiss Daddy Goodnight: A Speak-Out on Incest.* New York: Pocket Books, 1978

Ashe, Geoffrey. *The Virgin.* London: Routledge & Kegan Paul, 1976

Badgley, R. (Chairman). *Report on Sexual Offenses Against Children and Youths. Volumes I & II, "Summary."* By committee appointed by Minister of Justice and Attorney General of National Health and Welfare. Ottawa: Canadian Government Publishing Centre, 1984

Baker, Ian, ed. *Methods of Treatment in Analytical Psychology.* Dallas: Spring Publications, 1980

Barfoot, Jane. *Gaining Ground.* London: The Women's Press, Ltd., 1980

Barzun, Jacques. "Scholarship Versus Culture." In *The Atlantic Monthly,* 254, 5: 93-104, November 1984

Bateson, G. *Steps to an Etiology of Mind.* New York: Ballantine Books, 1972

Berry, Patricia. "Stopping: A Mode of Animation." In *Spring 1981.* Dallas: Spring Publications, 1981

Becker, Judith, Linda Skinner, Gene Abel, and Eileen Treacy. "Incidence and Types of Sexual Dysfunction in Rape and Incest Victims." In *Journal of Sex and Marital Therapy,* 8, 1:65-78, 1982

Bettelheim, Bruno. *The Uses of Enchantment: The Meaning and Importance of Fairy Tales.* New York: Random House, 1976

Boe, John. "Jack London, the Wolf and Jung." In *Psychological Perspectives,* 2,2:133-138, Fall, 1980

Bosselman, B.C. "Castration Anxiety and Phallus Envy: A Reformulation." In *Psychiatric Quarterly,* 34: 252-259, 1960

Brand, S. *Cybernetic Frontiers.* New York: Random House, 1974

Brod, Thomas N. "The Natural History of Eroticism." Lecture presented at Auburn Faith Hospital, Auburn, CA, on April 23, 1981

Brownmiller, Susan. *Against Our Will: Men, Women and Rape.* New York: Simon & Schuster, 1975

Broyles, William. "Why Men Love War." In *Esquire,* December 1984

Cameron, Anne. *Daughters of Copper Woman.* Vancouver: Press Gang Publishers, 1981

Campbell, Joseph. "The Power of Myth." PBS Broadcast, No. 4 in series "The Way of Beauty." Cassette of lecture presented at the San Francisco C.G. Jung Institute seminar "A Call to Beauty," May 17-18, 1980

Campbell, Joseph, ed. *The Mysteries: Papers From The Eranos Yearbooks.* Princeton: Princeton University Press, 1978

Carotenuto, Aldo. *A Secret Symmetry.* New York: Pantheon Books, 1982

Carr, Emily. *Growing Pains—The Autobiography of Emily Carr.* Toronto: Clarke, Irwin and Co., Ltd., 1966

Carson, Rachel. *The Edge of the Sea.* Boston: Houghton & Mifflin Co., 1979

Christ, Carol P. *Diving Deep and Surfacing: Women Writers on Spiritual Quest.* Boston: Beacon Press, 1980

Christ, Carol, and Maskow, J., eds. *Womanspirit Rising.* San Francisco: Harper & Row, 1979

Claremont de Castillejo, Irene. *Knowing Woman: A Feminine Psychology.* New York: Harper & Row, 1973

Coons, Philip M. "Child Abuse and Multiple Personality Disorder: Review of the Literature and Suggestions for Treatment." In *Child Abuse and Neglect,* 10, 4: 455-462, 1986

Cooper, Ingrid, and Bruno Cormier. "Inter-generational Transmission of Incest." In *Canadian Journal of Psychiatry,* 27, 4:231-235, April 1982

Cormier, B., Kennedy, M., and Sangowicz, J. "Psychodynamics of Father-Daughter Incest." In *Canadian Psychiatric Assoc. Journal,* 7:203-217, 1962

Cowan, Lyn. *Masochism: A Jungian View.* Dallas: Spring Publications, 1982

Dale-Green, Patricia. *The Archetypal Cat.* Dallas: Spring Publications, 1983

Davies, Robertson. *The Manticore.* Harmondsworth: Penguin Books, 1983

The Rebel Angels. Harmondsworth: Penguin Books, 1983

de Beauvoir, Simone. *Nature of the Second Sex.* London: Four Square Books by the New English Library, Ltd., 1964

de Rola, Stanislaw Klossowski. *The Secret Art of Alchemy.* New York: Avon Books, 1973

Dickson, Ken. "Characteristics of Offenders and Their Families." Talk at Forensic Assessment and Community Services (FACS), Spring 1984

"Incest Offender Subtypes." M. Ed. thesis, Education Library, The University of Alberta

Dietz, C., and Craft, J.L., "Family Dynamics of Incest: A New Perspective." In *Social Casework: The Journal of Contemporary Social Work.* Family Service Assoc. of America, 1980

Dourley, John. *The Ilness That We Are: A Jungian Critique of Christianity.* Toronto: Inner City Books, 1984

Downing, Christine. *The Goddess: Mythological Images of the Feminine.* New York: Crossroad Publishing, 1984

Dunwoody, Ellen. "Sexual Abuse of Children: A Serious, Widespread Problem." In *Response To Family Violence and Sexual Assault.* 5, 4:114, July-August 1982

Edinger, Edward. "An Outline of Analytical Psychology." In *Quadrant,* 1,1:8-19, Spring 1968

Ego and Archetype. Baltimore: Penguin Books, 1974

Eliade, Mircea. *The Forge and the Crucible.* England: Watford, Rider Co., 1964

Rites and Symbols of Initiation: The Mysteries of Birth and Rebirth. New York: Harper & Row, 1975

Elkes, Joel. "Behavioral Medicine: The Early Beginnings." In *Psychiatric Annals,* 11, 2, February 1981

Elkind, David. *The Hurried Child.* Reading: Addison-Wesley Publishing Co., 1982

Falk, Nancy Auer, and Gross, Rita M. *Unspoken Words: Women's Religious Lives in Non-Western Cultures.* San Francisco: Harper & Row,

1980

Fehmi, Lester, and Fritz, George. "The Attentional Foundation of Health and Well Being." In *Somatics,* Spring 1980

Fordham, Frieda. *An Introduction to Jung's Psychology.* Harmondsworth: Richard Clay & Co. Ltd., 1964

Fox, Matthew. *Compassion.* Minneapolis: Winston Press, 1979

Friday, Nancy. *My Mother/My Self: The Daughter's Search for Identity.* New York: Dell Publishing Co., 1978

Friedan, Betty. *The Feminine Mystique.* Harmondsworth: Penguin Books, 1965

Fromm, Erich. *The Forgotten Language: An Introduction to the Understanding of Dreams, Fairy Tales and Myths.* New York: Grover Press, 1957

Funk & Wagnalls Standard Dictionary of Folklore, Mythology and Legend. New York: Harper & Row, 1972

Gebard, Gagnon, Pomeroy, and Christenson. *Sex Offenders: An Analysis of Types.* New York: Harper & Row, 1965

Giaretto, H. "Humanistic Treatment of Father/Daughter Incest." In Helfer, R.E., and Kemp, C.H., eds., *Child Abuse and Neglect: The Family and the Community.* Cambridge: Ballinger Publications, 1976

"Humanistic Treatment of Father/Daughter Incest." In *Journal of Humanistic Psychology,* 18, 4:59-76, Fall 1978

"Treating Sexual Abuse—Working Together." Presented at Statewide Conference on *Child Abuse and Neglect,* Jefferson, Missouri, March 3, 1977

"A Comprehensive Child Sexual Abuse Treatment Program." In *Child Abuse and Neglect,* 6:1982

Gil, Eliana. *Outgrowing the Pain: A Book For and About Adults Abused as Children.* San Francisco: Launch Press, 1983

Gilbert, Lucy, and Webster, Paula. *Bound By Love: The Sweet Trap of Daughterhood.* Boston: Beacon Press, 1982

Gilligan, Carol. *In a Different Voice.* Cambridge: Harvard University

Press, 1982

"Why Should a Woman be More Like a Man?" In *Psychology To-day*, 16, 6:68-77, June 1984

Gimbutas, Marija. *The Goddesses and Gods of Old Europe: Myths and Cult Images.* Berkeley: University of California Press, 1982

Giory, A. *Psychology as a Human Science: A Phenomenologically Based Approach.* New York: Harper & Row, 1970

Glas, Norbert. "Red Riding Hood." In *Once Upon a Fairy Tale.* Spring Valley: St. George Book Service, 1977

Goldenberg, Naomi R. *Changing of the Gods: Feminism and the End of Traditional Religions.* Boston: Beacon Press, 1979

Goodwin, Jean, Simms, Mary, and Bergman, Robert. "Hysterical Seizures: A Sequel to Incest." In *American Journal of Orthopsychiatry*, 49,4:698703, October 1979

Graves, Robert. *Mammon and the Black Goddess.* New York: Doubleday & Co., 1965

"Introduction." *The New Larousse Encyclopedia of Mythology.* London: Hamlyn, 1979

Griffin, Susan. *Pornography and Silence: Culture's Revenge Against Nature.* New York: Harper & Row, 1982

Woman and Nature: The Roaring Inside Her. New York: Harper & Row, 1978

Groesbeck, C.J. "The Analyst's Myth: Freud and Jung as Each Other's Analyst." In *Quadrant*, 8, 1:28-55, Spring 1980

Gross, Meir. "Incestuous Rape: A Cause for Hysterical Seizure in Four Adolescent Girls." In *American Journal of Orthopsychiatry*, 49, 4:70-4708, October 1979

Groth, Nicholas, and Birnbaum, H.J. "Adult Sexual Orientation and Attraction to Underaged Persons." In *Archives of Sexual Behavior*, 7, 3:175-181, May, 1978

Men Who Rape: The Psychology of the Offender. New York: Plenum Publications, 1979

Groth, Nicholas. "The Incest Offender." In Sgroi, Suzanne, ed., *Handbook of Clinical Intervention in Child Sexual Abuse.* Toronto:

Lexington Books, 1983

Groth, Nicholas, and Laredo, D. "Juvenile Sexual Offenders: Guidelines for Treatment." In *International Journal of Offender Therapy and Comparative Criminology*, 25, 3:265-272, 1981.

Groth-Marnett, Barbara. "The Phenomenology of the Puella Aeterna." Doctoral thesis submitted at International College, Los Angeles, January 1987

Guggenbühl-Craig, Adolf. *Eros on Crutches: Reflections on Amorality and Psychopathy*. Irving: Spring Publications, 1980

Hadlock, Don. "Family Therapy for Incestuous Families." Talk presented at The Child Sexual Abuse Program, PO Box 952, San Jose CA, 95108

Hall, Nor. *The Moon and the Virgin: Reflections on the Archetypal Feminine*. New York: Harper & Row, 1980

Halliday, Linda. In *Edmonton Journal*, November 17, 1984

Harding, Esther. *The Way of All Women*. New York: Harper & Row, 1970 (reprint of 1932 edition)

Woman's Mysteries. New York: Harper Colophon, 1976

Harris, George. "The Criminal Personality: A Dialogue With Stanton Samenow." In *Journal of Counseling and Development*, 63:227-229, December 1984

Heller, Stuart. "Movement Psychology: Freeing 'Postural Beliefs.'" In *Brain/Mind Bulletin*, 8, 8, April 18, 1983

Herman, Judith. *Father-Daughter Incest*. Cambridge: Harvard University Press, 1981

Hillman, James "A Psychology of Transgression Drawn From an Incest Dream: Imagining the Case." In *Spring 1987*. Dallas: Spring Publications, 1987

Archetypal Psychology. Dallas: Spring Publications, 1983

"Betrayal." Talk presented at the Guild of Pastoral Psychology, 41 Radcliffe Gardens, London SW16. Guild Lecture No. 125, December 1964

Interviews. New York: Harper Colophon, 1983

The Myth of Analysis. New York: Harper & Row, 1978

Re-Visioning Psychology. New York: Harper & Row, 1975

"The Bad Mother, An Archetypal Approach." In *Spring 1984.* Dallas: Spring Publications, 1984

"The Thought of the Heart." In *Eranos 1979,* Vol. 48. Ascona: Eranos Foundation, 1981, pp. 133-182

"The Therapeutic Value of Alchemical Language." In Baker, I., ed., *Methods of Treatment in Analytical Psychology.* Dallas: Spring Publications, 1980

"Towards the Archetypal Model for the Masturbation Inhibition." In *Loose Ends.* Dallas: Spring Publications, 1975

Hillman, James, *et al. Facing the Gods.* Dallas: Spring Publications, 1980

Hopkins, Adam. *Crete: Its Past, Present and People.* London: Faber & Faber, 1977

Hull, R.F.C., and McGuire, William, eds. *C.G. Jung Speaking: Interviews and Encounters.* Princeton: Princeton University Press, 1977

Huxley, Aldous. *The Doors of Perception.* New York: Harper & Bros., 1954

James, Beverley, and Nasjleti, Maria. *Treating Sexually Abused Children and Their Families.* Palo Alto: Consulting Psychologists Press, 1983

Jenks, Kathleen. *Journey of a Dream Animal: A Human Search for Personal Identity.* New York: The Julian Press, 1975

Johnson, Brian D. "Women Behind Bars—This Is Not a Nice Place To Live." In *Equinox,* March-April 1984, pp. 50-67

Johnson, Robert A. *She: Understanding Feminine Psychology.* New York: Harper & Row, 1976

He: Understanding Masculine Psychology. New York: Harper & Row, 1977

Jung, C.G. *Collected Works,* Vols I-IXX. Princeton: Princeton University Press, Bollingen Series XXII

Analytical Psychology: Its Theory and Practice. New York: Vintage Books, 1968

"Approaching the Unconscious." In *Man and His Symbols*. New York: Doubleday and Co., 1964

Dreams. Princeton: Princeton University Press, 1974

Dream Analysis. Vol. II, Notes of the Seminars in Analytical Psychology. Zürich: October 29, 1929-June 30, 1930

Memories, Dreams, Reflections. New York: Vintage Books, 1965

Word and Image. Aniela Jaffé, ed. Princeton: Princeton University Press, 1979

Jung, Emma. *Animus and Anima*. New York: Spring Publications, 1970

Kerényi, Karl. "A Mythological Image of Girlhood." In Hillman, James, ed., *Facing the Gods*. Dallas: Spring Publications, 1980

Kinkead, G. "The Family Secret." In *Boston* Magazine, 69, 10:100-183, October 1977

Kluft, Richard, and Braun, Bennett. "Multiple Personality and Intrafamilial Abuse." In *International Journal of Family Psychiatry*, 5, 4: 283-301, 1984

Kluft, Richard. "An Update on Multiple Personality Disorder." In *Hospital and Community Psychiatry*, 38, 4: 363-373, April 1987

Koltuv, Barbara Black. "Lilith." In *Quadrant*, 16, 1:63-87, Spring 1983

Krishna, Gopi. *Kundalini: The Evolutionary Energy in Man*. With Psychological Commentary by James Hillman. Boulder: Shambhala, 1967

Kroth, J.A. *Child Sexual Abuse: Analysis of a Family Therapy Approach*. Springfield: C.C. Thomas, 1979

Kugler, P. "Childhood Seduction: Physical and Emotional." In *Spring 1987*. Dallas: Spring Publications, 1987

Larsen, Stephen. *The Shaman's Doorway*. New York: Harper & Row, 1976

Layard, John. *A Celtic Quest*. Dallas: Spring Publications, 1985

"The Incest Taboo and the Virgin Archetype." In Stroud, Joanne, and Thomas, Gail, eds., *Images of the Untouched*. Dallas: Spring Publications, 1982

Lederer, Wolfgang. *The Fear of Women*. New York and London: A Harvest/HBJ Book, 1968

Leonard, Linda Schierse. *The Wounded Woman.* Boston: Shambhala, 1983

Lewis, Stephen, ed. *Art Out of Agony.* Toronto: CBC Enterprises, 1984

Lindbergh, Anne Morrow. *Gift From the Sea.* New York: Random House, 1978

Linedecker, Gifford L. *Children in Chains.* New York: An Everest House Book, 1981

Lockhart, Russell, and Hillman, James, eds. *Soul and Money.* Dallas: Spring Publications, 1982

Lockhart, Russell. *Words as Eggs: Psyche in Language and Clinic.* Dallas: Spring Publications, 1983

Lopez, Barry H. *Of Wolves and Men.* New York: Charles Scribner's Sons, 1978

Luke, Helen M. *Woman, Earth and Spirit: The Feminine in Symbol and Myth.* New York: Crossroad Publishing, 1981

Mailer, Norman. *Marilyn: A Biography.* New York: Grosset & Dunlap, 1973

Malcolm, Janet. "Annals of Scholarship: Trouble in the Archives." In *The New Yorker.* Article Part I, 59, 42:59-152; Article Part II, 59, 43:60-119. December 5, December 12, 1983

Maslow, A.H. "The Creative Attitude." In Avila, D., Combs, A., and Perkey, W., eds., *The Helping Relationship Sourcebook,* 2nd ed. Newton: Allyn & Bacon, 1977

Masson, Jeffrey M. *The Assault on Truth.* New York: Farrar, Straus & Giroux, 1984

"Freud and the Seduction Theory." In *The Atlantic Monthly,* 253, 2:33-60, February 1984

"The Prosecution and Expulsion of Jeffrey Masson As Performed by Members of the Freudian Establishement and Reported by Janet Malcolm of The New Yorker." In *Mother Jones,* December 1984, pp. 34-47

May, Robert. "Sex Differences in Fantasy Patterns." In *Journal of Projective Techniques,* 30, 6:252-259, June 30, 1966

McCall, Cheryl. "The Cruelest Crime." In *Life Magazine*, December 5, 1984, pp. 35-62

McCombs, Phil. "Unlocking the Criminal Mind." In *The Washington Post*, Monday, March 5, 1984

McMahon, C.F., and Hastrip, J.L. "The Role of Imagination in the Disease Process: Post-Cartesian History." In *Journal of Behavioral Medicine*, 3, 2, 1980

Meador, Betty de Shong. "Transference/Countertransference Between Woman Analyst and the Wounded Girl Child." In *Chiron* 1984. Wilmette: Chiron Publications, 1984, pp. 163-174

Merchant, Carolyn. *The Death of Nature: Women, Ecology, and the Scientific Revolution*. San Francisco: Harper & Row, 1983

Metford, J.C.J. *Dictionary of Christian Love and Legend*. London: Thames and Hudson, 1983

Michaels, Walter Ben. "Masochism, Money and McTeague." In *The Threepenny Review*, No. 16, Winter 1984

Michlem, N. "Lightning Conduction and the Psychopathology of Convulsion." In *Spring 1983*. Dallas: Spring Publications, 1983

Miller, Alice. *The Drama of the Gifted Child: How Narcissistic Parents Form and Deform the Emotional Lives of Their Talented Children*. New York: Basic Books, 1981

Thou Shalt Not Be Aware. New York: Farrar, Straus & Giroux, 1984

Miller, David. "Womb of Gold." In Stroud, Joanne, and Thomas, Gail, eds., *Images of the Untouched*. Dallas: Spring Publications, 1982

Mindell, Arnold. *Dreambody: The Body's Role in Revealing the Psyche*. Boston: Sigo Press, 1982

Monaghan, Patricia. *The Book of Goddesses and Heroines*. New York: A Dutton Paperback, 1981

Nagy, Marilyn. "Menstruation and Shamanism." In *Psychological Perspectives*, 7, 1:52-68, Spring 1981

Neumann, Erich. *The Great Mother*. Princeton: Princeton University Press, 1972

"The Youngest Witness." In *Newsweek*, 105, 7:72-75, February 18, 1985

Pagels, Elaine. *The Gnostic Gospels.* New York: Vintage Books, 1981

Paris, Ginette. *Pagan Meditations.* Dallas: Spring Publications, 1986

Pearce, Joseph Chilton. *Magic Child.* New York: Bantam Books, 1977

Pelletier, K.R. *Mind As Healer — Mind As Slayer: A Holistic Approach to Preventing Stress Disorders.* New York: Dell Publishing, 1977

Perera, Sylvia Brinton. *Descent to the Goddess: A Way of Initiation for Women.* Toronto: Inner City Books, 1981

Pines, Maya. "Children's Winning Ways." In *Psychology Today,* 18, 12:58, December 1984

Powers, W.T. "Cybernetic Model for Research in Human Development." In Ozer, M.N., ed., *A Cybernetic Approach to the Assessment of Children: Towards a More Humane View of Human Beings.* Boulder: Westview Press, 1979

Preston, Robb. *Epilepsy: A Manual For Health Workers.* NIH Publications, No. 82-2350, September 1981

Progoff, Ira. *Jung, Synchronicity, and Human Destiny: Noncausal Dimensions of Human Experience.* New York: Dell Publishing, 1973

Rickles, W.H. "Biofeedback, Transitional Phenomena and Therapy of Psycho-Somatic Narcissistic Disorder." Paper presented at the 11th Annual Conference of the Biofeedback Society of America, Colorado Springs, 1980

Rist, Kate. "Incest: Theoretical and Clinical Views." In *American Journal of Orthopsychiatry,* 49, 4:680-691, October 1979

Roberts, Barbara. "All Our Lives: Sexual Assaults and Other Normal Activities." In *Canadian Woman Studies,* 4, 4:7-9, Summer 1983

Robertson, Seonaid. *Rose Garden and Labyrinth: A Study in Education.* Dallas: Spring Publications, 1982

Roscher, Wilhelm H., and Hillman, James. *Pan and the Nightmare.* Irving: Spring Publications, 1982

Rose, H.J. *Religion in Greece and Rome.* New York: Harper & Bros., 1959

Rosenfeld, A. "Sexual Misuse and the Family." In *Victimology: An International Journal,* 2, 2, 1977

Rossi, Ernest L. "As Above, So Below: The Holographic Mind." In *Psychological Perspectives,* 11, 2:155-169, Fall 1980

Rossman, Michael. *On Learning Social Change.* New York: Vintage Books, 1972

Rush, Florence. *The Best-Kept Secret: Sexual Abuse of Children.* New York: McGraw-Hill, 1980

Sanford, John A. *Dreams and Healing.* Ramsey: The Paulist Press, 1978

The Invisible Partners: How the Male and Female in Each of Us Affects Our Relationships. Ramsey: The Paulist Press, 1980

"The Problem of Evil in Christianity and Analytical Psychology." In *Psychological Perspectives,* 11,2:112-132, Fall 1980

Sardello, Robert. "The Suffering Body of the City: Cancer, Heart Attack and Herpes." In *Spring 1983.* Dallas: Spring Publications, 1983

Sayle, Hans. *The Stress of Life.* New York: McGraw-Hill, 1978

Schmidt, Lynda W. "How the Father's Daughter Found Her Mother." In *Psychological Perspectives,* 14, 1:8-19, Spring 1983

Schumaker, E.F. *Small is Beautiful: Economics As If People Mattered.* New York: Harper & Row, 1973

Schwarz-Salant, Nathan. "Archetypal Factors Underlying Sexual Acting Out in the Transference/Countertransference Process." In *Chiron 1984.* Wilmette: Chiron Publications, 1984

Severson, Randolph. "Puer's Wounded Wing: Reflections on the Psychology of Skin Disease." In Hillman, James, ed., *Puer Papers.* Dallas: Spring Publications, 1983

Sgroi, Suzanne M., ed. *Handbook of Clinical Intervention in Child Sexual Abuse.* Lexington: Lexington Books, 1982

Shinoda, Jean Bolen. *The Tao of Psychology.* New York: Harper & Row, 1979

Shuttle, Penelope, and Redgrove, Peter. *The Wise Wound: Menstruation and Every Woman.* Harmondsworth: Penguin Books Ltd., 1980

Sifneos, P.E. "The Prevalence of Alexithymic Characteristics in Psychosomatic Patients." Topics of Psychosomatic Research, 9th European Conference, Psychosomatic Res., Vienna, 1972. In *Psychother. Psy-*

chosom., 22:266-262, 1973

Silbert, Mimi. "Sexual Child Abuse as an Antecedent to Prostitution." In *Child Abuse and Neglect*, 5:407-411, 1981

Snyder-Ott, Joelynn. *Women and Creativity*. Milbrae CA: Les Femmes Publishing, 1978

Stein, Murray. "Power, Shamanism, and Maieutics in the Countertransference." In *Chiron 1984*. Wilmette Il: Chiron Publications, 1984

Stein, Robert. "Coupling/Uncoupling: Reflections on the Evolution of the Marriage Archetype." In *Spring 1981*. Dallas: Spring Publications, 1981
Incest and Human Love. Dallas: Spring Publications, 1983
"On Incest and Child Abuse." In *Spring 1987*. Dallas: Spring Publications, 1987

Stewart, Louis. "Affect and Archetype in Analysis." In *Chiron 1987*. Wilmette: Chiron Publications, 1987

Stone, Merlin. *When God Was A Woman*. New York: A Harvest/HBJ Book, 1976

Stroud, Joanne, and Thomas, Gail, eds. *Images of the Untouched*. Dallas: Spring Publications, 1982

Sullivan, Harry Stack. *The Interpersonal Theory of Psychiatry*. New York: W.W. Norton, 1953

Summit, Roland. *Typical Characteristics of Father/Daughter Incest — A Guide For Investigation*. Torrance CA: Harbor UCLA Medical Center

Summit, Roland, and Kryso, Jo Anne. "The Sexual Abuse of Children: A Clinical Spectrum." In *American Journal of Orthopsychiatry*, 48, 2:237251, April 1978

Sutton-Smith, B. "The Playful Mode of Knowing." In *Play: The Child Strives Toward Self-Realization*. Washington DC: The National Association for the Education of Young Children, 1971

Taylor, Charles. "Sexual Intimacy Between Patient and Analyst." In *Quadrant*, 15, 1:47-54, Spring 1982

TePaske, Bradley. *Rape and Ritual: A Psychological Study.* Toronto: Inner City Books, 1982

Thompson, Keith. "Talks With Robert Bly 'On Being a Man.'" In *Dromenon Journal,* 3, 4, Summer-Fall 1982

Thompson, William Irwin. *The Time Falling Bodies Take To Light.* New York: St. Martin's Press, 1981

Trudeau, Garry. "Child Sex Trade Big Business." In *The Edmonton Journal,* November 24, 1984

Tsai, Mavis, and Waggoner, Nathaniel. "Therapy Group for Women Sexually Molested as Children." In *Archives of Sexual Behavior,* 7, 5: 417-427, 1978

van der Post, Laurens. *Jung and the Story of Our Time.* New York: Penguin Books, 1976

"Vis-à-Vis Newsletter of the National Clearinghouse on Family Violence." In *Health and Welfare Canada,* 2, 2, Spring 1984

von Eschenbach, Wolfram. *Parzival.* New York: Vintage Books, 1961

von Franz, Marie-Louise. *The Problem of the Feminine in Fairytales.* Zürich: Spring Publications, 1972
  Shadow and Evil in Fairytales. Zürich: Spring Publications, 1974
  C.G. Jung: His Myth In Our Time. London: Hodder and Stoughton Ltd., 1975
  Puer Aeternus: A Psychological Study of the Adult Struggle With the Paradise of Childhood. Boston: Sigo Press, 1981

von Franz, Marie-Louise, and Hillman, James. *Jung's Typology.* New York: Spring Publications, 1971

Walker, Barbara G. *The Woman's Encyclopedia of Myths and Secrets.* San Francisco: Harper & Row, 1983

Walker, L.E. "Battered Women and Learned Helplessness." In *Victimology: An International Journal,* 2:3-4, 1978

Watson *et al.* "A Hidden Epidemic." In *Newsweek,* 103, 20:30-36, May 14, 1984

Weinberg, S.K. *Incest Behavior.* New York: Citadel Press, 1955

Wells, Jess. *A Herstory of Prostitution in Western Europe.* Berkeley: Shameless Hussy Press, 1982

Wheelwright, Joseph. *Psychological Types.* San Francisco: C.G. Jung Institute of San Francisco, 1973

Whitmont, Edward. *Return of the Goddess.* New York: Crossroad Publishing, 1984

Wiedemann, Florence. "Mother, Father, Teacher, Sister: Transference / Countertransference Issues With Women in the First Stage of Animus Development." In *Chiron 1984.* Wilmette: Chiron Publications, 1984

Winnicott, Donald W. *Playing and Reality.* London: Penguin Books, 1971

Wolowitz, Howard M. "Hysterical Character and Feminine Identity." In Bardwick, Judith, ed., *Readings on the Psychology of Women.* New York: Harper & Row, 1972

Woodman, Marion. *Addiction to Perfection: The Still Unravished Bride.* Toronto: Inner City Books, 1982

"Transference and Countertransference in Analysis Dealing With Eating Disorders." In *Chiron 1984.* Wilmette: Chiron Publications, 1984

Yates, Alayne. "Children Eroticized by Incest." In *American Journal of Psychiatry,* 139, 4:482-485, April 1982

Zabriskie, Beverly. "Incest and Myrrh: Father-Daughter Sex in Therapy." In *Quadrant,* 15, 2:5-24, Fall 1982

INDEX

219

RESOURCES

In Canada:

For additional information about Canadian resources in incest and/or sexual abuse research and treatment programs, contact:

> Vis-à-vis, Family Violence Program
> Canadian Council on Social Development
> 55 Parkdale Avenue, P.O. Box 3505
> Station C, Ottawa, Ontario K1Y 4GI
> (613) 728-1865

For information about local counseling centers and private practitioners specializing in the therapy of incest and/or sexual abuse victims, contact your area's Mental Health Services office. For the branch nearest you, please consult your local telephone directory.

In the U.S.A.:

The following organizations are able to answer your questions about incest and/or sexual abuse clearinghouses, resource programs, hotlines, and support groups throughout the U.S.A. and Canada. Each of these provides accurate, prompt, and confidential information to incest/sexual abuse victims, their families, and their loved ones.

Parents United International
  Adults Molested As Children United (AMACU)
  P.O. Box 952
  San Jose, CA 95108
  (408) 280-5055

Childhelp USA
1345 El Centro Avenue
P.O. Box 630
Hollywood, CA 90028
(213) 465-4016
(800) 4ACHILD (Hotline)

C. Henry Kempe Center
1205 Oneida Street
Denver, CO 80220
(303) 321-3963

Incest Resources, Inc.,
46 Pleasant Street
Cambridge, MA 02139
(please write for information)

Incest Survivors Resource Network International
P.O. Box 911
Hicksville, NY 11802
(516) 935-3031
(a resources as opposed to crisis network)

National Committe For the Prevention of Child Abuse
332 South Michigan Avenue, Suite 950
Chicago, IL 60604
(312) 663-3520
(provides a free catalogue of sources)

SIGO PRESS

SIGO PRESS publishes books in psychology
which continue the work of C.G. Jung, the great
Swiss psychoanalyst and founder of analytical
psychology. Each season SIGO brings out a small
but distinctive list of titles intended to make a
lasting contribution to psychology and human
thought. These books are invaluable reading for
Jungians, psychologists, students and scholars
and provide enrichment and insight to general
readers as well. In the Jungian Classics Series,
well-known Jungian works are brought back into
print in popular editions.